WITHDRA

UTSA LIBRARIES

DATE DUE

Karl Kraus and the Critics

Harry Zohn

Karl Kraus
and the Critics

CAMDEN HOUSE

Published by Camden House, Inc.
Drawer 2025
Columbia, SC 29202 USA

Printed on acid-free paper.
Binding materials are chosen for strength and
durability.

Printed in the United States of America

ISBN 1–57113–181–7

Library of Congress Cataloging-in-Publication Data

Zohn, Harry.
    Karl Kraus and the critics / Harry Zohn.
        p.   cm. – (Studies in German Literature, Linguistics, and
    culture. Literary criticism in perspective)
    Includes bibliographical references and index.
    ISBN 1-57113-181-7 (akl. Paper)
    1. Kraus, Karl, 1874-1936—Criticism and interpretation.
I. Title. II. Series: Studies in German literature, linguistics,
and culture (Unnumbered). Literary criticism in perspective.
PT2621.R27Z96 1997
838'.91209—dc21   97-14409
                                                            CIP

Contents

To the memory of
Ernst Křenek,
consummate Krausian
and fatherly friend

Introduction

In an article whose title is almost identical with that of this book (I chose *Karl Kraus and* the *Critics* because the satirist would surely have balked at the notion that they were his, or he theirs), the Czech-born American scholar Wilma Abeles Iggers, who has the distinction of having produced one of the first major studies of Kraus in English, displays a becoming sense of the difficulty of writing about Karl Kraus, particularly in a language other than his, and of reducing the enormous critical literature on him to manageable dimensions. "To give an adequate picture of the literature on Kraus to the present time," she writes, "would be a gigantic task probably occupying more space than Kraus's entire work" (1975, 26). Such a statement would be extravagant even today, two decades after the centennial of the satirist's birth and six decades after his death, but it is difficult to fault Iggers' conclusion that Kraus's sometimes paradoxical stance has resulted in a body of criticism that "generally lacks passionate detachment and is itself deeply immersed in the issues of the day and in the charges and countercharges of Kraus polemics" (27). Iggers correctly points out that the satirist's readership has changed since World War II, but when she claims that "the core of Kraus's following during his lifetime consisted largely of young Jews with some intellectual aspirations" (28) and that these young people, who lived comfortable upper-class lives, delighted in rebelling against their bourgeois background, this is at best a half-truth reminiscent of the early Berlin performances of the Brecht-Weill *Threepenny Opera*, which attracted high society in all its finery.

Karl Kraus is hardly a household name today, but one does encounter it in a great variety of contexts in the English-speaking realm alone. His life and works are discussed in some detail in such dissimilar books as *The Portable Curmudgeon*, *Wittgenstein's Vienna*, *Makers of Modern Culture*, *Brecht's Tradition*, *The Cynic's Lexicon*, *The Vienna Coffeehouse Wits*, and *Schönberg and His Circle*. This relative prominence is disproportionate to the minuscule percentage of his writings that is available in English translation. In his lifetime Kraus, that implacable foe of the press, was bedeviled by what has been called the *Totschweigetaktik* of the public prints, which gave him the silent treatment, "killing him with silence," but there is ample evidence of a Kraus renaissance during the past forty or fifty years. While most of the dyed-in-the-wool *Krausianer* (somehow the English word "Krausians" does not convey the full unquestioning and even militant passion of his adherents) are no longer around, emotions still tend to run high in the critical discourse about Kraus. His contemporary critics may be divided, on the one hand, into those who are convinced of his uniqueness and greatness, regard him as a satirist sui generis and are willing to concede to the art of satire, and particularly the "total satire" practiced by Kraus, a special status and special privileges; and, on the other, those who seem to expect of a satirist like Kraus balance, fairness, restraint, consistency, tact, taste, verisimilitude, and general right-mindedness. If the former are sometimes decried as uncritical eulogists or "positivists," the latter often wind up reading Kraus against the grain, as it were.

If special privileges or considerations need to be claimed in a critical assessment of the satirist Karl Kraus, I must also excuse (though, I hope, not accuse) myself for not consistently following the general guidelines or practices of the series in which this book appears. My task would have been far easier, and I might have exposed myself to less controversy and criticism, if I had found it possible to divide Kraus's oeuvre neatly into prose, poetry, and drama; sound a Krausian note; and then cue in a chorus of critical voices, discussing the published criticism of each work within these categories in chronological order and indicating the evolution and changing perspectives of Kraus criticism. However, in the case of Kraus, relatively few studies have been devoted to individual works; most critics have seen and presented Kraus's work as all of a piece, as a continuum, and have commented on its totality even when they have concentrated on one or another aspect of it. Because Kraus scholarship is largely a matter of the past half-century and is still very much in flux, it is hardly possible to identify or demonstrate the evolution of particular "schools" of criticism.

As for the difficulties of reducing a mass of material to manageable and surveyable dimensions and culling, for purposes of inclusion or exclusion, an enormous amount of material (in English and German only), I must beg my readers' indulgence for what is sometimes bound to seem undue subjectivity. I can only express the hope that despite all such obstacles I am presenting the kind of typology of Kraus criticism that will illuminate his work and stimulate further reading and research.

Right at the outset I shall mention three books that provide keys to Kraus, at least for those able to read German, and not only because they contain extensive bibliographical information.

Friedrich Jenaczek's book *Zeittafeln zur Fackel* (1965; The *Fackel*: Chronological Tables, subtitled "Themes, Aims, Problems") performed an important function before the reprint editions of Kraus's journal (first by Kösel in the late 1960s, then by Zweitausendeins in an inexpensive reprint), and it is still a useful reference and a valuable guide, being replete with statistics and biographical data. Agreeing with Heinrich Fischer,

Kraus's literary executor, that the satirist's autonomous texts should take precedence over any commentary, Jenaczek sets out to provide an inventory and presents these chronological divisions of the *Fackel*, which runs to around 30,000 pages, some 5,000 of which contain the contributions of other authors:

1. The period of social ethics, 1899ff.
2. The turn toward aestheticism, 1902–5ff.
3. In the service of language, 1909ff.
4. Between orientations, 1914ff.
5. Pro-Democracy, Pro-Republic, 1919ff.
6. Break with the Social Democratic Leadership, 1930ff.

Paul Schick's pictorial biography of Karl Kraus also appeared in 1965 and has been reprinted numerous times. This study by the longtime director of the Kraus Archive in the Vienna Municipal Library, a collection that has been in existence since 1954, is as accurate and balanced as it is informative and authoritative.

An equally valuable handbook is Jens Malte Fischer's 1974 contribution to the series Realien zur Literatur, a book that clearly and succinctly sets forth the various stages of Kraus's life and the significant aspects of his work in addition to giving a wealth of bibliographical information for further reading and research.

In this book a Karl Kraus chronology that is intended to provide a framework for the various critical voices is followed by a chapter entitled "When Vienna Saw Red: Some Early Themes" that deals with early reactions to Kraus's journal *Die Fackel* (The Torch) as well as recent critical studies of *Sittlichkeit und Kriminalität* (Morality and Criminal Justice) and the sexual question in fin-de-siècle Vienna. Critical views of Kraus's controversial prewar essay on Heine are followed by a brief discussion of an even more controversial aspect of the satirist's life and work, his attitude toward Judaism, the Jews, and his own Jewishness. A more positive note is sounded in a discussion of groups of theologians, philosophers, and musicians that came under Kraus's spell. Succeeding chapters present some of the historical and political background as well as Kraus's relationship to psychoanalysis and the theater. Kraus scholarship has not yet rivaled Goethe philology (some years ago a reputable scholarly journal published an article entitled "Goethe and the Yo-Yo," based on one of the poet's *Venetian Epigrams*), but the chapter entitled "Karl Kraus and . . . " ranges, in possibly parodistic fashion, from a key Krausian concept to more trivial topics. A chapter on translation in a book of this kind may strike some readers as strange, but I would point out that in a very real sense translation is interpretation, and thus a critical discussion of Kraus as both a translator and a "translatee" may be justified. The concluding chapters deal with what has been described as the Kraus renaissance of the past half-century.

Unless otherwise noted, translations from the German are my own.

A Karl Kraus Chronology

1874   Karl Kraus is born at Jičin (Bohemia) on April 28, the ninth child (and fifth son) of Jacob Kraus, a well-to-do paper manufacturer, and Ernestine Kantor Kraus.

1877   The Kraus family moves to Vienna, where Karl Kraus is to spend the rest of his life ("My hatred of Vienna is not love gone astray. It's just that I've discovered a completely new way of finding it unbearable").

1884–92   Kraus attends secondary school, the Franz-Josephs-Gymnasium, where he is a mediocre student.

1891   Kraus's mother dies on October 24.

1892–98   Kraus studies law, philosophy, and German literature at the University of Vienna but attends few lectures and does not take a degree.

1892–99   Kraus contributes book reviews, drama criticism, and satirical sketches to such periodicals and newspapers as *Die Gesellschaft* (Leipzig); *Magazin für Literatur* (Berlin); *Neue literarische Blätter* (Bremen); *Wiener Literatur-Zeitung, Wiener Rundschau, Liebelei, Die Wage,* and *Neue Freie Presse* (all Vienna).

1893   In January Kraus makes an unsuccessful debut as an actor at a theater in suburban Vienna.

1896   Kraus's first major work, *Die demolirte Literatur* (A Literature Demolished), appears in the *Wiener Rundschau* and as a pamphlet the following year. In the form of a witty obituary of the Café Griensteidl, the headquarters of Austria's men of letters, particularly the "Young Vienna" circle, the work lampoons many of Kraus's literary contemporaries.

1898   Kraus's pamphlet *Eine Krone für Zion* (A Crown for Zion) attacks political Zionism and its leader Theodor Herzl from the standpoint of an assimilated European Jew in sympathy with socialism.

1899   Kraus turns down an editorial position offered him by the *Neue Freie Presse,* a newspaper he is to attack for the rest of his life. ("There are two fine things in the world," he said: "to be part of the *Neue Freie Presse* or to despise it. I did not hesitate for one moment as to what my choice had to be.") Kraus founds his own aggressive periodical, *Die Fackel* (The Torch), the first issue of which appears on April 1. The journal soon becomes a Viennese institution. Initially it is published three times a month; after 1904 it appears at irregular intervals and with a fluctuating number of pages. Some fifty noted writers and artists contribute to the journal during its first decade. Setting out to "drain a swamp of clichés," Kraus announces as his motto not the usual "Was wir bringen" (What We Shall Do) but "Was wir umbringen" (What We Shall Undo). "May the *Fackel* provide light for a land in which — unlike the empire of Charles the Fifth — the sun never rises." On October 12 Kraus leaves the Jewish fold and becomes *konfessionslos* (religiously unaffiliated).

1900 Kraus's father dies on April 5. Kraus detaches himself from his family, from which he continues to receive a subvention, and goes to live in a bachelor apartment.

1901 Kraus mourns the death, on May 2, of Annie Kalmar, a young actress for whom he had great admiration and affection.

1902 Kraus's essay "Sittlichkeit und Kriminalität" (Morality and Criminal Justice) focuses on the glaring contrast between private and public morality and exposes the hypocrisy inherent in the administration of justice in Austria.

1903–07 The satirist conducts polemics with the German-Jewish essayist Maximilian Harden, his one-time mentor.

1908 The book edition of *Sittlichkeit und Kriminalität* appears with forty-one essays on the above theme drawn from the pages of the *Fackel*.

1909 Kraus's first collection of aphorisms appears under the title *Sprüche und Widersprüche* (Dicta and Contradictions).

1910 Kraus gives his first public reading from his writings and the works of others ("When I read, it is not acted literature; but what I write is written acting"). In his pamphlet *Heine und die Folgen* (Heine and the Consequences) Kraus attacks the German-Jewish writer for establishing the deleterious tradition of feuilletonistic journalism, a dangerous intermediary between art and life and a parasite on both ("To write a feuilleton is to curl locks on a bald head — but the public likes such curls better than a lion's mane of thought"; "Heinrich Heine so loosened the corsets of the German language that today every little salesman can fondle her breasts").

1911   Kraus carries on a polemic with the Berlin critic Alfred Kerr. On April 8 Kraus is secretly baptized and joins the Catholic Church. Starting with the *Fackel* no. 338 in December, Kraus writes the entire contents of the journal himself. ("I no longer have collaborators. I used to be envious of them. They repel those readers whom I want to lose myself.")

1912   With his address (and pamphlet) *Nestroy und die Nachwelt* (Nestroy and Posterity), Kraus revives interest in the nineteenth-century Viennese comic playwright and actor, whom he presents in his full stature as a great German dramatist and social satirist who, like Kraus himself, achieves his critical and satirical effects through an inspired use of language. Kraus's second collection of aphorisms, *Pro domo et mundo*, appears.

1913   Kraus meets Baroness Sidonie Nádherný and unsuccessfully proposes marriage to her on several occasions. Despite her engagement to an Italian and her brief marriage to an Austrian fellow aristocrat in 1920, Kraus's affectionate relationship with her continues (with a few periods of estrangement) for the rest of his life. ("To love, to be deceived, to be jealous — that's easy enough," he writes. "The other way is less comfortable: to be jealous, to be deceived, and to love!") For many years Kraus finds relaxation and inspiration at Sidonie's family estate at Janowitz (Janovice, south of Prague) and on trips taken with her.

1914   The outbreak of World War I inspires the outraged pacifist and humanitarian to produce his most powerful and characteristic work, beginning with the address "In dieser großen Zeit" (In These Great Times), delivered in Vienna on November 19.

1915   Kraus begins work on his mammoth drama *Die letzten Tage der Menschheit* (The Last Days of Mankind) and reads parts of it at numerous wartime recitals. The publisher Kurt Wolff founds the Verlag der Schriften von Karl Kraus for the dissemination of the satirist's work.

1916   The first collection of Kraus's poetry appears. By 1930 eight additional volumes are published under the collective title *Worte in Versen* (Words in Verse).

1918   Kraus publishes *Nachts* (At Night), his third and last collection
          of aphorisms.

1918–19   *Die letzten Tage der Menschheit* appears in special issues of the
          Fackel.

1919   A two-volume compilation of *Fackel* articles appears as *Weltge-
          richt* (Last Judgment).

1921   Kraus publishes *Literatur oder Man wird doch da sehn* (Litera-
          ture or We Shall See About That), a "magical operetta" sati-
          rizing literary expressionism in general and Franz Werfel, one of
          several apostles turned apostates, in particular. ("A poem is
          good until one knows by whom it is," he writes. And "Some-
          thing I cannot get over: that a whole line could be written by
          half a man. That a work could be built on the quicksand of a
          character.") Kraus breaks with Kurt Wolff, and his writings
          henceforth appear in the Verlag *Die Fackel*, Vienna.

1922   In the collection *Untergang der Welt durch schwarze Magie*
          (End of the World by Black Magic), Kraus concentrates on the
          pernicious press and its deleterious mixture of intellect and in-
          formation. At Christmastime he writes his one-act verse play
          Traumstück (Dream Play), a surrealistic dramatic fantasy.

1923   On March 7 Kraus officially (and publicly) leaves the Catholic
          Church in protest against the perceived collusion between the
          church and dubious artistic, journalistic, and commercial as-
          pects of the Salzburg Festival. He publishes *Wolkenkuckucks-
          heim* (Cloudcuckooland), a "fantastic verse play in three acts"
          based on Aristophanes' *The Birds*.

1924   Kraus publishes *Traumtheater* (Dream Theater), a one-act phil-
          osophical-dramatic vignette about the nature of theater, and
          dedicates it to the memory of Annie Kalmar.

1925   Kraus designates his recitals as "Theater der Dichtung" (Thea-
          ter of Poetry, or Literary Theater) and regularly puts on one-
          man performances of plays by Nestroy, operettas by Offenbach,
          and Shakespeare dramas in his adaptation. He polemicizes
          against the "Buda pest," Imre Békessy, Vienna's corrupt press
          czar, and the following year manages to "kick the crook out of
          Vienna." Several professors at the Sorbonne in Paris propose
          Kraus for the Nobel Prize in literature.

1927   Kraus concerns himself with the bloody police riot touched off
          by the burning of the Ministry of Justice in response to the ac-

quittal of killers in a clash of two Austrian paramilitary organizations.

1927–28   Kraus writes *Die Unüberwindlichen* (The Unconquerable), a four-act documentary drama about Johannes Schober, Vienna's chief of police (and sometime Austrian prime minister), and his collusion with Békessy.

1927–30   Polemics and litigation with Alfred Kerr.

1929   Kraus's collection *Literatur und Lüge* (Literature and Lies) appears.

1930–32   Kraus's adaptations of Offenbach and Shakespeare are broadcast by the Berlin and Vienna radio.

1931   Kraus publishes *Zeitstrophen,* a collection of topical stanzas that he interpolated in Offenbach operettas and Nestroy plays.

1932   Kraus attends an international pacifist congress in Amsterdam.

1933   Kraus works on *Die Dritte Walpurgisnacht* (The Third Walpurgis Night). He delivers the funeral oration for his friend, the architect Adolf Loos.

1933–35   Kraus's versions of Shakespeare are published as *Sonette* and *Dramen.*

1936   The last *Fackel* (no. 922) appears in February. On April 2 Kraus gives his seven hundredth (and last) public reading. He dies of heart failure on June 12.

1: When Vienna Saw Red:
Some Early Themes

Karl Kraus's early success and a degree of prominence are indicated by his inclusion in *Das geistige Wien* (Intellectual Vienna), a lexicon of writers and artists published in 1893, when Kraus was still a teenager. Its editor, Ludwig Eisenberg, described Kraus as being "active in the areas of drama criticism and satire." Such early notice was uncommon in an age that did not ordinarily accord recognition to young intellectuals in the arts. Thus the composer-conductor Robert Stolz felt he had to grow a beard at age twenty-five in order to preside authoritatively over the early perform- ances of Franz Lehár's operetta *The Merry Widow*. Eisenberg's compen- dium listed Kraus as the editor of a *Satirenanthologie*. Kraus had actually planned an annual anthology of satire together with Anton Lindner and had actively solicited contributions — in the pages of the journal *Die Ge- sellschaft* (January 1893) and elsewhere — but the project was stillborn, and not a single volume appeared, presumably owing to a dearth of suit- able material. A scant six years later, however, Kraus established himself as Vienna's preeminent satirist by founding his own journal, *Die Fackel* (The Torch). Robert Scheu's description of Vienna's reaction to the historic first issue of this periodical makes it plain that from April 1, 1899, on, Karl Kraus was a Viennese institution.

> One day, as far as the eye could see, everything was — red. Vienna has not seen such a day since. What murmuring, whispering, spine-tingling! In the streets, on the streetcars, in the City Park, everyone was reading a red magazine . . . Originally designed to flutter into the provinces in a few hundred copies, the little brochure had to be reprinted within a few days in tens of thousands of copies. And this whole issue, which was so chock- full of wit that, as the *Arbeiter-Zeitung* put it, one had to read it carefully in order not to miss any of those glittering pearls, had been written by one man. (4)

Scheu's rapturous description of a city that saw red in more ways than one appeared in 1909, on the occasion of the tenth anniversary of the *Fackel*, when Kraus still had some fifty writers and artists as collaborators. Scheu's essay was the first assessment of Kraus to appear in book form, and the fact that it was published by Jahoda and Siegel, the longtime printers of the *Fackel*, in addition to being printed in the journal itself (*Fackel*, 277– 78, March 31, 1909), indicates that Scheu was an insightful and friendly, though not uncritical, commentator. "Who could have suspected fifteen years ago," he writes, "in this cheerful-looking blond boyish head such a volcanic personality with its capability for suffering, this consuming flame, the insatiable destructive urge, the passionate intellectuality?" (3). Scheu points out that Kraus chose a dangerous adversary, the powerful daily *Neue Freie Presse*, and he defends Kraus against the canard that his opposition stemmed from his failure to gain an editorship on that daily. The "printed reign of terror" of the "red monster" (4) has affected many people, both those praised (or tolerated) and those censured. Young people in particular have come under the spell of the *Fackel*, which they often read on the topmost (and cheapest) seats of the Burgtheater, and they derive from this journal a sense of intellectual superiority but also the satisfaction of their crueler impulses. Scheu comments knowingly on Kraus's splendid isolation in his fight against the press and on two recent books by the satirist, *Sittlichkeit und Kriminalität* (1909 — a collection of forty-one *Fackel* articles) and *Sprüche und Widersprüche* (Dicta and Contradictions, 1909 — the first of Kraus's three collections of aphorisms), "Karl Kraus discovered those who happen to own printer's ink and pointed to the colossal power that they possess" (12). In appointing himself a watchdog over the press, Kraus is waging a real *Kulturkampf* and performing a valuable educational function. Proceeding from social criticism to cultural criticism and championing "the right of the nerves," Kraus is fighting for privacy and the inviolability of the personality. Being neither a patriarch nor a paterfamilias, Kraus has a penchant for isolation that has led him to negate politics and spurn democracy. Scheu wonders, however, whether the satirist can be fruitful if he detaches himself from his soil, nation, territory, or state. He effusively praises Kraus's aphorisms, which give free rein to his linguistic prowess and artistry. "Language to him is like a garden full of unexpected roses that burst forth from every arbor . . . In these aphorisms I discern a perfect free spirit who has shed all slags, an unexpected, noble finish of a tempestuous decade" (37–39). Somewhat paradoxically, Kraus manages to deride what is popular and achieve popularity thereby: "He is indispensable to the Viennese" (33).

That *Sittlichkeit und Kriminalität*, a seminal work of Kraus, is of undiminished topicality and relevance for our time as well is indicated by two relatively recent studies. In an article that forms part of his *Noten zur Literatur iii* (1965) T. W. Adorno (Theodor Wiesengrund-Adorno) states that Kraus's insights and formulations were often prophetic. Even though Kraus, an "antipsychological psychologist" (60), was an unsystematic thinker not really interested in philosophy, he "single-handedly discovered the principle of immanent criticism, which, according to Hegel, is the only fruitful one" (12). In his essays on criminal justice Kraus insists on one basic question:

To what extent does society guarantee an individual rights in its administration of justice? Does it perhaps pounce upon an individual in the name of threadbare ideals as soon as he tries to practice his freedom? Kraus, at any rate, was determined to keep the two spheres of private morality and legality separate. Adorno concerns himself with Kraus's Jewish heritage when he states that his morality was self-righteousness, the intellectualization of the heritage of persecuted and pleading Jews: "Kraus is the Shylock who gives his own heart's blood, whereas Shakespeare's Shylock would like to cut out the heart of the guarantor" (62). Kraus is seen as the great litigator who brings suit against the despoilers of language, using the pathos of truth to fight subjective reason. In a lighter vein, Adorno characterizes the court cases of Theodor Beer, accused of homosexual abuse of two boys, and of the madam Regine Riehl, whose trial included a demand that a prostitute prove total moral depravity to be licensed to practice her "shameful" profession, as Viennese Offenbachiads.

In a wide-ranging study entitled *Strafrecht und Satire im Werk von Karl Kraus* (Criminal Law and Satire in the Work of Karl Kraus, 1994) Reinhard Merkel points out that *Strafrecht* (criminal justice) was one of the major themes of the *Fackel* over a period of three decades. In five substantial, variously subdivided chapters Merkel deals with the politicosocial background of Austrian and German criminal law; the political aspects of *Die Fackel*; the influence of Franz von Liszt (a Liberal), Heinrich Lammasch (a Catholic Conservative), and Hugo Heinemann (a Social Democrat) on Kraus's thought; the philosophical theories on which Kraus's critique of criminal justice was based; and the concrete use made by Kraus of those theories over a long period of time. Merkel believes that the satirist's personal acquaintance (and even friendship) with these legal theorists entitle him to "intercede, as a layman and with the absoluteness characteristic of him, in the labyrinthine discussions relating to a reform of contemporary criminal law" (124). The author sees as the basis of Kraus's thought the primacy of justice and autonomy, derived from the classical age and the Enlightenment, in its clash with the social flaws of a falsely liberal system of criminal justice. Kraus, who repeatedly characterized himself as a "*Strafrechtler*," insisted on the formalization of the rationality of criminal law.

Among the most valuable feature of Merkel's occasionally rather technical study (produced as a doctoral dissertation at the University of Munich School of Law) is an "Excursus on Satire." One of its important insights is the age-old notion of satire complementing the law (Swift, Kant, Schiller), and Kraus's stance was indeed that of an abstractly moralistic satiric "*Complementär*" of the law. On the twentieth anniversary of the *Fackel*, Karl Kraus described his literary activity as a decades-long judgment, but after World War I his interest in the law was largely limited to his old foe, the press. Kraus made a distinction, one based on normative rather than semiotic or stylistic considerations, between satire (which Merkel defines as a "symbolic stabilization of the norm," 345) and polemics, with personal attacks deemed to belong to the latter. The author identifies two problematic cases of "punishing satire" (in Schiller's sense) in Kraus's writings that had devastating and even tragic effects — those of Alice Schalek, a war correspondent who became a lifelong subject of ridicule, and Georg Kulka, who committed suicide after Kraus had exposed his plagiarism.

Merkel provides ample evidence to refute Walter Benjamin's statement about Kraus that in his writings the satirist ignored sociological considerations. He also denies that Kraus spurned politics, for he believes that an apolitical stance determined by politics is a political act of wellcalculated public symbolism. However, the author is not uncritical of Kraus's attitudes and statements, some of which are deemed contradictory and based on misinformation or false premises.

In her wide-ranging, meticulously documented study *Geist und Geschlecht: Karl Kraus und die Erotik der Wiener Moderne* (Intellect and Sexuality: Karl Kraus and the Eroticism of Viennese Modernism, 1982), Nike Wagner places Kraus in the context of the sexual question and sexual emancipation in a city that boasted such thinkers on the subject as Sigmund Freud, Otto Weininger, Peter Altenberg, Arthur Schnitzler, and Gustav Klimt. In the early years of the *Fackel*, where the phrase *Geist und Geschlecht* first appeared in 1908, Kraus participated in the discussion about the special nature and culture of women and the role of eroticism and sexuality in society, as well as the nature of sexuality and its significance for the male mind. Concentrating on the period between 1899 and 1914, the author points out that concern with erotic and sexual subjects was only one aspect of Kraus's thought and creativity and that it was largely limited to the prewar period and expressed primarily in polemics and aphorisms. Later Kraus concerned himself mainly with political polemics, while his eroticism was integrated into his lyric poetry and linguistic theory.

In her first chapter, "Eros and Doxa," Wagner shows that in 1908 Kraus spoke about reflecting on "erotic life" rather than on "love" and that he sometimes used "erotic" and "sexual" interchangeably, indicating a physiology of love. In so doing he broke through the wall of silence in the bourgeois society of his day. At the upper end of the scale the beautiful aristocratic female was enthroned; at the bottom there was the prostitute, the woman whose only possession was her body. Turning away from the bourgeois world enabled Kraus to see its moral contradictions and conflicts. A wave of antirepressive impulses produced naturalism, the earliest and most aggressive current of burgeoning modernism, which was in opposition to the social indifference and intellectual smugness of the *Grün-*

derzeit, the period of rapid economic and industrial expansion. The desire for change and renewal manifested itself in literary and satirical periodicals as well as in social-reform movements and secessionist artistic associations. Kraus appreciated such apostles of muckraking as Ibsen, Zola, and Hauptmann, and his sympathies for German naturalism were expressed in his very first public reading of 1892 ("Im Reiche der Kothpoeten," In the Realm of the Muckraking Poets). Yet naturalism never got a foothold in Vienna — because of a social climate more conducive to compromise, the polyglot cultural atmosphere, and a general tendency to solve problems by means of a sort of benign neglect. By 1894 Kraus withdrew from the movement because it seemed to work with clichés rather than artistry, and he turned his attention to the Viennese brand of modernism, with its cult of beauty and decadence, its aestheticization of life, and its psychological introspection. "With the exception of the, if anything, thick-skinned Bahr," writes Wagner, "who liked to wear *lederhosen,* the 'Young Vienna' café clique consisted of men with highly sensitive nerves — neurasthenics, in the imprecise fashionable jargon of the times" (29). The author believes that, constitutionally, Kraus was a neurasthenic, as evidenced by his very delicate, nervous hands, his frail figure, and his curvature of the spine. Daily living was a problem for these writers, and so the hothouse atmosphere of the cafés offered them a refuge. Women were often identified with this life: alien, enigmatic, and threatening. Despite several aspects that might have attracted Kraus — nightly visits to cafés, aesthetic values, opposition to the bourgeois world — he dared to swim against the tide of modernism and early on rejected the decadent modernists and their coffeehouse culture by writing *Die demolirte Literatur* (about the razing of the Café Griensteidl). Kraus did not like artistic modernism any more than he did the literary kind, and he rejected the Young Vienna-*Sezession* dream of a blending of, or mediation between, art and life, its mixing of spheres in which ornamentation and atmosphere loomed large. While he agreed with some aspects of Young Vienna's critique and rejection of bourgeois society and with the idea of *Sezession,* his satiric impulses resisted the aestheticization of life and these writers' and artists' papering over of problems. Kraus wanted to retain an art of emotional directness as well as clear contrasts and polarities rather than seeing them intermingled and blurred with style and symbols. Furthermore, he was looking for true eroticism, which he discerned neither in the sensibilities and nervousness of the modernists nor in the unimaginative erudition of the philistines. Kraus longed for a pure, pleasurable abandonment and surrender, which he regarded as attributes of the feminine. He appreciated Klimt as an impressionistic artist but not as a painter of women or as a depicter of allegorical ideas (as in his university frescoes). Furthermore, Kraus suspected that the artists of the *Sezession* were in collusion with commercial interests. After his return from the United States the architect Adolf Loos preached an upright lifestyle based on reason, truthfulness, hygiene, and timesaving, and "Kraus and Loos became permanent antipodes of both the traditional philistine taste and the neosensual orientation of Vienna" (57).

Nike Wagner analyzes "Vor dem Springbrunnen" (Before the Fountain), in her view one of Kraus's biographically most important poems (dedicated to Sidonie Nádherný, Rome, 1915). Its last line, "O schöne Überflüssigkeit" (Oh beautiful overflow/superfluity), may be regarded as symbolizing the act of love, for Kraus uses the metaphor of the (male) fountain and the (female) basin. Beauty is equated with superfluity. There is a realm in which the beautiful can enjoy an uninhibited self-sufficiency free from censorship and achieve a true union of art and life without recourse to societal morality. Referring to Gustav Klimt, the author writes: "Seldom has a painter identified woman with excess, with flow and overflow, and rarely has one been able to depict the asocial, purposeless self-seeking nature of eros to such an extent. Was Kraus unaware of this secret kinship?" (64). Nike Wagner opines that Kraus's optical faculties and visual sensitivity were not as developed as his auditory faculties and that he was apparently unable to distinguish between the garden variety of *Jugendstil* (the Austro-German version of art nouveau) and Klimt's genius.

For the second chapter of her book Wagner uses Kraus's working title for his *Sittlichkeit und Kriminalität*: "Eros and Themis." In connection with Otto Weininger's *Sex and Character* she briefly discusses the work of early sexologists like Havelock Ellis, Iwan Bloch, Albert Moll, Magnus Hirschfeld, Eduard Fuchs, Richard von Krafft-Ebing, and Auguste Forel as well as such early feminist writers and activists as Franziska Reventlow, Bertha von Suttner, Helene Böhlau, Adelheid Popp, Rosa Mayreder, Ellen Key, and Grete Meisel-Hess. Rejecting "scientific" concerns with the mysteries of sexuality and opposing jurists and doctors, Kraus was bent on saving "true" eroticism, which meant that he had to work simultaneously against the modern tendencies to reveal and the traditional tendencies to conceal. The author points out that Kraus shared in the erotic dilemma of young men of that time: how to gratify their sexual drive within the limitations imposed by morality, society, or hygiene. This dilemma drove many of them into the arms of prostitutes. Kraus's relationship with the young actress Annie Kalmar, whom he met in 1900, is significant here. He defended her against exploitation by other men, and after her early death from tuberculosis in 1901 he presided over a veritable cult intended to fight the desecration of her memory. "He owed to her his gratitude to women — even those who deceived him with other men . . . [and his acceptance of] a component of female sexuality that excludes the idea of possession and elevates the phantom of the pollyannish woman, as ideally incorporated in an actress, to the quintessence of femininity" (102). In *Sittlichkeit und Kriminalität*, the author points out, Kraus comes to the paradoxical conclusion that public morality and the unimaginative rigorousness of the bourgeois ideal of morality, as typified in "sting" operations of the police, produce criminality. In this connection Wagner disputes Ernest Jones's assertion that Kraus was one of the bitterest adversaries of Freud. Before 1907 the two men admired each other, and at the time of *Sittlichkeit und Kriminalität* Kraus must be regarded as a Freudian, a fellow fighter against sexual hypocrisy. Freud's adherent Fritz Wittels published thirteen articles in the *Fackel* between February 1907 and May 1908, but on January 12, 1910 he mounted an attack on Kraus at a meeting of the Mittwochgesellschaft, the Vienna Psychoanalytic Society. Nike Wagner points out that Kraus never attacked Freud satirically, though in *Nachts* (At Night), a collection of his aphorisms issued in 1919, there are many capsule critiques of psychoanalysis and its practitioners.

In her third chapter, "Eros and Logos," the author concerns herself with shifting ideals of women and femininity. She considers it significant that instead of *Frau* the word *Weib*, with its natural, earthy, and mythic overtones, was used. "Promiscuity and woman-swapping were among the erotic customs in which Kraus participated," she writes (135) as she details his relationship with the actresses Irma Karczewska, Berthe Maria Denk, and Kate Parsenow, all of whom he shared with other men and helped professionally and financially. "In that 'erotomanic' *fin-de-siècle* period, literature and life, fiction and reality fructified one another in unusual fashion" (136). In contrast to such empathic admirers and apotheosizers of "pure," soulful, almost disembodied *femmes fragiles* as Hofmannsthal, Rilke, and Altenberg, there was a group of ideologues of virility that favored the type of demonic *femme fatale*. Nike Wagner places Kraus in that group, which also included Wedekind, Heinrich Mann (both of whom Kraus printed in the *Fackel*), Bahr, Dehmel, Sacher-Masoch, Strindberg, and Weininger. Kraus was fascinated by the literary figure of the hetaera. Yet the author is aware of Kraus's contradictory attitude in encompassing both types of men and women and becoming "a paradoxical combination of misogynist and troubadour: There are Kraus aphorisms that reflect the most cruel contempt for women and others that praise woman humbly and hymnically" (150). In her view, *Die Fackel* clearly participated in an antimodernist current with a masculine orientation that reflected a rejection of all symptoms regarded as feminine. Femininity, to be sure, was a very vague and general concept, including a softening of forms and values in literature, painting, language, and culture generally. Kraus agreed with Weininger on a concept of masculinity that seemed threatened by the female principle, and both men called for a maximal separation of the male and female realms. In particular, Kraus regarded the field of satire as an exclusively male preserve. In Wedekind he saw the incarnation of the masculine poet, the "new Shakespeare." Kraus, Wedekind, and Weininger thus share a theory of woman, though both Kraus and Wedekind rejected Weininger's proposed solution of the "female question," which called for a masculinization of the female gender. Kraus appreciated the figure of the sensual prostitute because he felt that a man derived an intellectual, spiritual, and artistic renewal from an ecstatic encounter with her. The author does not regard the "unity between misogyny and gynolatry" (163) discerned in Kraus as paradoxical, for he may have believed that a solidarity between an artist and a whore constituted a subversion of bourgeois morality. She even finds a broader application of this attitude: "In a way that has largely escaped attention, Kraus participated in the anarchistic tendency that around the turn of the century produced numerous murders of monarchs" (165).

In Kraus's aphorisms about women, some of which betray the influence of Weininger, she sees an "inimitable mixture of irony, wit, malice, and tomfoolery" (164), and she analyzes two of them in support of her dual hypothesis "that Kraus was a symbolic double of the pimp and that the alliance between a prostitute and her procurer is the only pattern of love that promises a solution of the problem of jealousy" (165). The author claims that in 1915 Kraus made an agreement with Sidonie Nádherný: She was to marry *standesgemäß* (in accordance with her class), and this marriage was to serve as a cover for their trysts based on true love. However, she "cheated" on him with numerous other lovers. Though Kraus never felt fully accepted by her because of his lower-class birth and his Jewishness, he continued to hope for a purer existence as the aristocratic *femme fatale* supplanted the ideal type of the actress. Sidonie's indecisiveness, ambiguity, and half-heartedness kept Kraus's passion for her and his paradisiac *buen retiro* at Janovice Castle alive.

Discussing such other women in Kraus's life as the sexually promiscuous Gina (called "Vagina") Kaus, Wagner agrees with the latter, who said that Kraus was more of a voyeur, a confidant, a discussant, and an adviser than a lover or sex partner, that he enjoyed picturing women in whom he was interested with other men. Wagner believes that Kraus was a *Ritter* and *Retter* (chivalrous savior or rescuer) of women from his youth on. Since he was convinced of the superhuman dimensions of female sexuality as an inevitable force of nature, the powerful satirist often assumed a humble position as a vulnerable, sensitive, patient, and long-suffering servant of women. Kraus's attitude toward men and their virility was ambiguous: certainly he had no use for the type of "macho man." While he did not agree with Weininger's glorification of platonic love, he felt that the eroticist and the artist were closely related. Another *compagnon de route* for Kraus in this sense was the exquisitely effeminate Peter Altenberg, who also rejected male sexuality and was uncommonly attuned to feminine feelings and a beauty that must not be violated by brutish male voluptuaries. In discussing Wedekind's Lulu, a favorite literary figure of Kraus, the author points out that Kraus accused Wedekind of siding with "macho man," the enemy of creativity, and of favoring the possessor (and ultimate destroyer) of woman over her admirer. Yet the sexual woman, such as Lulu, is attracted to sexual men like Jack the Ripper, and her very sexuality seems to demand that she be killed in a symbolic, sacral act. Kraus agreed with Weininger that the idea of (self-)destruction is part of the nature of prostitution and that death is extreme voluptuousness. Only the selfless, unfulfilled, self-abnegating, renunciatory love of an Alwa or Kraus could save a woman from the infernal consequences of her nature. In line with psychoanalytic interpretations of Margarete Mitscherlich-Nielsen and Manfred Schneider, Nike Wagner believes that Kraus compensated for his dependence on women by narcissistically heightening his own ego; his artistry had to help him overcome his anxieties, disappointments, and frustrations. To women he assigned the task of reflecting his projected image. Later Kraus toned down his (apparently) misogynistic remarks and came to appreciate female intellectuals as well as truly creative women like Else Lasker-Schüler.

Nike Wagner also discerns a relationship between Kraus's sexual theory and language. In her view, language has dual determinants: ethical-male and erotic-female. Its ethical dimension derives from a critique of societal, political, and intellectual conditions, especially as they are manifested through language. The erotic dimension is sufficient unto itself, autonomous by virtue of its poetic and semantic potential. The author states that what eluded Weininger and Altenberg — an acceptance of the male and female tendencies in themselves — may be observed in Kraus: action and reaction, domination and submission, calling and hearing, giving and receiving, impregnating and procreating. It is a kind of bisexuality realized metaphorically, on the plane of language, and many aphorisms work with the image of impregnating and procreating.

Toward the end of her study Nike Wagner gives the following stages of Kraus's "erotic biography:" "Erotic experiences, defense of eros in the societal sphere, reflection of erotic problems on the cultural level, integration of basic erotic concepts into art" (201). "Being clairvoyant and sensitive," she concludes, "Kraus is in conflict with the eroticism, styled by morality, of the philistine world and the eroticism, devoured by ornamentation, of the art world" (208). He proclaims intellectuality as the purest form of masculinity and sexuality as the purest form of femininity. *Geist* and *Ge-*

schlecht, then, are cerebral figures of passion, of a passionate thinking in language, and "Kraus is happy only when he is writing/loving" (213).

Karl Kraus repeatedly reprinted notices of his work in the *Fackel* — favorable ones usually without comment, unfavorable or controversial ones often as an occasion for a polemic. *Die Fackel* 321–22 (April 29, 1911) carries (on pages 55–56) a review of *Sittlichkeit und Kriminalität* by Adalbert Albrecht (South Easton, Massachusetts) that had appeared in the *Journal of the American Institute of Criminal Law and Criminology* in March 1911. This appreciative review was probably the first positive notice Kraus had received in the English-speaking world:

> Kraus is considered by many Germans to be the most eminent living satirist in the sense of Swift and Rabelais. This means, of course, without raising Mr. Kraus to the same plane as these two giants, that his wit is not displayed for wit's sake, but that there lies in it a criticism of society as sharp, caustic, and deadly as criticism can well be . . . In the above volume he takes his aim first of all at the sexual falsehood and sham saintliness of modern society and describes the desperate efforts made by the antiquated Austrian penal law to protect this falsehood and sham saintliness. Treating in detail several of the greatest Austrian sensational trials of recent years, he shows, above all, how much mischief a bureaucracy (particularly a police) that is too firmly convinced of its own importance may do by sniffling about among the private affairs of citizens and dragging people before the courts and into publicity . . . A glance at the regions of sexual perversity (especially homosexualism) and the state-taxed prostitution shows clearly that antiquated laws, framed without criminal-political or psycho-physiological insight, not only do not protect public morality, but even pave the way for "chantage," blackmail, etc. Even if some of Mr. Kraus's proposed reforms are too radical, if his large and genuine humanity imagines the difficult tasks of the legislators to be simpler than they are, yet his combative book has certainly done much good. Probably never, for instance, has the scandal-mongering press with its speculations on the basest sexual instincts been arraigned in such stinging terms and judged with such iron severity. For this reason alone this book should merit recognition. (56)

In the *Fackel* 389–90 (December 1913) Kraus reprinted the following appreciation by the Polish-born writer Amalie von Ende (from *Bookman*, New York, October 1913:

> At mention of the latter name [Karl Kraus] the average Vienna citizen is likely to exclaim: "Ach, der Fackel-Kraus!" — this being the limit of his knowledge. The resident with some pretence of being well informed may add: "Der Narr!" But to men and women of independent judgment Karl Kraus, the editor of *Die Fackel* (The Torch) is one of those sublime "fools" from the ranks of which come the champions, the heroes and the

martyrs of truth and justice. As such he is recognized by Germany's greatest writers, Dehmel, Thomas Mann, Frank Wedekind and others. Fifteen years ago his little magazine for the first time threw its glaring flashlight upon the Hydra of journalistic corruption in Vienna, and made the malefactors writhe and turn upon him in frantic wrath. It speaks for the moral fibre of the man that no amount of persecution has hindered him from continuing the fight, which he gradually directed against everything in the social structure and in municipal management that was a disgrace to modern humanity. The little one-man magazine has found its way upon all news-stands of Austria and Germany, and the author of it has made for himself a unique reputation as a writer and as a speaker. When a lecture by Kraus is announced in any German-speaking community, the auditorium is crowded, and when he appears upon the platform, his face illumined with the eyes of a seeker and the fearlessness of a fighter for an ideal, there is reverence in the silence which falls upon the audience. He has fervour reflected in the unforgettable head of Michelangelo's Moses. To meet the man whom the choicest minds among his contemporaries consider the greatest ethical force in German letters today, and one of his Viennese colleagues calls the conscience of our time, was a great temptation. But the man who is so much in the public eye is in his private life of an almost morbid reserve, and beyond a few intimate friends, is personally unknown to the wide circle of admirers which he has won through his books of aphorisms, keen-edged like blades of Damascene steel, yet coming down with the force of a sledgehammer, and essays, plain and unadorned in diction, yet radiant with the light of genius.

In his book *The Hapsburg Monarchy*, published shortly before World War I (1914) Henry Wickham Steed refers to the *Die Fackel* as

a biting, stinging, sometimes scurrilous periodical pamphlet called the *Fackel*, which keeps a vigilant eye upon the follies and failings of daily journalism and pillories them mercilessly. The editor, proprietor and staff of the *Fackel* consist of one and the same person, Karl Kraus, a Jewish writer of remarkable talent. The daily press maintains a conspiracy of silence in regard to his very existence but he has nevertheless a faithful public of readers who enjoy his mordant satire and find in his brilliant style relief from the pomposities and bathos of Austrian journalese . . . He is an Ishmael, courting and requiting the hostility of his contemporaries but rarely allowing their shortcomings to pass unpunished. In one respect his efforts deserve specially honourable mention. He has encouraged by precept and practice the tendency of modern writers of German to react against the artificial clumsiness of the language and to prove that German can be written harmoniously. (192.)

More recently, J. P. Stern has attempted to assess the uniqueness and significance of the *Fackel* by stating (1966, 73):

> To delimit the intellectual region in which to place this journal, one would have to think of Péguy minus his Catholicism and patriotism; of F. R. Leavis uninvolved in any educational "establishment" plus genius; of the satirist in G. B. Shaw as milk-and-water to Kraus's vitriol; of the early Wittgenstein's equation of "language" and "world"; of H. L. Mencken's criticism of the leisure class; of the poet Siegfried Sassoon's "scarlet major at the base"; of the early Evelyn Waugh's satirical typecasting — and all this would have to be translated into the peculiar medium of Vienna.

2:   "Heine and the Consequences"

In her study *Ein Angriff auf Heinrich Heine: Kritische Betrachtungen zu Karl Kraus* (An Attack on Heinrich Heine: Critical Reflections on Karl Kraus, 1971, originally a 1969 University of Munich dissertation), Mechthild Borries is aware that she is dealing with a precarious subject: "the artistic and moral defamation of one writer by another" (7). Believing that Kraus's reaction to the German-Jewish poet, or what he regards as his "consequences," can be the basis for historically significant criteria, she makes an attempt to "correct" Kraus's view of Heine in the light of modern scholarship and to take a detached, unimpassioned, skeptical view of Kraus's stature. After World War II, she writes, "the experience that the masses can be manipulated by a linguistic mode of expression distorted to the point of inhumanity suddenly gave Kraus's struggle, which was based on a critique of language, an aura of unassailable validity" (13). However, as Kraus's linguistic criteria were turned into absolutes, they rigidified into dogmas with a claim to infallibility. Sociologists like Max Horkheimer thought that Kraus's experience of language could form the basis of a critical social theory, yet Walter Benjamin had written that Kraus never understood sociological matters.

Borries points out that Heine was mentioned in the *Fackel* as early as 1899 and that in the succeeding years Kraus tended to defend him against defamation by the poet's frequently anti-Semitic detractors. A few years later, however, Kraus read his essay "Heine und die Folgen" (Heine and the Consequences) in Vienna on May 3, 1910, and published it as a pamphlet shortly thereafter. In her analysis of this critique Borries states that Kraus was convinced of Heine's transgression against his own principle that the form and the substance of a work of art should constitute a harmonious whole. Instead, according to Kraus, Heine invented superficially dazzling and effective forms that were an end in themselves; he was an artistic technician who used language irresponsibly and had insufficient reverence for tradition. Kraus rejected Heine's conflation of prose and poetry; as a poet he was too shallow, too prone to imitation, too exchangeable, too "singable." Above all, Kraus held Heine responsible for his pernicious consequences, regarding him as the father of a corrupt and corrupting feuilletonistic newspaper style and an ancestor of the horrendous linguistic decline, typified and fostered by the press of his own day, which he discerned fifty years after the poet's death. Borries quotes Franz Pfemfert as typical of the largely negative reactions to Kraus's essay: "The cultural critic Karl Kraus will wince when Adolf Bartels, the scourge of our time, applauds him for this deed. And Bartels will applaud him. Even if Kraus tried to put up ten Great Walls of China between himself and the Teutonic literary travesty, the Bartels clan will not stop hailing him as a fellow fighter" (*Demokrat*, Berlin 1911; reprinted in *Fackel*, 315–16, 50). According to the author, Kraus was unconcerned because he thought that Bartels and his Jew-baiting associates were not smart enough to understand his artistic intent. Bent on demonstrating Kraus's insufficient understanding of history and socioeconomic forces, Borries claims that

> Kraus prophesied the decline of mankind in apocalyptic visions of horror, but what was really imminent was the decline of the Austrian monarchy and bourgeois culture. Since Kraus stubbornly declined to take a historical point of view, he was blind to such connections. Thus he defined the melancholy and morbid mood of Viennese writers as the expression of a general and final cultural decline, as an irreparable intellectual and characterological loss of substance. Even though he was absolutely convinced that this process could not be halted, he resisted this morbid mood by invoking traditional ethical standards that needed to be preserved. (37)

As a response to anti-Semitic nationalism and a Teutonic cult of "Aryanism," Zionist organizations sprang up. Far from recognizing the historical necessity of such endeavors, Kraus, the assimilated Jew, thought he could refrain from being in either camp and was "so busy despising the liberalism infected by the 'Jewish spirit' that he underestimated the effectiveness of the inhumanity threatening from the anti-Semites" (39).

As a defender of Heine the author has to come to terms with Kraus's poetry and also compare the motivations of the two satirist-poets. In her view, Kraus's lyric poetry is based on obsolete ideas and linguistic models, and it is anachronistic because it reflects a private, subjective longing for childhood, nature, and an unchanging harmony, a timeless rapture expressed with preformed or ready-made poetic means. Heine and Kraus only *seem* to be united in their fight against prejudice, sham values, oppression, and inhumanity, for they start from entirely different premises: Kraus bases himself less on an analysis of the existing political power structure than on a suprahistorical notion of humanitarianism projected onto an eternal plane, whereas Heine believes that the present can be understood only by a politically aware artist. In Heine's view, freedom comes from politics as a representation of social reality, whereas Kraus believes that his rebellion against hypocrisy and intellectual stultification is incompatible with politics. Borries points out that Kraus's despair over mankind makes him take refuge in a notion of art where the world is still whole and intact: "Kraus defamed Heine as the author of the journalistic style he abhorred, but at the same time he capitulated before the misfortune of his time. Such an ahistorical despair of the present cannot vouchsafe any hope for the future; such hope is reserved for all those who, like Heine, believe that regenerative forces are always at work in history" (100). In contrast to Kraus, Heine is seen as someone who attempted to mediate between the traditional and the modern, allowing the present to illuminate the past and seeing a future in a new world dialectically reshaped on that basis. Borries views in that context what has been widely perceived as a misjudgment by Kraus in the 1930s: "Kraus's critique of Heine's character (or lack of it) and his dubious support of Dollfuß and Austrian clerico-fascism shows how private ethical honesty can be dialectically transformed into its inhumane opposite if this honesty is not based on political and societal reality. . . . Evidently Kraus was deceived by his belief that subjective moral integrity sufficed for diagnosing syndromes of his age" (92–93).

Commenting on Kraus's relationship with Stefan George and his circle, Borries points out that the satirist was originally very interested in this group and did not turn away from it until 1928. He felt akin to George in rejecting any connection between literature and commercialism, the very thing he criticized in Heine, but he was later repelled by George's aestheticism and totalitarianism. The author discerns the latter in Kraus, believing that his technique of quoting out of context is a totalitarian process. *Heine and the Consequences* is, in her view, a pastiche of falsifications, ready-made motifs, and aphorisms. "By virtue of his scorning of history Kraus seems predestined for the aphoristic form, because it need not concern itself with causes and experiences but sometimes presents results or diagnoses effects without elucidating the thought process behind it" (87). The author views Kraus's attacks on Heine as a linguistic product composed of aphoristic and other apodictic statements that are not really related to Heine's work as a whole. "One is left with a feeling of having experienced the prestidigitation of a verbal virtuoso that one marvels at — and forgets" (87).

Mechthild Borries has produced a thorough, well-documented study that is written with great energy (though perhaps also with a bit of frustration), but because she is bent on refuting and "correcting" Kraus "scientifically," her expostulations somehow seem pointless and even naive, for she reveals little appreciation of the special nature and characteristic techniques of Kraus's satire. An occasional statement affords both the author and the reader a disarming glimpse into the ultimate futility of her undertaking — for example, when she writes that "Kraus's admission of conscious partisanship and an absolute capriciousness is so radical that it cannot be objectivized in scientific terms. . . . Historical justice is replaced by the satirical principle of absolute judgments" (80–81). She is aware that Kraus's criteria are predominantly linguistic in nature and that this very selective reader seldom proceeds from a thorough knowledge of texts. His satire is usually fed by "occasions," and facts are often swamped by his brilliant style. In her view, Kraus never questions his own insights and never recognizes any inconsistency or injustice in his evaluations.

Two leading American Kraus scholars have also commented on *Heine and the Consequences*. What makes Leo A. Lensing's article "Heine's Body, Heine's Corpus: Sexuality and Jewish Identity in Karl Kraus's Literary Polemics Against Heinrich Heine" (1992) particularly notable is that Lensing connects Kraus's controversial essay not only with the two satirists' Jewishness but also with Kraus's relationship with Sigmund Freud. Lensing believes that critics have paid insufficient attention to the "genesis of Kraus's critical attitudes in the ideologically charged atmosphere of *fin-de-siècle* literary politics, or to the way in which issues of sexuality and Jewish identity . . . contributed to the rhetorical vehemence of this particular text" (95). The critic argues that *Heine und die Folgen* has never been analyzed from the viewpoint of the development of Kraus's critical persona, and he attempts to disprove Kraus's claim that he was not among those who came under Heine's spell in their youth by showing that Kraus was more influenced by Heine's satiric methods and style than he admitted. The early Kraus, Lensing writes, shared Heine's "deeply ambivalent attitude toward Judaism and . . . the predicament of the Jewish writer within German culture" (98). Lensing describes the two satirists as "sufferers who surmounted the fate of being German-Jewish poets" (110). Heine became a touchstone for Jewish writers in Germany, and in the very first issue of *Die Fackel* "Heine figures prominently in the oppositional program formulated by the young satirist" (99). In an effort to lay bare the unconscious motives behind the Austrian's increasingly negative appraisal of the German's literary legacy, Lensing points out that Kraus's essay "Um Heine" (1906) was still positive, as was his support of a Heine monument in the same year, the fiftieth anniversary of Heine's death. The image of Heine's grave and corpse figures prominently in Kraus's early writings, but Kraus soon began to identify the poet's corpse with his poetic corpus. Heine came to represent to Kraus all the evils of modern journalism. In *Heine and the Consequences* Kraus did not claim to have disposed of Heine but aimed only at demolishing the Heine cult and "feuilletonism." Lensing argues that Kraus's literary identity demanded the disintegration of Heine's and that he had a basic need to disassociate himself from Heine's Jewishness. Near the end of his essay, however, Lensing cites a Yiddish writer, Shlomo Bickel, who, in an attempt to mediate between Heine and Kraus in his book *Inzich un Arumzich* (Introspection and Circumspection, 1936), calls Kraus the heir of all Jewish prophets and points out that Heine's "consequences" also included the work of great Yiddish poets and thinkers.

Lensing notes that near the beginning of his essay Kraus uses a "metaphor of sexual pathology to describe these consequences: the feuilleton, which embellishes factual reporting with literary pretensions, is called '*die Franzosenkrankheit*' [the French disease — that is, syphilis]" (102), which Heine imported to Germany. His essay, then, reflects Kraus's opposition to any attempts to pathologize artistic creativity and his rejection of reductionistic interpretations and explanations. As he establishes a connection between the Heine essay and his relationship with psychoanalysis and its eminent practitioners Sigmund Freud and Fritz Wittels, Lensing marshals evidence that "a critical reappraisal of Freud and psychoanalytic theory belongs to the previously unrecognized motivations behind the essay" (105). In other words, the idea of Heine offered the satirist, among other things, an opportunity to attack Freud, who had named Heine as one of his favorite writers, for Kraus discerned a connection between Heineism and Freudianism. Kraus must have known that Freud had given Heine pride of place in his book *Jokes and Their Relation to the Unconscious* (where Heine and Kraus are even bracketed in one passage), but he was bound to regard those quotations as bad jokes and bad puns. Certain parts of this essay, which may be regarded as "a covert reckoning with Freud and his veneration of Heine" (106), contain a more or less subtle message to the psychoanalyst.

Jay F. Bodine's substantial article "Heinrich Heine, Karl Kraus and 'die Folgen': A Test Case of Literary Texts, Historical Reception and Receptive Aesthetics" (1984) is comparable to Lensing's only in that both far transcend the proximate occasion, Mechthild Borries's defense of Heine, which both critics find unsound. Equating "consequences" with "reception," Bodine argues that an appreciation (or adequate reading) of Kraus need not entail a condemnation of Heine and sets out to promote "a positive appreciation of both within the framework of both men's thinking as well as an actualization of both in our present aesthetic and socio-political contexts" (16). He points out that although for several decades since World War II the predominant school of Kraus criticism in the Western world has incorporated anticommunistic, conservative thinking and attempted to stereotype the satirist along ideological lines, Marxists have displayed a certain legitimate understanding of Kraus as well. "In order to understand Kraus," writes Bodine, "in order to approach the level of the ideal reader . . . one must respect Kraus's representation of his views and believe him when he avers that he must not contradict himself in essence. . . . By perceiving the full sense behind Kraus's intentional hindrances to the reader — the aphoristic over- and understatement, the paradoxes, complex syntax, and overloaded semantics — one will determine a specific '*Sehweise*' [paradigm, or way of looking at things] and many subtle differentiations. . . . Kraus's critique of language and literature is ultimately a verifica-

tion procedure; it checks for the truth content of an expression. . . . His
having pointed out the motivation and private interests in the discourse
and aesthetic enterprises of his world . . . is what makes Kraus even today
for many a Marxist and capitalist, for many a Liberal and Conservative,
Christian and Jew, a persona non grata" (22, 26).

In assessing the critical reaction to Kraus's Heine essay, Bodine says
that it is difficult to "fathom the implications and limits of Kraus's half-
truths and one-and-a-half truths'" (33) and that it is easy to miss Kraus's
unique "*Sehweise*." What Kraus finds objectionable in Heine is the lack of
"creative necessity" — that is, of the need to "express vital human, social
concerns along with the manipulation (rather than creativity) of language
to obtain an artificial, affected, or interested style" (32). Bodine's definition of the feuilleton is pertinent here: "The mellifluous, chatty but empty,
usually veiling yet often stinging style, one that induces the reader to go
hurriedly on rather than pondering the content (or lack of content) and
the implied (often shallow) system of values in each formulation" (32).
Briefly discussing Borries's study, Bodine finds it flawed in its perspective
and approach, faults that may be due to the author's inadequate knowledge of Kraus's work. He seems to agree with Lensing's view that far from
representing an artistic and moral defamation of the German-Jewish poet,
Kraus's polemic concerns itself with the deleterious consequences of a veritable Heine cult that prizes above all easily consumed entertainment for
philistines that masquerades as literature or art.

3: "Arch-Jew" or "Shining Exemplar of Jewish Self-Hatred"?

In an article entitled "Karl Kraus: 'Jüdischer Selbsthasser' oder 'Erzjude'?" (1975) I undertook the difficult task of sketching Kraus's relationship to Judaism, Jewry, and his own Jewishness. Both before and after its publication most critics of Kraus, no matter what their special subject, have felt impelled to comment on, or come to terms with, Kraus's convoluted Jewishness. When Kraus wrote that "According to the plebiscite, Vienna has 2,030,834 inhabitants — that is, 2,030,833 souls and me" (*Die Fackel* 315–16, January 26, 1911, 13) he was undoubtedly trying to indicate that he was unique, a *homo pro se* in the Erasmian sense, and unwilling to be counted as a member of *any* group, be it religious, ethnic, or social. That was the year in which Kraus, who had left the Jewish fold in 1899 and become *konfessionslos* (religiously unaffiliated), was secretly baptized and joined the Catholic Church, which he left again in 1923, this time publicly, because of its less than admirable attitude during the war and its perceived collusion with artistically and commercially dubious interests.

An "*Erzjude*" is what Martin Buber called himself, and in his appreciative study of the satirist (1921) Berthold Viertel writes: "There is no doubt: Karl Kraus is an arch-Jew" (56). Viertel is aware that Kraus the arch-Jew may seem like a heretic, a betrayer of the material interests and international success of his fellow Jews, but quoting Buber on the combative genius of the prophets and teachers of Israel, he views Kraus as "the timeless arch-Jew against a latter-day Korah's band" (89). With a reference to Otto Weininger, and foreshadowing Theodor Lessing, Viertel argues that "Kraus was able to alleviate self-hatred by fairly distributing it over all children of his time, Jews and non-Jews" (60). As he rejects the values and successes of his Jewish contemporaries, "a man like Karl Kraus is not yet the direct, believing, metaphysical Jew . . . not yet the great righteous man, the fulfiller. Satire is not yet truth or humaneness, art and intellect are not yet religion" (61). To Viertel, the satirist's philosophy of language is a religious ritual, and he refers to the Hasidic attitude toward language: words contain worlds, souls, and godliness. In his afterword, in which he comments on Kraus's wartime writings, Viertel writes: "Aware of his Jewish origin, his orientation is anti-Jewish; guarding German cultural values, he is anti-German; with his soul rooted in the Austrian landscape he is the representative anti-Austriacus" (89). Viertel concludes his picture of an evolving but incomplete Kraus by still tying him to the Jewish community and tradition. "In the sophistication of his European arts he is ineffably poorer in messianic attitude than those impoverished Yiddish-speaking Jews who were able to realize their dream of Hasidism, the most soulful Judaism. But the more distant the answer must remain, the more inexorable and more urgent is the necessity of his questions!" (94)

In his 1920 book Leopold Liegler, who praised Kraus for overcoming his own Jewishness, at least what he regarded as its inferior aspects ("In all periods individual Jews have managed to neutralize the Semitic poison within themselves, which has been so harmful to the Western spirit, and to develop voluntarily a free, ethical humanitarianism beyond a strictly circumscribed ethnicity" [47]), polemicizes against Viertel's description of Kraus as an "arch-Jew." If Kraus is an arch-Jew, and thus an oriental figure, why is he concerned with saving European, Western civilization? At any rate, Liegler denies that Kraus still feels as a Jew. If Kraus were an arch-Jew, he would have to be another Buber trying to lift the idea of Judaism from the mud. But, like Otto Weininger, he put the torch to Judaism, and he is thus closer to Weininger. Liegler believes Viertel 's attempt to view Kraus's linguistic phenomenon as specifically Jewish to be a failure. He describes Kraus's break with Judaism as "the most momentous decision of his life" (152). His detachment from the Jewish fold gave him great freedom and autonomy.

On the other extreme of the spectrum is the German-Jewish philosopher Theodor Lessing, an early victim of the Nazis even though he was living in Czechoslovakia, who presented Kraus as a "shining exemplar of Jewish self-hatred" in his classic study *Der jüdische Selbsthaß* (1930). Pointing out that Kraus embodies the self-hatred of ethically motivated persons in a particularly tragic form, he writes:

> Here a fine, pure natural force has been wasted on a basically fruitless work of which after two or three generations nothing can remain but a mountain of printed paper. This Hercules cannot be reproached with cleaning out the Augean stables of his time but with . . . lighting his torches merely to show the filth on the paths of small people. . . . He is the most serious among today's Jew-haters. . . . All the great foes of the Jews in Germany — Lagarde or Treitschke, Dühring or Chamberlain — hated because of an ecumenical will to power. They did not want to concede intellectual leadership to the Jews because they themselves desired only to be the intellectual leaders of the world. (43)

It should be noted that while Lessing groups Kraus with the exemplary monomaniacs and self-haters, he mentions him by name only once and does not include him among the six men whose biographies he presents, even though Kraus's relationship to two of these — Otto Weininger and

Maximilian Harden — would have given Lessing an opportunity to draw interesting comparisons and buttress his main thesis.

"Arch-Jew" or "Shining Exemplar of Jewish Self-Hatred"? In Kraus's life and work there is ample evidence for each of these extreme characterizations, and for many in between. Hans Weigel (1968) calls Kraus "an Old Testament prophet who pours cataracts of wrath over his people" (61), and to Frank Field (1967), "the fact that Kraus was Jewish is of vital importance in understanding the particular extremism, the *Angst*, the sense of the apocalyptic which pervades his work" (x). Field believes that Kraus was and remained intensely Jewish, and he places him in the tradition of the masochistic anti-Semitism that was a characteristic feature of many German and Austrian Jews. Like Gustav Mahler, Field argues, Kraus was full of contradictions, "a Jew who had renounced Judaism and yet, for that very reason, felt even more acutely Jewish than before" (8). His view that Kraus "attacked his own people in the same way that the prophets of the Old Testament had castigated the unworthiness of the Israelites for the trust which God had placed in them" (68) is supported by one of Kraus's own statements: "I believe I can say about myself that I go along with the development of Judaism up to the Exodus, but that I don't participate in the dance around the Golden Calf and, from that point on, share only in those characteristics which were also found in the defenders of God and in the avengers of a people gone astray" (*Fackel* 386, October 24, 1913). "Kraus's 'anti-Semitism,'" writes Erich Heller, "in all its problem-ridden complexity, was a new form of the prophet's indignation at the worshippers of the Golden Calf" (1973, 37). Sol Liptzin, by contrast, regards Kraus's "failure as a human being" as a "result of his estrangement from his Jewish roots and his inability to grow roots in non-Jewish soil. . . . His masochistic anti-Semitism led him to vilify Heine, to applaud Otto Weininger, to attack the defenders of Dreyfus, and to refuse to speak out against Hitler in 1933" (1972, 15, 14). Paul Neumarkt, on the other hand, agrees with Viertel and Field when he writes: "Kraus remained thoroughly committed to the prophetic tradition of the Old Testament. . . . The moralist assumes the stance of Jeremiah and Isaiah. His call for social justice and compassion with our fellow men has the ring of the Old Testament" (1973, 39, 41). Neumarkt also points, somewhat extravagantly, to an unintended effect of some of Kraus's writings: "His works were not included in the *auto da fé* of 1933. He, in an ironical twist of fate, became Hitler's 'decent' Jew, whose writings were spared because he had exposed the international conspiracy of world Jewish finance" (39). In his book *Wer ist Jude? Ein Selbstgespräch* (Who is a Jew? A Conversation with Myself, 1964) William Siegmund Schlamm calls the satirist "the most Jewish intellect among the great Germans" and continues: "That Karl Kraus was an anti-

Semite was probably the most inevitable of the many misinterpretations to which Karl Kraus exposed himself. In their immoderation Jewish intellectuals did not stop at the phenomenon of the Jew; on the contrary, this made them particularly shrill" (32, 33). In an essay published in a collection entitled *Über Ruhestörer* (About Disturbers of the Peace, 1973) the critic Marcel Reich-Ranicki seems to agree with Theodor Lessing when he writes: "The always dogged and at times tragicomic fight that Karl Kraus all his life waged against the Austrian press turns out, upon closer inspection, to be his secret struggle against the Jewish elements in himself, or what he regarded as such. This struggle was nothing but a painful and highly dramatic coming to terms with himself" (25). Max Brod saw Kraus as an altogether destructive force when he wrote in a letter to Richard Dehmel dated December 1913: "I am disgusted and repelled by such types of my race [*sic*] as Karl Kraus because I regard them as the embodiment of everything that has abased my people for thousands of years" (in *Max Brod-Bibliographie*, edited by W. Kayser and H. Gronemayer, 1972, 29). Brod clearly regarded Kraus as the very antipode of those who, like Martin Buber, were striving to translate the messianic and prophetic elements of the Jewish soul into action.

In "*Incognito ergo sum*: Zur jüdischen Frage bei Karl Kraus" (1987) Nike Wagner deals with the paradox of the assimilated Jew. As the satirist's Jewish heritage she sees "his biblical pathos, his stance of an advocate, his ethical rigorism, his relationship to the 'word,' and his Old Testament ability to curse" (387). It is the author's thesis that Kraus was really unable or unwilling to address what has been called the Jewish Question and that only outside pressure, such as the myriad manifestations of anti-Semitism, forced him to come out of his hiding place and take a stand. Wagner quotes a passage from Kraus's article "Warum die Fackel nicht erscheint," written in January and February 1934 (published in *Fackel* 890–905, July 1934, 36), in which Kraus denies that his critique of Judaism and Jewry contains even a trace of self-hatred and that he greatly appreciates the natural strength (or force) of a Judaism (*Judentum*, which can refer to the religion, the religious community, or Jews in general) that cannot be compromised and is not swayed by "*Rasse und Kasse . . . Klasse, Gasse und Masse . . . Hasse*" (race and finances, class, "the street" and the mob, hatred), and since Kraus did not define *Judentum* ethnically, nationally, socially, or spiritually, she asks what he might have meant. Is it religion? The Jewish *Geist* (mind/intellect/spirit)? In any case, Kraus seems to have accepted and used all the current anti-Semitic clichés about money changers in the temple, capitalistic speculators, rootlessness, and the corrosiveness of the Jewish mind — possibly internalizing the picture that others have of Jews. "It is not Kraus," she writes, "who is perverse when he manifests anti-Semitism, but his situation of advanced assimilation and Jew-hatred; seen in this light, his anti-Semitism is a sign of mental health, or at least a saving of his own self" (396). Through the externalization and excoriation of "bad" Jews like Moriz Benedikt, the author argues, he abreacted various psychological complexes and kept "good" Jews positive and inviolate. In her view, Kraus concentrated his fire on what he perceived to be corrupting Jewish influences on his beloved German language, the nefarious discourse of journalists and stock-exchange speculators to which terms like *Jargon*, *Jüdeln*, and *Mauscheln* have been applied by such scholars as Sander Gilman who have attempted to analyze what has been perceived as the "corrupted" language of the Jews.

The French critic Jacques Le Rider deals with Kraus's Jewish identity in his study *Modernité Viennoise et crises de l'identité* (1990. American edition: *Modernity and Crises of Identity: Culture and Society in Fin-de-Siècle Vienna*, 1993). Taking it for granted that Kraus was a self-hating Jew, Le Rider describes Kraus's early diatribe *A Crown for Zion*, with its extreme assimilationism and incomprehension of historical and contemporaneous anti-Semitism, as shortsighted and unreadable. He points out that in Kraus's view the Jews had an important share in many of the cultural phenomena that the satirist excoriated: liberalism, the corruption of the press and the economy, a bourgeois morality that had strayed too far from nature, pseudoscholarship, the excrescences of psychoanalysis, and a "progress" that was in actuality rushing toward the last days of mankind. In what might be called his Judaeophobia, Kraus used racist language (for example, calling the Jews a "*Rasse*" — a nefarious practice that has persisted to this day). In his discussion of Kraus's relationship with Otto Weininger, Houston Stewart Chamberlain (whom he repeatedly printed in *Die Fackel*), and Jörg Lanz von Liebenfels (a curious pseudoscholar and anti-Semite who hailed Kraus as the savior and benefactor of the *Ariogermanentum*, the Aryan Germanic spirit), the author expresses surprise at the fact that the last-named enjoyed such esteem in fin-de-siècle Vienna, and he feels this shows that in the early part of this century anti-Semitism was a sort of language game that was attempted and more or less zestfully played by certain leading intellectuals.

Le Rider regards Kraus's essay on Heine and his consequences as one of the satirist's most unfair writings and a document of his Jewish self-hatred. In his view, Kraus could not bear to be compared to his German-Jewish ancestor or predecessor and thus distanced himself from him as he lashed out at this Doppelgänger and declared his language to be corrupt. Such fears on the satirist's part that slumber in the soul of every assimilated Jew are reminiscent of Theodor Herzl's term *Mauschel* for servile, inauthentic Jews who opposed his Zionist idea. Le Rider likens such writings to Richard

Wagner's invectives against Felix Mendelssohn in his tract *Das Judentum in der Musik* and argues that in a certain sense Kraus was a Wagnerian Jew.

In his novel *Badenheim 1939* (Boston: David R. Godine, 1980) the Romanian-born Israeli storyteller Aharon Appelfeld has one of his characters, Professor Fussholdt, make this striking statement: "If anyone deserved the title of a great Jew . . . it was Karl Kraus: he had revived satire . . . the only art form appropriate to our lives" (62). When I met the author several years ago, I asked him whether this statement was just a fictional conceit, and he assured me that it represented his personal conviction. Appelfeld, who was born in the Bukovina in 1932, is the youngest and presumably the last of the Jewish writers of that region (part of the Austro-Hungarian Empire until 1918), who regarded Kraus as their "rebbe" (rabbi). Most of these poets — Alfred Margul-Sperber, Rose Ausländer, Alfred Kittner, Immanuel Weissglass, and many others — wrote in German and decisively shaped the culture of the city of Czernowitz (later Cernauti and presently known as Chernovtsy). In her book on the most famous of these poets, *Paul Celan: Holograms of Darkness* (1991), Amy Colin, herself Romanian-born, writes: "Karl Kraus, along with Stefan George, provided Bukovina poets with linguistic theories which justified and reinforced their attachment to tradition" (19). She also quotes from an essay by Rose Ausländer that comments on Kraus's "magical fascination" for these Czernowitz-based poets, for whom German remained the mother tongue and language of culture until the end of World War II. "Through the influence of so many languages, and especially Yiddish (over one-third of the population was Jewish)," Ausländer writes, "an idiom emerged from which the cultured and linguistically fastidious — taking their cue from Vienna — distanced themselves. . . . Our capital was Vienna, not Bucharest. Oh, how the Viennese scorned that 'Buko-Viennese' German! We suffered from a sense of inferiority due to our language. To this complex, I believe, Karl Kraus owes the admiration (bordering on adoration) of his followers. The great stylist and satirist was more than anything our language teacher. Every sentence in *Die Fackel* was thoroughly discussed down to the last detail of its language and thought" (20, translated by J. Sheldon). A more detailed discussion of Kraus's influence on these Jewish writers may be found in Amy Colin's article "Karl Kraus und die Bukowina" (1990).

The most comprehensive and most searching treatment of the subject is contained in *The Paper Ghetto: Karl Kraus and Anti-Semitism* by the British scholar John Theobald (1996). The title of this study derives from Kraus's own description of assimilated Viennese Jews and their reliance on a press that inadequately shielded them from a broader reality. "It may also, with some irony," writes Theobald, "be possible to see *Die Fackel* as Kraus's own private paper ghetto, intended, but ultimately failing, to shield him from racism" (16). The author's subtitle seems to be a misnomer — until he makes his basic points that Kraus's work "is deeply penetrated by the effect on him of the anti-Semitism of the society and period in which he lived" (13) and that the satirist's "identity as an Austrian Jew was determined by a deep fear of anti-Semitism" (81). Displaying a becoming awareness that he is painting a paradoxical picture as well as a lively sense of the controversial nature of his subject, Theobald quotes from an undated letter from Gershom Scholem to Sigurd Paul Scheichl: "In dealing with the question of Kraus and his relationship to Jewish issues [*zum Judentum*], one can in my estimation *only* commit errors, something for which Kraus himself made sure there was plenty of scope" (13–14).

The author views his book as "a narrative of the personal contortions undergone by one creative individual in his struggle to transcend racial [*sic*] discrimination, and of his controversial life-long campaign against the linguistic and cultural cause of barbarism" (13). While Theobald does refer to Theodor Lessing's study of Jewish self-hatred, he does not view Kraus in this light; rather, he operates with the infelicitous locution "the Jewish," which derives from Otto Weininger. Curiously enough, he says nothing about the motivations and implications of Kraus's conversion to Catholicism, but keeps referring to "Kraus, the Jew." As he sketches the historical, political, and social background of Viennese Jewry, the author presents a typology of Jewish identities, attitudes, and reactions to persecutions by giving capsule biographies of Freud, Schnitzler, Herzl, Buber, Weininger, and Viktor Adler. "Excluded from any easy acceptance in the majority culture by the growth of anti-Semitism," he writes, "[the Jews] were drawn either to the collective solution offered by socialism or to the individual solution of distancing themselves from all that was 'Jewish' to the extent of adopting aspects of anti-Semitic propaganda. While Kraus's earlier instincts took him towards the former, his persona as independent satirist and critic increasingly drew him to the latter" (77). Kraus's solution (if it was one) was to react as a Jew against Jews who seemed to perpetuate anti-Semitic stereotypes, to attempt to be the exact opposite of the anti-Semitic notion of the Jews, to dissociate himself from Jewish liberalism, and to embrace German culture wholeheartedly. "It was only on rare occasions," Theobald writes, "that his definition of what was Jewish penetrated beyond his observation of what was a small minority of Jews" (198). The idea of "the Jewish" occupied a pivotal place in Kraus's cultural criticism, and he regarded the Jews, who dominated the press, as a central cause of the cultural decline that he discerned and opposed, though he also excoriated the anti-Semitic press.

According to Theobald, Kraus viewed World War I as "the catastrophic consequence of an ever-expanding materialism which, aided by capitalism, technology, the press and the military, was destroying nature, humanity, and culture to the profit of a ruthless minority" (112); and the author describes *The Last Days of Mankind* as "a dramatized chronicle of the victory of 'Jewish' forces over positive forces of German culture (113). By the unexorcised "ghosts" of the postwar Austrian Republic Kraus meant those Jewish forces, and for over a decade "we see Kraus, the Jew, struggling to fit a preformed cultural analysis which made Jews responsible for cultural decay, into a situation in which Jews were . . . clearly decreasingly influential and increasingly the victims of violent and irrational prejudice" (170). In the author's view, Kraus continued to espouse a conservative anti-Semitism that was directed against those who continued to perform a dance around the "golden calf" of materialism and served to corrupt language, an anti-Semitism to which a Jew could subscribe without contradiction and fear of being accused of self-hatred.

In *The Third Walpurgis Night* ("essentially a comic work, although comedy was never blacker," 191) and other writings of the time, Theobald discerns "the desperate moves of a Jew, grasping at what he saw to be the last straw of hope that Austria might remain free from Hitler's anti-Semitism" (181). With "cultural guerilla tactics" (183) Karl Kraus simultaneously attacked the Social Democrats, the Jews, and the Nazis; and although the author describes Kraus's special kind of anti-Semitism as relatively benign, he feels that the satirist "must be criticized for the anti-Semitic aspect of his polemic and censured for sustaining it into the Nazi era while fully conscious of what Nazi barbarism meant" (198).

Not the least virtues of Theobald's cogently argued book are his clear conclusions after each chapter and his copious quotations from Kraus, both in the original and in his serviceable English translation, which add up to a somewhat disturbing Kraus sampler of sorts.

4: Two Support Systems: The Brenner Circle and the Second Viennese School

Mutual respect bound Kraus, who was neither a philosophical nor a religious thinker, to the periodical *Der Brenner*, published in Innsbruck and often favorably mentioned in *Die Fackel*, to its longtime editor Ludwig von Ficker, the poet Georg Trakl, and the philosophers and scholars Theodor Haecker, Carl Dallago, Karl Borromäus Heinrich, and Ferdinand Ebner — Christian thinkers who appreciated Kraus's eschatological orientation. An evening with Karl Kraus sponsored by *Der Brenner* in Munich on March 19, 1913, was unfavorably reviewed by a local weekly, *Zeit im Bild*, which claimed that Kraus was virtually unknown and ineffective outside Vienna. To refute this negative view, Ludwig von Ficker organized an *Umfrage* (what the French call an *enquête*, a survey or poll) about Kraus, which elicited thirty statements by such renowned writers, academicians, and artists as Else Lasker-Schüler, Richard Dehmel, Frank Wedekind, Thomas Mann, Adolf Loos, Georg Trakl, Peter Altenberg, Hermann Broch, Franz Werfel, Oskar Kokoschka, Arnold Schönberg, and Stefan Zweig. These statements, which were intended to counteract the *Totschweigetaktik*, or silent treatment, accorded Kraus by most of the press, appeared in 1913 in numbers 18, 19, and 20 of volume 3 of *Der Brenner*, and they were republished during the war as a booklet edited by Ficker (*Rundfrage über Karl Kraus*, 1917). In his preface the editor says that "the true and only world war that the intellect may still fight enthusiastically continues to be waged and decided by one individual in the red issues of *Die Fackel*" (5).

Among the statements appearing in the collection, Frank Wedekind hails Kraus as "Austria's bravest fighter" (14), and Thomas Mann, after attending a Kraus reading, stresses the passionate involvement, the satiric pathos, and the spiritual quality of this "anti-journalist" (15), Adolf Loos sees Kraus standing at the threshold of a new age and pointing the way for a mankind that has strayed far from God and nature; "some day this mankind will owe its life to Karl Kraus" (17). Arnold Schönberg recalls the dedication of his *Harmonielehre* to the satirist: "I have perhaps learned more from you than one should if one wants to remain independent" (21). Georg Trakl apostrophizes Kraus in a few lines of poetry:

White high priest of truth.
Crystal voice in which God's icy breath dwells.
Angry magician
Under whose black cloak clangs the blue armor of the warrior. (17)

Stefan Zweig's pained statement deserves to be reprinted here in its entirety, for it is typical of the reactions of numerous anti-Krausians or non-Krausians. Even the uncharacteristically guarded, labored, and stiff style of the author indicates that Zweig was performing a task distasteful to him:

> I believe that those who have an inwardly or outwardly aggressive attitude toward Karl Kraus and strongly negate him by their words or their silence have a more valuable relationship to him than the crowds that fill his readings and pass the *Fackel* from hand to hand. The former at least direct the resistance against the core of his personality, whereas the latter hide their petty, impotent, unproductive venom behind his explosive hatred — envious marauders on his battlefields. These followers who amuse themselves past him, as it were, greedily absorbing a mockery of productive personalities that he hardly has a right to practice, and they have no right whatever — for this effect of his nature I have the utmost possible antipathy, and he is to blame for this audience, because far from despising it as a misunderstanding of his inner intention or disparaging it as a side effect, he keeps seeking it out and presents it as a confirmation, something that would only speak against him. Cheers in Bielitz, large editions of his writings, and full lecture halls are the arguments of an Otto Ernst but not those of a writer who aims at the intrinsic forms of inner value that are not so painfully distinct and who desires the rarest and most precious kind of fame: the lonely kind, which has not yet been given voice in real life and is only a force fermenting beneath the surface. Thus my strongest positive impression of Karl Kraus was merely a relative one — when I chanced to compare the first volume of the *Fackel* with recent issues. To be sure, there has been no change in his personality, for which I can have no sympathy, but the level of his attacks has changed, and so has his artistic intensity, which I esteem to the extent possible to my nature, which values manifestations of life that serve to a considerable degree to arouse enthusiasm and enhance joy — which means that I can appreciate these only with my artistic intellect, but not with what is all-important to me, my innermost nature. (38–39)

In his *Nachwort des Herausgebers* (editor's afterword) Ludwig von Ficker comments on Zweig's contribution and defends Kraus against Zweig's assertion, or accusation, that Kraus pandered to his adherents in cheap fashion and cared mostly about full houses and big sales of his books.

In a collection of his essays and addresses (1910–66) that appeared in the year of his death, 1967, Ficker includes several essays on Karl Kraus. The title, *Denkzettel und Danksagungen*, might be rendered as "Memorabilia and Thanksgiving," though the word *Denkzettel* also indicates a warning. In a rhapsodic essay that first appeared under the pseudonym Fortunat in volume 1, number 2 of *Der Brenner* (June 15, 1910), Ficker displays a becoming awareness of the fact that Kraus is not easy to classify, but he does characterize him as a solid, almost pedantically industrious smasher of facades who managed to expose a world full of empty horrors that has been hiding behind the decorative plaster of an age that traditionally believes in progress. However, Kraus cannot be written off as a nihilistic destroyer, for he has proved strong and creative enough to fashion a new way of viewing the world. His frequently paradoxical irony is not mere playfulness but is based on the demonism of an almost ascetic intellectual-spiritual intoxication.

In a review of a reading by Kraus under the auspices of the *Brenner* (Innsbruck, January 4, 1912, published in *Der Brenner* on January 15) Ficker states that the age refuses to accept the satiric portrayer of its lack of culture as a thinker or an artist. The graphic wit of a Hogarth or Goya may be appreciated, but the verbal wit of Karl Kraus is not. Ficker sounds a warning about the satirist's success as a reciter: This appreciation is too facile, based on too ready an understanding of what is presented by a "humorist," and in such a setting there is nothing to indicate that behind this instant success there is "the serious and lonely cultural peak of 13 volumes of *Die Fackel*" (19).

In 1913 the Brenner publishing house issued *Studien über Karl Kraus*, a booklet containing appreciative essays by Carl Dallago ("Karl Kraus the Man"), Ludwig von Ficker ("Notes on a Reading by Karl Kraus" — his first presentation in Innsbruck, January 1912), and Karl Borromäus Heinrich ("Karl Kraus as an Educator," inspired by his second reading in Innsbruck a year later). These essays had appeared in *Der Brenner* earlier, and their publication in book form was intended to "bring light and assurance into the chaos of hatred and veneration that still surround . . . the figure of the greatest and only satirist of our day" (3).

In his book *Der Brenner und die Fackel* (1976) Gerald Stieg points out that for a quarter of a century the journal *Der Brenner* was patterned after *Die Fackel*, and he draws attention to the dual sense of the title: the name of an important mountain pass and "The Burner." In the prewar period the two journals shared a number of satiric objects, but after World War I their aims diverged. Ludwig von Ficker increasingly devoted his journal to the problems and aims of Christianity in a devastated intellectual Europe, and a distancing began. For Ficker and his associates, especially Ferdinand Ebner and Theodor Haecker, Kraus now was the last representative of an idealism that equated ethics with aesthetics. In the postwar period Ficker's personal admiration for Kraus conflicted with his newly won religious position. He tried to bridge this by regarding Kraus as a representative of the Old Testament and himself, his circle, and his journal as the bearers of the New Testament. Ficker became more interested in Kraus's poetry and de-emphasized the more questionable destructive role of the *Fackel*. In his analysis of Kraus's influence on *Der Brenner*, a journal that the satirist repeatedly extolled, Stieg draws on Ficker's letters and notes. Among the most useful features of his study are lists of meetings between Ficker and Kraus from 1912 to 1934 and Kraus readings sponsored by *Der Brenner*, mostly in Innsbruck from January 1911 to February 1920.

When Arnold Schönberg published his *Harmonielehre* in late 1911, he dedicated his book to the memory of the recently deceased Gustav Mahler, but the composer sent a copy to Karl Kraus, to whom it was presumably a book with at least seven seals: "To Karl Kraus, from whom I have perhaps learned more than one should if one wants to remain independent." A few years after sending that famously inscribed copy, Schönberg had occasion to express his appreciation in public when he was asked to participate in Ludwig von Ficker's *Rundfrage über Karl Kraus*. In these pages Schönberg repeated his inscription from memory and added that this sentiment and these words expressed the scope but not the high level of his appreciation of Kraus (whom he had met through his future brother-in-law, the composer Alexander von Zemlinsky, at the legendary Café Griensteidl in 1895). In an as yet unpublished presentation at a Schönberg Festival at the University of Minnesota in May 1996, I asked this question: What was it that Schönberg had learned from a determined nonmusician, at best a musical amateur, though he was professional in almost everything else that he undertook (with the possible exception of affairs of the heart), who could not read music, played no musical instrument, and did not have much of a singing voice, a voice that was more of a *Sprechstimme* in Schönberg's sense, a man who repeatedly averred that he knew nothing about music and certainly could have no artistic appreciation of the avant-garde in that field, least of all twelve-tone composition? It should be noted, however, that Kraus never called these new composers *Neutöner* (new-sounders), a derogatory term that he applied with less logic to the expressionist poets, whose linguistic foreshortenings and surrealistic mannerisms he viewed with dismay and contempt. At any rate, the so-called Second Viennese School, consisting mainly of Arnold Schönberg, Alban Berg, and Anton von Webern, constituted a second support system for Kraus, though it was almost entirely on a personal, human plane and can hardly be compared to the benefits Kraus derived from the Brenner Circle.

Schönberg was not only among the subscribers to *Die Fackel* but also among its contributors before 1911. The composer sent Kraus a presentation copy of number 14 of his opus 15, settings of fifteen poems from Stefan George's collection *Das Buch der hängenden Garten* (The Book of the Hanging Gardens), and in April 1910 Kraus devoted a page of the *Fackel* to a facsimile of that very brief song ("Sprich nicht immer von dem Laub . . . Windesraub . . . " — Do not always speak about the leaves that are the prey of the wind) without any commentary. Why, so I asked, did Schönberg send Kraus that particular song? Was he trying to convey the message that Kraus should stop concentrating on evanescence and infirmity and not be a destroyer all the time? Having declined to publish some aphorisms by Schönberg as well as a polemical essay about Viennese music critics, Kraus did print (in the *Fackel*, 272–73, February 15, 1909, 34–35) the composer's open letter to the critic Ludwig Karpath regarding the latter's critique of his Second String Quartet.

Only two post-Griensteidl meetings between the two men are documented, but they did exchange several letters from which it is clear that Schönberg discerned a kindred spirit in Kraus, a fellow outsider with the unflagging courage of his convictions. Surely the relationship between them was rather one-sided. Kraus did not understand Schönberg's work, but he was an encouragement to the composer whenever the latter felt misunderstood by his contemporaries. Schönberg interpreted Kraus's judgments in a very personal way, which means that he was more dependent on Kraus's thought than he realized. What Schönberg might have derived from Kraus, so I opined, was an education in how to be an outsider, in the *Haßliebe* for, or love-hate relationship with, Vienna that the composer and the satirist shared with so many other creative spirits, most notably Sigmund Freud. For another thing, it was surely Kraus's iconoclastic courage and uncompromising stance, his moral rigorism, his stylistic precision and linguistic punctiliousness, his concern for clarity and exact meaning, his attention to detail and his general integrity that served as a model for the Second Viennese School. This is confirmed by the interviews that Joan Allen Smith conducted for her "Viennese portrait" *Schönberg and His Circle* (1986). For example, when the author asked the violinist Rudolf Kolisch whether Schönberg had somehow applied Kraus's use of the German language to a musical language, he denied this and instead pointed to the ethical categories connected with Kraus's style. Writing about Alban Berg's operas, George Perle points out that "Schönberg, Berg, and Webern saw Kraus as one whose work in the domain of language paralleled theirs in the domain of music" (1985, 288–89). Another commentator on Berg, the Viennese-born Mosco Carner, even argues that it is not difficult to see the Krausian influence in Schönberg's opera *Moses und Aron*, believing that Kraus's high moral view of language may have derived from the Old Testament. "Kraus's insistence that great art can only be achieved on the basis of truthfulness, authenticity, and sincerity," he writes, "is reflected in the *integer* music of the Second Viennese School" (1983, 37). It was Kraus's example and public life, his practical thought, and his almost mystical relationship to language rather than any system or theory that influenced these musicians.

Kraus's influence on Alban Berg was, if anything, stronger, more direct, and more specifically documented. From his youth Berg was a voracious reader of the *Fackel,* particularly enjoyed the symmetrical construction of each issue, and frequently commented on it in his letters. It undoubtedly helped to shape his pessimistic Weltanschauung as well as his polemical, ironic literary style. On May 29, 1905, Berg attended a memorable private performance of *Die Büchse der Pandora* (Pandora's Box), the second of Frank Wedekind's Lulu plays, at the tiny Trianontheater in Vienna. "In marked contrast to Wedekind," writes Carner, "Kraus saw feminine sexuality not in terms of destructive power but as an element fecundating and inspiring masculine reason" (38). Under the influence of Kraus's introductory talk Berg adopted Kraus's view. The composer and the satirist met in 1909 through their mutual friend Peter Altenberg. Berg mentioned Kraus in numerous letters, and as an ardent antimilitarist he particularly appreciated the pacifist stance of Kraus, one of the few Austrian or German writers who had not rushed to the ramparts of rhyme or boarded the bandwagon of banality when the guns of August started shooting in 1914. Mosco Carner believes that Berg derived his negative view of psychoanalysis from Kraus (23). Though the composer did not reject the theory of the unconscious and at one time consulted Alfred Adler about the supposed psychosomatic origin of his asthma, he had no use for the theories of wish fulfillment and the repression of the sexual drives. Like Elias Canetti and others, Berg adopted a number of Kraus's biases — for example, against the later Gerhart Hauptmann and Hugo von Hofmannsthal. In his article "Opera, Apocalypse and the Dance of Death: Berg's Indebtedness to Kraus," David P. Schroeder writes: "Through his sympathetic response to the work of Vienna's most trenchant satirist, Berg was aided in devising operatic means for treating complex issues, such as apocalypse, despair, and the possibility of redemption, allowing him to arrive at his stunning operatic achievement in *Wozzeck*" (1991, 92). Berg saw Büchner's play *Woyzeck* in 1914, and in wartime the figures of the German and the Austrian dramatists coalesced for him. Schroeder also points to the deconstruction of a powerful Viennese symbol of security, the dance, especially the waltz, which is turned into a *danse macabre,* a dance of death. (In this connection, it should be pointed out that the original title for Maurice Ravel's wartime tone poem *La Valse* was *Vienne*). The supernatural final scene of *The Last Days of Mankind* is set in a ballroom, and in *Wozzeck* Berg uses a *Ländler* just before the apprentices' scene as a symbol of disintegration and chaos. Kraus's use of verse at the end of his play and his operatic, or cinematic, phantasmagoric reprise of earlier themes, scenes, and figures may have influenced Berg's interlude, or musical reprise, after the protagonist's suicide. Kraus's pacifist play seems to consist of disjointed scenes, yet there is a formal structure involving cycles and repetitions that could be described as musical, thematic, or rhythmic. "If Kraus played a role in solving the problem of opera," writes Schroeder, "it was entirely unintentional on his part. Concerning the music of Schönberg and Berg, Kraus remained entirely baffled, but he took a benign view with the assumption that this music probably served some higher purpose" (103).

Susanne Rode's meticulously researched, exhaustively documented, and copiously illustrated book *Alban Berg und Karl Kraus* (1988) is the standard work on the subject, for it presents and interprets valuable source material, often in the form of facsimiles or tables. In this intellectual biography of the composer, Karl Kraus is given pride of place as the great model, inspirer, inner support, and literary-aesthetic guide. Berg's intellectual attitude toward the libretti of his two operas, which he based on nineteenth-century plays, resembled Kraus's championship of half-forgotten poets of past generations. The author analyzes *Lulu* to show how Berg expressed his reception of Kraus in musical terms, and she also tries to demonstrate that the carefully wrought structure of each issue of *Die Fackel* influenced the architectonic form of Berg's compositions. "Language as the bearer of intellect and humaneness," she writes, "language as expression, and the conditionality [*Bedingtheit*] of expression and thought — these are the three central aspects frequently recurring in Kraus's thinking through language that Berg adopted and anchored in his own aesthetics" (65).

As already indicated, Karl Kraus could not read music and had a flexible voice that was more suited to *Sprechgesang* than to singing. Yet his was, by all accounts, a kind of by-the-seat-of-his-pants musicality that made him a quick study, even though he refused to take voice lessons, and allowed him to memorize, with just a few run-throughs, all the songs from the fourteen Offenbach operettas that he presented in 123 of his 700 public recitals in programmatic opposition to the Viennese operetta of his time, which he considered inane, meretricious, and harmful, whereas he hailed Offenbach as a consummate social critic and valued fellow satirist. Kraus sang every part in German translation, his own or someone else's, with the accompaniment of a pianist who, however, had to play the vocal line as well, for otherwise Kraus would have sung the "oompapa oompapa" of the accompaniment. Georg Knepler and Franz Mittler, who served Kraus in the last half-dozen years of his musical-literary evenings, have written knowingly and appreciatively about this experience, Knepler in a wide-ranging book and Mittler in an article published in *Forum* (Vienna) in June 1956 and included in English translation ("It Wasn't Easy, But It Was Nice") in Diana Mittler Battipaglia's book *Franz Mittler* (1993). (See also the same author's article "Some Notes on the Musical Association of Karl Kraus and Franz Mittler," *Modern Austrian Literature* viii, 1–2, 1975, 20–25). One critical voice was raised by the composer Paul Amadeus Pisk, the music critic of the Social Democratic *Arbeiter-Zeitung*, who attended four of Kraus's eight Offenbach presentations in one week in 1929. Kraus reprinted Pisk's review in *Die Fackel* 811–19, August 1929, 85–87:

> It takes but a few measures for a musician to realize that the performer lacks the ability to express melody and rhythm with his singing. The accompaniment to the *Sprechgesang* is bumpy piano playing by Georg Knepler behind a screen. . . . Every intellectual gladly acknowledges Kraus's fight against the *kitsch* and frippery of the operetta, but it must not be overlooked that by distorting the music, thus depriving it of its real means of expression, Kraus does not do justice to the most important artistic element of Offenbach's operettas. Kraus's assumption of all the roles only directs the listener's attention to the performer and away from the music, shifting the focus from the musical to the literary sphere. Kraus does not really care about the music, just about the text, which he often modernizes by referring to Schober, Békessy, Kerr, etc. One would speak of book operettas in analogy to book dramas, plays intended to be read rather than staged. Offenbach's music is and will remain alive, but only in an orchestra and on a stage for which it was written, not at the lectern, where Offenbach is crowded out by Karl Kraus. (87)

Kraus's rather pained reply in the same issue of the *Fackel* is followed by a letter from Eduard Steuermann, dated July 1929, in which the noted pianist claims to be speaking in the names of Alban Berg and Rudolf Kolisch as well. These musicians, Steuermann points out, do not need the opulent sound of an orchestra and a chorus to hear the "inner voice" of the music. Putting Offenbach in the framework of Kraus's readings, with its musical values, might be the only possibility of keeping him alive. "I very deliberately call it *Musizieren* (music-making)," adds Steuermann, "though it happens to be known that you cannot read music. Notes are not music, and they can slumber in popular works until someone comes along and awakens them. You have taught us that there can be music without notes" (91–93).

To speak about Ernst Křenek in the context of the Second Viennese School may be a bit of a stretch, because he was born in 1900 and thus was a quarter of a century younger than Schönberg and fifteen years younger than Berg. Yet he belongs in this context, for he was probably the youngest musical member of Kraus's circle, regarded the satirist as his most important extramusical influence, and spoke and wrote about him on a number of occasions. Together with the music critic Willi Reich and the jurist Wolfgang Ploderer, Křenek founded a lively musical journal called *23. Eine Wiener Musikzeitschrift*. The number refers to the clause in Austria's press law that dealt with the correction of false statements in the public prints. Between 1932 and 1937 thirty-three issues appeared, and the journal's noble aim was to do for Vienna's music what Kraus was doing for, or against, that city's literature, culture, and politics in the *Fackel*. The press was, of course, regarded as the main adversary by both journals. Among the contributors to *23* were, in addition to the three founders, Theodor Wiesengrund-Adorno (under the pseudonym Hector Rottweiler), Heinrich Jalowetz, Alfred Einstein, and Siegfried Kracauer. Křenek, who was as resourceful a writer as he was a composer, was the only musician or critic who undertook to establish a connection between Kraus's *Sprachgedanke*, his thinking in and through language, and ideas in the realm of music. The article "Karl Kraus und Arnold Schönberg" which Křenek published in *23* in October 1934, was reprinted in Křenek's *Zur Sprache gebracht: Essays über Musik* (1958) and included in an English translation (by Margaret Shenfield and Geoffrey Skelton) in *Exploring Music: Essays by Ernst Křenek* (1966). There Křenek speaks of the "streak of inexorability and intransigence" and "strange position of public solitude" that the two men share (83). While Kraus is primarily a conservative, Schönberg is

> usually venerated or execrated as a revolutionary destroyer of the current codes of law, and yet in his own way he too may be called a conservative spirit, for what is thought of as his avant-garde quality is only the most complete, the truest possible fulfillment of the law. . . . He resembles Karl Kraus in that he, too, wages his war against "the existing order" on its own ground, and, by insisting on a complete and utter faithfulness to the prevailing code, aims at taking it *ad absurdum*, showing how it contradicts the higher laws of absolute morality. (83)

However, Schönberg's fight is primarily an aesthetic rather than a moral one. Being the vehicle of thought, language is part of the moral counterworld to the world of wickedness and immorality. Because of the opposition to his artistic course that Schönberg encountered, there has been an increasing rapprochement between the aesthetic sphere of a Schönberg and the moral sphere of a Kraus, and "Schönberg approaches Kraus's creative law, according to which the two spheres are completely and inseparably identical from the beginning, although this cannot be true for Schönberg, since he is a musician" (85).

Křenek continues this train of thought in "Erinnerung an Karl Kraus" (Memoir of Karl Kraus) and his "Ansprache bei der Trauerfeier für Karl Kraus" (Address at the Karl Kraus Memorial), both dated November 1936 and included in *Zur Sprache gebracht*. On the latter occasion Křenek said:

"Music is the prehistoric, prelogical existence of thought, embedded in its mystery like an enchanted bug preserved in amber" (224). Was Kraus, he asks, a stranger in the land of music because his linguistic form had achieved such perfection that it has strayed too far from that (musical) origin of thought? No, Kraus's thinking had so much language, such form and such reality that it had arrived at that goal which is intertwined with the origin (*Ursprung*), where the darkness of music is transformed into the light of language and language is transformed into the muteness of fulfillment. In other words, comments Werner Kraft (who features and interprets Křenek's views in his 1956 book on Kraus), there is a relationship between music and language that is mediated by thought, and this thought belongs to both realms. In his "Memoir" Křenek writes:

> To us Kraus was the originator of a concrete doctrine of general artistic validity which was like no other designed to illuminate our particular musical path and to give intellectual substance to our production. . . . The analogy of Kraus's thinking in terms of language (*Sprachdenken*) with musical thought lies mainly in the fact that Kraus neatly separated the subject matter of his linguistic works from their thought content, and that only this ideational content determined the linguistic form derived from the verbal material. (231)

"The surprising thing about this linguistic theory," Křenek goes on to say, "is that it anticipates a musical theory that really ought to have been the basis of this linguistic theory, for music, which has no extra-musical content, should always have been conceived of in that way" (231).

Křenek's thinking about the relationship between Kraus and Schönberg is perhaps best summed up by the last paragraph of his article on the two men (in my translation, for that in *Exploring Music* is mangled): "It is remarkable and significant that the Austrian decadence should have produced these two men in the same year, 1874 — both of them destined to cause in countless generations a truly salutary disturbance of vital importance to European culture. This, too, is a manifestation of Austria's mission" (86).

5: Viewing Kraus Against the Historical and Political Background

The British historian Frank Field shares with the American Germanist Wilma Abeles Iggers the distinction of having published one of the first major books on Kraus in English (*The Last Days of Mankind: Karl Kraus and His Vienna*, 1967). His perceptive study proceeds from the author's belief that it is "fitting that the personality and achievement of Karl Kraus should be used as a focus for a study of Vienna in the first four decades of this century" (ix). In that regard this book is comparable to Harold Poor's study of Kurt Tucholsky, the other great German-speaking satirist of our time (*Kurt Tucholsky and the Ordeal of Germany*), and in his historical commentary the author never loses sight of the figure of Kraus, his thoughts and reactions. Field points out that "it is easy . . . for a present-day reader of *The Last Days of Mankind* and the *Fackel* of the First World War to mistake the real significance of Kraus's achievement" (133). Responding to criticism, whether real or expected, that the truths of Kraus's great wartime drama, which Field characterizes as "basically a play for voices" (103), may be regarded by some as only half-truths, the historian writes: "Although he took his material from real speeches and newspaper accounts, it was the satirist who shaped the material into a final picture. It was inevitable that, in the process, the relentless and neurotic logic of the satirist should have ignored the complexities of human behavior and the conditions which govern that behavior" (133). The years after 1919, the "Republican Interlude" that Field discusses as a "melancholy, if fascinating and lengthy postscript to the career of Karl Kraus" (139), brought the Békessy affair, which, according to the historian, "throws light upon the extraordinary laxity and lack of fibre in Austrian society" (167) as well as the events of July 1927, in connection with which Field erroneously states (175) that "two members of the Schutzbund" (rather than innocent bystanders) were killed. In his comments on Kraus's controversial book *The Third Walpurgis Night*, Field points out that "the mirror of satire is a distorting mirror. Kraus was not a historian, and the full significance of his writings on Nazism does not lie in the realm of historical analysis" (211). The author also has cogent things to say about Kraus's Jewishness. "In the twelve years that followed the accession of Hitler to power in Germany," he concludes, "things were to happen that surpassed the most pessimistic insights of the satirist: the building of the concentration camp at Buchen-

wald around Goethe's beech tree, and the processions that took place into
the extermination chambers of Auschwitz while elsewhere in the camp the
orchestra played selections from Viennese light music — all this only becomes a little more explicable after reading the work of Kraus" (212).

Alfred Pfabigan's book *Karl Kraus und der Sozialismus*, subtitled *Eine
politische Biographie* (1976), is a companion volume to Frank Field's study
in that it attempts to place the essentially apolitical, casuistic satirist in the
context of the politics and culture of his time, but it is considerably more
wide-ranging than the earlier book by the British historian. Pfabigan clearly
wants to go beyond tracing Kraus's relationship with the political realm
and to provide a new interpretation of Kraus's life, work, and thought.
However, the author's well-documented and absorbing study sometimes
strays from its subject and is marred by excessive psychologizing and sec-
ond-guessing. For example, the lengthy third chapter, "The Hellish Sexual
Morality of the *Fackel*," makes for fascinating reading but is only tangential
to Pfabigan's subject.

In his introduction Pfabigan speaks of Kraus's overwrought subjectiv-
ism that led the satirist to create a world of his own and to suggest to the
reader that it was the only real and true world. In discussing Kraus's hyp-
notic effect on his readers and biographers, he points out that the development of a consistent critical attitude has been impeded by what may be
described as Kraus's immunization strategies, such as the satiric anticipation
and refutation of possible critiques. As a result, Kraus's biographers, notably Leopold Liegler and Heinrich Fischer, have usually interpreted him in
accordance with his own wishes and ignored the social context. Pfabigan
calls the eschewing of explanatory notes "a foolish principle" (20). In the
author's view, the astonishing Kraus renaissance after 1945 was possible
only through a sort of foreshortening or truncation of his work: the "radical" Kraus, the man with leftist leanings of the 1920s who may be characterized as an aesthetic agnostic, refused to integrate his writings into a social context. Displaying a becoming sense of the satirist's adaptability and
evolution, Pfabigan writes that "the political development of the satirist
was a complex and contradictory social process" (24).

The author points out that as an Austrian, a Jew, and a member of the
middle class, Kraus had a lifelong ambivalent attitude toward all three identities. He agrees with the psychiatrist Margarete Mitscherlich that the widely disseminated reports of Kraus's warmth, sociability, virility, and mental
health are incorrect. His childhood angst led him to develop a mechanism
for coping with unpleasantness: In his recollection, things that made him
suffer, such as the authoritarian school system and his physical defect (curvature of the spine), became positive experiences. Kraus's celebrated German style was a hard-won possession; Pfabigan speaks of the obsessive,

masochistic *Sprachlust* with which Kraus took on all the hidden difficulties of the German language and even created new ones. Continuing his facile psychologizing, Pfabigan believes that "when he had loved someone and either he or the other person had changed, Kraus as a rule executed the break with almost ritualistic cruelty" (31) and that "his silence on certain social phenomena can be explained by the fact that they contained nothing that he rejected in himself" (32). Pfabigan is on somewhat firmer ground when he points out that a phenomenon like Karl Kraus would have been unthinkable without a long Jewish tradition and that "in his polemics he projected onto other Jews precisely those Jewish characteristics that he repressed in himself" (34). Tending to agree with Berthold Viertel's view of Kraus as an "arch-Jew," Pfabigan rejects the label of Jewish self-hatred on the grounds that Kraus's "anti-Semitism" was too differentiated for that.

Warming to his real subject, the author points out that the early fighter against corruption stayed on the surface and mounted campaigns against individuals rather than identifying and combating root causes. For example, the press was not the independent forum that Kraus discerned in it but the willing tool of other forces. Thus, in his manic opposition to it, he did not penetrate to the roots of its evils. Furthermore, his fight was not differentiated; he opposed not only the bourgeois press with all its venality but also the publications of the workers' movement. His confusion of persons with institutions and his inability, or at least unwillingness, to integrate single phenomena into a system brought about many distortions. "From the founding of the *Fackel* to Kraus's death," writes Pfabigan, "there was an intensive emotional relationship between him and Social Democracy [the form socialism took in Kraus's Austria], and it was manifested on both sides alternately in passionate rejection, neutrality, and considerable identification. . . . Had Kraus been a disciplined member of the party, he could never have developed as he did, and a Social Democratic Party that Kraus could have joined without abandoning his convictions would have been . . . a romantic but politically . . . inefficient structure" (52–53).

Since Kraus was not an analytical thinker or a theorist of historical materialism, it is hard to place him on a particular socialist track, though it may be safe to say that he was closer to Lassalle than to Marx. The prewar Kraus felt closest to the workers' movement, which he expected to be an uncompromising, ethically unobjectionable counterpoise to the rejected bourgeoisie, but he became increasingly aware that the Social Democracy was led oligarchically and bureaucratically.

Pfabigan's general psychological approach may be in conflict with his own insight that "Kraus's critical mode of thought, in which such phenomena as self-reflection, self-criticism, personal guilt feelings, and the like hardly played a role, was diametrically opposed to psychoanalysis" (110), but it has yielded a cogent discussion of Peter Altenberg, Otto Weininger, and the satirist's personal relationship with women. Kraus always saw himself as an advocate of the female gender, yet he opposed women's quest for self-realization (except in the sexual sphere). "If we want to use the terminology of the American feminist movement," writes Pfabigan, "the polemical designation 'male chauvinist' is undoubtedly apt for Kraus" (119). His sensitive discussion of Kraus's love for Sidonie Nádherný leads him to conclude that it was not a happy relationship but did meet Kraus's needs, his "longing for intercourse [in every sense of the word] with aristocrats" (124).

Proceeding to World War I, Pfabigan discusses Kraus's essay "Franz Ferdinand und die Talente" (*Fackel* 400–403) as one of the last great documents of Kraus's prewar conservatism. Though he was unable to see the social background of the assassination of the successor to the Habsburg throne, Kraus was "a prophet of detail who, basing himself on his magnificent imagination, managed to use trivial occasions to predict catastrophes years before they actually transpired. However, just before the catastrophe, his imaginative faculties failed him. The pessimist was suddenly transformed into a blind optimist who refused to believe that his frightful vision could soon become reality" (170). In Pfabigan's view, Kraus missed the opportunity of turning his obituary of Franz Ferdinand into a call for peace. The author actually seems to hold the satirist responsible when he adds that "Kraus was not spared the suffering he caused" (171–72) — because his friends and relatives Franz Grüner, Franz Janowitz, Stefan Fridezko, and Franz Koch fell in the war and his friends Elisabeth Reitler and Georg Trakl committed suicide. Unlike most biographers and other critics, Pfabigan does not see a harmonious transition of the satirist from the prewar period to wartime, pointing out that the war met many demands of the prewar *Fackel*, such as the abandonment of parliamentarianism, absolute government, nationalization of the economy, and domination by the aristocracy and the military. The author denies that the satirist was a pacifist from the first moment on, though the carnage soon enough made him one. "We cannot entirely absolve Karl Kraus, who dreamt of a conservative revolution under Franz Ferdinand and polemicized against parliamentarianism and progress and shortly before the war extolled the military type, of all responsibility for the world war" (176). Pfabigan does concede that Kraus's guilt is minimal as compared to that of other great German and Austrian intellectuals and that Kraus did penance by revoking some of his earlier statements, showing genuine remorse, and thereafter rejecting all forms of violence. In the author's view, *The Last Days of Mankind* conveys the misleading impression that the satirist's attitude toward the war was a unified one. Early on war was a possible value for Kraus, and only later did he realize that the world had corrupted war, too, that far from being a fight against existing rottenness, it was conducted by that very evil. As Kraus shifted from a fixation on the aristocratic spirit to an all-encompassing humanism, his anti-capitalistic orientation filled him with greater sympathy for the proletariat. Though he was still far from socialism, he now began to take cognizance of the societal or sociological dimension in political manifestations and acquired a greater understanding of the economic foundations of power. The erstwhile monarchist and admirer of Emperor Franz Joseph now rejected the potentate and began to attack the Germans and the German spirit. Pfabigan regards Kraus's intellectual development as complete by the end of the war.

For Kraus the defeat of old Austria was a victory. Unlike the majority of the population — the politicians, the press, and the poets — he hailed the Republic and became a republican, though never a democrat. In fact, Pfabigan calls him one of the intellectual founders of the Republic and as such the possessor of a new identify that, according to Pfabigan, made for the happiest years of his life, though he soon became disillusioned with the Republic and increasingly critical of it after 1924. For a time, however, the educational activities of the Republic with its Social Democratic government seemed like a favorable framework for the improvement of the body politic. If his programmatic poem "Nach 20 Jahren" defined his satiric mission, the poem entitled "25 Jahre" is expressive of resignation. The Austrian press in general continued to ignore Kraus, but the Social Democratic *Arbeiter-Zeitung* now regularly reported about his activities. When Karl Seitz, a prominent Social Democratic politician and future mayor of Vienna, congratulated Kraus on his fiftieth birthday and the twenty-fifth anniversary of *Die Fackel*, this was the only honor ever bestowed on Kraus by official Austria. He was also appreciated by some younger Social Democrats, but soon enough Kraus was back in his isolation, splendid or otherwise, as a one-man party.

In a chapter entitled "An Artist and Fighter" Pfabigan points out that one reason for Kraus's sometime closeness to the Social Democrats was that he felt they could keep the press and the monarchists in check. He had no use for the social analysis of the Austro-Marxists, and some members of the party who believed that the ideas in the *Fackel* were identical with the political program of socialism were mistaken. Of the Social Democratic leadership, Friedrich Austerlitz, the editor of the *Arbeiter-Zeitung*, appreciated Kraus, while his successor, Oskar Pollak, was usually in the anti-Kraus camp, polemicizing against the satirist in the monthly *Der Kampf*. Kraus's most important link to the Social Democrats were his readings before appreciative audiences of workers, though his sophisticated and complex presentations could not have been easy to follow. Pfabigan believes that "Kraus constructed for himself a mythical view of the proletariat whose representatives would make all his dreams come true" (232). However, in his article "Ein Künstler und Kämpfer" (*Der Kampf*, 16, 1923, 31–36) Pollak concludes that Kraus was never a socialist, that he was clinging to the past and not changing his goals or methods, that he was reactionary rather than revolutionary or progressive, and that he would not be in the forefront in the coming struggle against capitalism. Pollak even claimed, in the face of much evidence to the contrary, that Kraus was not popular with the working class. In the same issue of *Der Kampf*, David Josef Bach, the head of the Kunststelle (cultural office) that sponsored Kraus's readings, published a more pragmatic and more conciliatory article. The following year Friedrich Austerlitz presented Kraus as a "genuine revolutionary" and "touchstone for the literati" (*Arbeiter-Zeitung*, April 27, 1924, 3). Many old "Krausians" were now leftists, but he did not support them, regarding those on the radical left as part of the "ghosts" that still bedeviled and threatened the Republic — though Pfabigan points out that Kraus had a great deal of personal respect for such martyred revolutionaries as Rosa Luxemburg.

Oskar Pollak's resentment of Karl Kraus survived the critic's exile and the war. In an article published in the *Arbeiter-Zeitung* on August 18, 1946, Pollak set out to destroy what he called the Kraus legend by describing Kraus as a peculiar saint whose cult was being foisted on the Austrians by patriotic clubmen and communist literati (the latter presumably a reference to Viktor Matejka, a communist member of the Vienna City Council, who took the initiative in proposing a Karl Kraus Society). Punning on Kraus's name, Pollak averred that Austria did not owe the satirist more than a muddled (*krause*) critique of bourgeois progress that only produced a muddled praise of reactionary ideas. Fear and cowardice turned Kraus into a short-sighted lickspittle who supported the Austro-Fascists, and Pollak even brings himself to report a rumor that Karl Kraus would have accepted the Nazis, too, if they had allowed him to sit at his desk and write his *Fackel*.

According to Pfabigan, the Békessy affair (January 1924 to August 1926) represented the last straw that sank Kraus's relationship with the Social Democrats. Because the authorities and political parties ignored the corrupt Hungarian-born press czar or even colluded with him, Kraus once again was alone in his fight. The badly divided leadership of the party claimed that Békessy was not one of their top priorities, and it did not even respond when the "Buda pest" claimed that the Kunststelle had been forcing Kraus and his readings on the workers. Pfabigan gives a detailed account of the motivations on all sides and points out that a debate about Kraus, that outsider and gadfly, was carried on in the pages of *Der Kampf* in 1926, after Kraus had succeeded in his quest to "kick the crook out of

Vienna." While Friedrich Austerlitz and Hans Menziger regarded Kraus as a revolutionary, Oskar Pollak criticized the Kraus cult. Pfabigan sees symbolic significance in Kraus's cancellation of his subscription to the *Arbeiter-Zeitung* on May 1, 1926. After all, he did this publicly, like his withdrawal from the Catholic Church in March 1923. (Pfabigan believes that "he remained a Christian but was outside the church organization, which had sided with his adversaries" [217]).

The events of July 1927 marked the last time that Kraus shared a viewpoint with the Social Democrats, though it also cemented his estrangement from them. Kraus had once admired Johannes Schober, the police chief of Vienna (and sometime Austrian chancellor), but he now held him responsible for the police riot that claimed ninety lives; and until his death in 1932 the elusive Schober was one of his prime satiric targets, since he also resented him for his fecklessness, deceitfulness, and abuse of power in the Békessy affair. Kraus's play *Die Unüberwindlichen* (The Unconquerable) combines a Bekessiad with a Schoberiad. After the year of shared mourning for the victims was over, the years 1928 to 1936 again brought great bitterness between the satirist and the Social Democrats. Pfabigan passes a particularly harsh judgment on Kraus when he writes: "None of his polemics were carried on with such hate and aggressiveness, in none did he use such dishonest methods, and in none was he as wrong historically as in this struggle" (311). The Social Democrats regarded Schober as only partly responsible for the police riot, and in the face of the threatening fascist forces they could not afford to alienate Schober.

A Vereinigung Karl Kraus (K. K. Association) was founded by Fritz König and associates in an attempt to mediate between the satirist and the party leadership, and it attracted two hundred members. Between March 1930 and January 1932 it published a bulletin that may be regarded as an attempt at a socialist *Fackel*. As they tried to reform the party from within in Kraus's spirit, they only disturbed its unity, and with the death of Friedrich Austerlitz in 1931 the last link between Kraus and the Social Democrats was gone. In a speech made in September 1932 Kraus blamed the Social Democrats for the emergence of the Nazis.

Pfabigan, who often chides Kraus for his ahistorical and apolitical attitude, believes that the satirist was wrong in equating the Social Democracy with the bourgeoisie. He has particularly harsh words for Kraus's attitudes, activities, and writings in his last years. If Kraus had died or fallen silent in October 1933, he argues, his memory and his readers would have been spared the embarrassment of his last writings. That month marked the appearance of a very thin *Fackel*, after a hiatus of ten months, which contained only a eulogy of the architect Adolf Loos and Kraus's last poem with its poignant last line "The word expired when that world awoke." As

Pfabigan points out, Bertolt Brecht was one of the few who interpreted that poem correctly. In his own poem "On the Significance of the Ten-Line Poem in No. 888 of the Fackel," he wrote:

> When the Third Reich had been founded
> Only a short message came from the eloquent one.
> In a ten-line poem
> He raised his voice to complain
> That it was not adequate.
>
> When the eloquent one excused himself
> That his voice had failed him,
> Silence stepped forward to the seat of judgment,
> Removed her veil
> And revealed herself as a witness.
>> (*Stimmen über Karl Kraus zum 60. Geburtstag*, Vienna:
>> Richard Lányi, 1934, 11–12)

Yet by the time this poem appeared in a *Festschrift* for Kraus, Brecht had responded to the satirist's support of the Austrian government's repressive measures during the riots of February 1934 and its proscription of the Social Democratic Party by writing a sad supplementary poem entitled "About the Quick Fall of the Good Innocent":

> He testified against those whose lips had been sealed
> And broke his staff over those who had been killed.
> He praised the murderers. He accused the murdered . . .
>
> . . . What an age, we said, shuddering.
> When the man of good will but no understanding
> Cannot even wait to perform his misdeed
> Until praise for his good deed has reached him!
>> (Brecht, *Gesammelte Werke*. Frankfurt: Suhrkamp, 1967, 4,
>> 505)

Pfabigan believes that Kraus should not have disregarded Social Democracy, and in particular the workers' movement, as a political force, and he does not accept the argument "Anything but Hitler!" that led the satirist to throw in his lot with "the little savior Dollfuß." "The profound tragedy of the great satirist's relationship to politics," he writes, "is that the changeable naysayer, who was also a great yeasayer but often vehemently abandoned objects of which he approved, was unable to revoke his final yea. . . . The man who harshly criticized Social Democracy because of trivial faults never uttered a word of criticism of Austro-Fascism, under which he lived for three years" (345). Pfabigan points to the great fear of the Jew

Karl Kraus: In contrast to many Jews, Kraus knew exactly what he would face if Hitlerism was victorious, and in this regard Austro-Fascism was decidedly the lesser evil, one tempered, moreover, by his personal regard for Dollfuß. Kraus's hatred of the workers' movement had become so irrational that he regarded its smashing, along with that of communism, as a sine qua non for stopping Hitler. Pfabigan views Kraus's late support of the Austrian brand of fascism as a product of decades of development, of Kraus's tendency toward an enlightened absolutism. "His assumption that the Third Reich did not need a satirist," Pfabigan concludes, "is surely erroneous, though it is true that he was not that satirist. . . . For him, the 'innocent,' fascism was devoid of history and tradition, an inexplicable, unfathomable phenomenon" (356).

In an article entitled "Kraus's Shakespearean Politics" (1991) Edward Timms, the doyen of British Kraus scholars, concerns himself with the satirist's public stances and political action as influenced, directly or indirectly, by his lifelong occupation with Shakespeare. As Kraus attempted to address the tragic dichotomy or disjunction between culture and politics, "he engaged in public affairs more intensively than any other Austrian writer of his generation. But the qualities of imagination he brought to bear on politics reflected an essentially literary disposition — a mind nurtured not on Karl Marx or Theodor Herzl, but on Goethe and Shakespeare" (345). As the satirist's essential technique in his struggle against authoritarian ideologies, Timms identifies "subversive intertextuality" (345), the juxtaposition of documentary material culled from newspapers with a wealth of cultural references, ranging from the Bible to the operettas of Offenbach, which were often capable of outwitting censors. These references were intended to serve and disseminate classical German, to Kraus the carrier of norms for a civilized society. But how were cultural values to provide guidelines for political conduct? Kraus turned concert halls into cultural-political forums, and his public platforms became tribunals presided over by the self-styled conscience of a great cultural tradition.

His crusade against the Vienna police chief Johannes Schober was Kraus's most explicitly political campaign, one that aligned him with the Social Democratic Party. Even though Schober was ethically and culturally discredited, he prevailed politically and became the Austrian chancellor. At that point Kraus realized that he was able to be victorious only in the imaginative (dramatic, poetic, musical, artistic) sphere and transformed Schober into a literary figure (in his play *Die Unüberwindlichen*). Disenchanted with politics, he declared that he was no longer interested in the convolutions of the ugly Austrian political system and shifted from practical to Shakespearean politics.

Timms points out that as early as 1902 Kraus defined the ideal legal system as "Shakespearean ideas couched in legal terms." In the same issue of *Die Fackel* (no. 115) Kraus wrote, "Shakespeare had foreknowledge of everything." "Shakespeare was important for Kraus," according to Timms, "because his plays seemed so prophetically to interact with the follies and disasters of the 20th century . . . to provide a kind of masterplot, linking political conflict with moral retribution" (354). Different Shakespeare plays were important at different times in Kraus's life. In 1905 it was *Measure for Measure*, set in a sort of mystical Vienna, where the disguised duke says "I have seen corruption boil and bubble / Till it o'er-ran the stew" (act 5, scene 1). After World War I *Hamlet* helped Kraus hail the downfall of what he regarded as a corrupt empire; he saw himself as Horatio, the bearer of witness and restorer of order. Kraus's strategy of silence began in 1930, after Schober's political triumph, when Kraus despaired of a politics based on ethical principles. Kraus now identified with Timon of Athens, and, as Timms points out, Prince Rüdiger von Starhemberg, the head of the rightist paramilitary organization Heimwehr, was reminiscent of Alcibiades, who threatened to sack fair Athens. After the assassination of Chancellor Dollfuß in 1934, *Macbeth* became particularly relevant. Timms comes to the conclusion that "Kraus never abandoned the quest for a moral meaning in political events, even after acknowledging his own powerlessness to affect the outcome" (357).

In his wide-ranging book *Karl Kraus: Studien zum "Theater der Dichtung" und Kulturkonservatismus* (1973) Jens Malte Fischer places Kraus in the political and cultural context of his time. He also concerns himself with Kraus's relation to Shakespeare and tells a revealing anecdote about one of Kraus's recitals. When his first reading of *A Winter's Tale* attracted only an audience of 150, Kraus announced a reading from his own works and then treated the 900 people who had shown up to *Timon of Athens*, ostensibly by way of punishment. In his discussion of the "Theater of Poetry," Fischer attempts to demonstrate that Kraus's endeavors were based on a certain tradition and had specific parallels — for example, the readings of Stefan George. Kraus's presentations are deemed to be in line with a postnaturalistic or antinaturalistic trend and were designed to focus attention again on dramatic works and their creators. Fischer also points to the similarity of Kraus's voice and style to those of Josef Kainz and Alexander Moissi, actors whom Kraus disliked.

Citing Kraus's poem "My Contradiction," Fischer points out that he did not set out to defend Kraus against his leftist critics or present him as a stylite [*Säulenheiliger*] of neoconservatism. "What fascinates [about Kraus]," he concludes, "is the mixture of receptivity and spontaneity in his espousal of tradition, the rescue of the past in the present that he undertook. What he concerned himself with was not the representation of the past but the realization of a bygone hope" (191).

In an article entitled "Karl Kraus und Shakespeare: Die Macht des Epigonen" (1990) the Portuguese scholar António Ribeiro relates Kraus's translations and presentations of Shakespeare plays to the idea of epigonism: "To him, an epigone is someone who completes an assignment that others have been unable to handle, thus forcibly establishing a new order" (247). The idea of epigonism in Kraus means that a "natural" and peaceful relationship to tradition is no longer possible; "what can be inherited is primarily the tradition of a struggle . . . that has to be carried on over and over again" (248). Ribeiro believes that Kraus's *Nachdichtungen* are guided by "a search for an idea where it seems to be expressed in the most Shakespearean fashion" (251).

6: "The Last Days of Mankind" and "The Third Walpurgis Night"

What *The Last Days of Mankind* and *The Third Walpurgis Night*, two works separated in time by almost two decades, have in common is a powerful satiric indictment of man's inhumanity to man. It has long been the consensus of critical opinion that Kraus's mammoth World War I drama *Die letzten Tage der Menschheit* (The Last Days of Mankind) is a forerunner of the post-World War II documentary drama, but Kraus's play has also been regarded, more proximately, as a major influence on the drama of the 1920s, specifically the political theater of Erwin Piscator and the epic theater of Bertolt Brecht.

In his book *Brecht's Tradition* (1967) Max Spalter devotes a chapter to Kraus and his best-known work, which he characterizes as "a panoramic, episodic play about World War I that is as much a satire prompted by the pettiness of those who made the war possible as it is a tragedy of European man rushing suicidally into oblivion" (138). "What, in the final analysis," he asks, "is *The Last Days of Mankind* but a series of character analyses on the basis of the spoken word? . . . Whether the language is bureaucratically dense or resonates with the peculiar accents and intonations of colloquial usage, Kraus carries through brilliantly his aim to make language the moral index of a dying way of life. A world literally talks its way to perdition" (155, 149). Another useful point made by Spalter is that both Kraus and Brecht favored a highly theatrical style of acting, emphasizing physical expressiveness, and that Kraus's predilection may have stemmed from performances he witnessed at the old Burgtheater in Vienna. Kraus never used the term *Verfremdung* (alienation — a key concept of Brecht's theater), yet "there is in his concept of satire the same desire to keep art from deteriorating into mere entertainment. . . . This mode of satire breaks sharply with Schiller's idea that drama has a moral effect precisely because it does not make sinners too self-conscious" (154–55).

Two shorter articles that, so to speak, reliably walk the reader through Kraus's play are by Mary Snell and Franz H. Mautner. Both are entitled "Karl Kraus's *The Last Days of Mankind*"; Snell's appeared in *Forum for Modern Language Studies 4* (July 1968), and Mautner's critical analysis is the afterword of Frederick Ungar's abridged edition of *The Last Days of Mankind* (1974) and a shortened version (in Sue Ellen Wright's translation) of his article in *Das deutsche Drama*, 1958. Characterizing Kraus's play as one of "the most intimidating satirical works that have ever come into existence" (234) and a work that "hovers grimly between grotesque phantasy, tragedy, and reality" (235), Snell points out that "Kraus selects his victims from all sections of the populace, from Emperor to prostitute, from the journalist to the starving soldier: no stone was to be left unturned, nor was any fool, tyrant, egoist or sadist to go unpunished" (235). The author concludes that "fifty years after Kraus wrote his monster-satire his words are as dramatically intense and as alive as on the day when they were still new" (247).

Like many other critics, Mautner views *The Last Days of Mankind* as a unique work of art. "As a whole, in its mingling of tragedy and wit, of dialectic and low humor, in its monumentality, in its technique of making a document into a dramatic character, in its multiplicity of style and forms, the drama is comparable to nothing else. In many respects it reminds one of the tragedy of the baroque age, in other respects of Nestroy, here and there of Offenbach and Gilbert and Sullivan" (262–63). Mautner believes that despite the universality of its subject matter the play is in some ways bound to its time and place, for local references, such as its "sanguinary jokes" (240), are not always fully understood. "Local color is almost nowhere the object," he writes, "but rather, emphasis is upon the types of people acting and speaking in each place, their manner of speech, and what is going on in their minds" (240). Pointing out that almost a third of the drama is identical with its raw material, Mautner writes: "That Kraus succeeded in utilizing this raw material in such a manner that it took shape as a work of art is an accomplishment that runs counter to all conventional aesthetic laws" (244). In line with his belief that "here, as in all Kraus's works, language has a religious dimension" (258), Mautner names as the primary object of the satirist's wrath "apostasy from the true spirit, from true ethos, from pure humanity, the turning away from the idealized origin to the worldly goal" (245).

The most searching analysis of Kraus's play to have appeared to date is contained in the concluding chapters of Edward Timms's book *Karl Kraus, Apocalyptic Satirist* (1986). Calling *The Last Days of Mankind* "the submerged masterpiece of the twentieth-century theater" (387), Timms sets out to answer these three questions: When exactly was the play written? What kind of play is it? How can it be staged? Since the play was begun in the summer of 1914 and did not appear in print in definitive form until 1922, the long gestation period reflects a radical reorientation on the part of its conservative author: "A play begun . . . by a 'loyal' satirist was completed by a radical republican with strong socialist sympathies" (372). Kraus's revisions indicate the author's progression from cultural to political satire and cause certain breaks and discontinuities in the text. Addressing his second question, Timms discerns an "unstable text whose disjunctive angles of vision generate a radical incongruity. . . . The satirical vision projects documentary materials on to the plane of apocalyptic myth" (372). Timms does agree with most critics that *The Last Days of Mankind* is a documentary drama and points out that, "unlike subsequent imitators, [Kraus] does not play fast and loose with the facts" (376). However, "the basic documentary form is . . . refracted through a series of intersecting paradigms which seem mutually incompatible" (377). Despite its basically Shakespearean tragic mode, Kraus's technique is actually closer to that of Georg Büchner (particularly his *Danton's Death*) in its fractured form and its characters buffeted about by anonymous historical forces. With a fine eye for the martial masquerade and carnival of carnage that are depicted in the play, Timms attempts to show that the form of tragedy is compromised by elements associated with operettas, cabarets, carnivals, and puppet theaters and that Kraus's satiric techniques of reduction, inflation, and montage lead to incongruities and ambiguities. "*The Last Days of Mankind* is a faulted masterpiece," Timms writes, "faulted in a geological sense. The seismic shift of history — and of Kraus's own response — means that the different strata of his play are no longer aligned. And the reader has to dig through accrued layers of meaning to find underlying coherence" (380).

Disagreeing with the critical consensus, Timms makes a strong case for the desirability of having Kraus's play staged. "It is . . . a play not for a static *theatrum mundi* but for a dynamic revolving stage. . . . The claim that *The Last Days of Mankind* is unperformable is a myth" (380). Those who make that claim are more purist than Kraus himself, who thought that a theater of the future, which would not be primarily bent on entertainment, might do it justice. In Timms's view, the play is essentially acoustic, with important physical and visionary motifs, scenic gestures, and visual effects. Its theatricality is enhanced by the inclusion of music and songs, and these fairly cry out for performance on the stage. "Verbal complexity need not preclude theatrical impact" (387), and even extensive pruning would not compromise its formal integrity.

Timms also has interesting things to say about the figure of the Grumbler (*Nörgler*) that has been widely regarded as the mouthpiece of the satirist and is even identified with him. The author believes that the Grumbler is a character that serves a literary purpose, not a mirror image of the satirist or Kraus himself. "It is clear that the character of the Grumbler is by no means an accurate reflection of Kraus's own stance as a publicist [*sic*]" (390), and to regard him in this light is to disregard the perspectival complexities of the play. For example, Kraus's antiwar position in 1914 was by no means as radical as the Grumbler's, and Timms estimates that only about one-third of the dialogue spoken by the Grumbler has a textual basis in the wartime *Fackel*. However, the author's admission that this character is "a simplified version of Kraus's satirical self" (391) would seem to indicate that his disagreement with other commentators is more apparent than real. The author also comments on the Grumbler's counterpart, the Optimist, an invented character, and believes that readers and critics would be well advised to look for literary correspondences rather than real-life prototypes.

Friedrich Torberg disagrees on the performability of Kraus's play. Born in 1908, he considers himself the youngest person whom Kraus admitted to his *Stammtisch* at the cafés he frequented (and, as a matter of fact, the dispenser of the last literary fruits of what has been called the German-Jewish symbiosis). After his return from his American exile Torberg became the editor of the journal *Forum* in Vienna and printed numerous articles on Karl Kraus, including his own. In "Das Wort gegen die Bühne" (*Forum* 11, 128, August 1964) he concerns himself with the first staged production of *The Last Days of Mankind* in Vienna, for which Heinrich Fischer and Leopold Lindtberg had reduced Kraus's two hundred scenes to forty-two. Reversing himself on what he had written the year before in connection with Helmut Qualtinger's readings from the play (in person and on records), Torberg concludes that Kraus's play can be read (aloud) but not performed. He reminds his readers that Kraus himself approved of the staging of the epilogue, "The Last Night," and in 1930 produced a stage version for two evenings that he read publicly in Vienna and elsewhere, but Torberg argues that a staging of the play would detract from the all-important words and language, which would, so to speak, be watered down by other ingredients. Then, too, our time is not propitious for a performance of the play, for people who have survived World War II, the concentration camps and gas chambers, and have lived with the atom bomb might find *The Last Days of Mankind* relatively tame. Who would mourn twelve hundred drowned horses? And, after all, those were not the last days of mankind! Torberg adds that "the superdimensional, eerie timelessness of the work is reduced by a three-dimensional stage presentation" (384).

"In his use of photomontage and cinematographic motifs," writes Timms, "Kraus was a pioneer in technical innovation" (384). "*Kinodramatisch*," a word used by Kraus in a pejorative sense (*Fackel* 360–63, November 7, 1912, 3) provided Leo A. Lensing with part of the title of his article "'Kinodramatisch': Cinema in Karl Kraus's *Die Fackel* and *Die letzten Tage der Menschheit*" (1982). Pointing out that the role of film in the play, as both a satirical object and a theatrical device, as an important part of the overall dramatic conception of the play, has largely escaped critical attention, Lensing believes that Kraus was more open-minded about films than is usually assumed. His disdainful comments on the cinema in the prewar *Fackel* were not in keeping with his private enjoyment of this then-new form, which experienced a great upswing in Austria during the war, as witness the 150 movie theaters that existed in Vienna by 1915. Lensing demonstrates that "Kraus's monumental anti-war drama contains characters connected with the Austrian film industry [in particular Count Sascha Kolowrat], scenes set in movie theaters . . . and an experimental use of the film as a theatrical device" (485–86). A particular target of Kraus's satire was the propagandistic documentary film, which Kraus regarded as a reprehensible misuse of the form, and he was bent on exposing the moral depravity of both filmmakers and moviegoers. Lensing shows that in several scenes of the play "the cinema and especially its abuse as deceptive entertainment and political indoctrination serve as the butt of Kraus's satire" (489). In a more positive sense, "Kraus progressed to seeing the cinema as a metaphor for the apocalyptic spectacle of the war's end" (485). Kraus's use of cinematic elements toward the end of the play, particularly in the Epilogue, indicates that he was aware of the film's satiric possibilities, and "the rapid scene changes and the *couplet*-like monologues [in the epilogue] suggest that Kraus may have intended to parody the typically Viennese combination of the operetta and the film" (491). Yet Kraus, ever the advocate of the word, continued to view the play as an exclusively verbal work of art and, repudiating the idea of documentary theater, insisted on its essential unperformability. Kraus turned down offers by Max Reinhardt and Erwin Piscator to stage the play, and he particularly objected to the latter's employment of projections and filmed interludes. At any rate, Bertolt Brecht, who was especially attracted by the play's filmic qualities, took it as a theatrical model, and Lensing believes that Brecht's *Furcht und Elend des Dritten Reiches* (first published in English as *The Private Life of the Master Race*) and *Schwejk im Zweiten Weltkrieg* ([The Good Soldier] *Schweik in the Second World War*) betray the influence of Kraus's play. Pointing to the need for a fresh evaluation of the play's scenic structure and theatrical appeal, Lensing concludes that "the drama's very early and innovative use of the cinema on the stage, Kraus's use of projections as disillusioning documents and as epic interruptions anticipated similar techniques employed by Piscator in his early agitatorial revues . . . and pointed forward to Brecht's deliberations about the place of the cinema in his epic theater" (493–94).

Jochen Stremmel's book *Dritte Walpurgisnacht: Über einen Text von Karl Kraus* (The Third Walpurgis Night. About a Work of Karl Kraus, 1982) is one of the relatively few studies dealing with a single work of the satirist. The title of Kraus's book, which did not appear in its entirety until 1952, alludes to the "romantic" and the "classical" Walpurgis Nights in parts 1 and 2 of Goethe's *Faust* as well as to the Third Reich. Stremmel's study is less an interpretation or evaluation of Kraus's text than a philological companion to a close reading of what is, as the author correctly points out, one of the least known and most misunderstood works of Kraus. Somewhat extravagantly, the author feels that this enigmatic and encoded work pre-supposes an acquaintance with the preceding thirty-four volumes of *Die Fackel* and thus fairly cries out for a critical edition. The misunderstanding on the part of some contemporaneous critics began with Kraus's striking first sentence: "Mir fällt zu Hitler nichts ein" ("I cannot think of anything to say about Hitler" — or "What can I say about Hitler?"). As it turned out, the apocalyptic visionary did have a great deal to say about Hitler and Hitlerism, and thus it is clear that his words, far from being indicative of resignation, really constituted a heuristic device for depicting the witches' sabbath of the time, highlighting the incommensurability of the intellect and human spirit with the horrors being perpetrated by the mindless and brutal regime across the German border.

The first section of Stremmel's book is entitled "Satirical Polemic or Polemic Satire," an allusion to the fact that Kraus himself classified this work as a polemical work of art or a polemical satire. On the basis of his ex-amination of characteristic stylistic elements, Stremmel concludes that this work has been less popular or effective than Kraus's other writings because its syntactically dense structure and apodictic, allusive language make it hard to read. Considerable interest attaches to the author's account of the genesis of this work and of the way it has been edited and presented to the public. In this case Kraus made a unique technical concession. Because of the length of his manuscript and in an effort to save time, he spoke the text into a dictaphone, presumably in the late summer of 1933, thus enabling all printers of the house of Jahoda and Siegel (and not just the two who were able to decipher his minuscule handwriting) to work on it. Unfortu-nately, this recording has not been preserved. Disagreeing with Heinrich Fischer, who states in his 1952 edition (Munich: Kösel, 308) that Kraus decided not to publish this work after it had been typeset, Stremmel at-tempts to demonstrate that this decision (to prevent bloody reprisals by the Nazis) had been made before the manuscript had been set, when Kraus left for Janovice Castle in early September of that year. (Parts of the work, chiefly those dealing with Austria rather than Germany, appeared in an is-sue of the *Fackel* in 1934). According to Stremmel, the satirist gave or sent copies of the galleys to Sidonie Nádherný and his American disciple and sometime translator Albert Bloch, which indicates that he regarded this work as his intellectual legacy. However, more recent research tells a differ-ent story. In her 1986 article "Zur Überlieferung der *Dritten Walpurgis-nacht*," Erika Wimmer-Webhofer states that in the fall of 1939 Oskar Sa-mek made three typescript copies on the basis of the galleys (with Kraus's handwritten corrections), one of which he sent to Albert Bloch for safe-keeping. This copy is now part of the Bloch papers at the Brenner Archiv in Innsbruck. Samek sent the corrected galleys to Switzerland, then took them with him to the United States, and eventually donated them to the Jewish National and University Library in Jerusalem. Kraus's original manuscript is lost.

In criticizing Heinrich Fischer's edition of *The Third Walpurgis Night* Stremmel speaks of an "ominous dematerialization" (52), meaning the absence of explanatory notes. Stremmel realizes that this is a "work in progress" and that an important Kraus aphorism seems to sanction this approach: "An understanding of my work is impeded by a knowledge of my material. People don't realize that what is there must first be invented, and that it is worth inventing. Nor do they see that a satirist for whom people exist as though he had invented them needs more strength than one who invents persons as though they existed." However, Fischer was inconsistent; for example, he added some first names to Kraus's text (Theodor to Lessing, for instance, presumably to prevent confusion with Gotthold Ephraim Lessing). Stremmel stops short of suggesting that the numerous quotations in the text (one hundred from Goethe, mainly from *Faust,* and twenty-seven from Shakespeare's "bloody" tragedies: *Macbeth, King Lear,* and *Hamlet*) should have been identified.

In providing what the Germans call a *Rezeptionsgeschichte* of the work, Stremmel discusses favorable reactions by Erich Pfeiffer-Belli, Paul Schal-lück, Edwin Hartl, Kurt Krolop, Helmut Arntzen, and Michael Scharang as well as negative assessments by Willy Haas and Hans Mayer. "The polemic is weak and diffuse," writes Mayer, "the language strangely colorless and unfocused. The events of early 1933 had struck the great journalist dumb in the most literal sense of the word" (1957, 58). More appreciatively the author cites and comments on the six theses of the German critic Wolfgang Frühwald (1971):

> 1. Kraus's linguistic, moral, and social satire is intended to have an ennobling effect on readers and listeners that is inherent in the art form satire. 2. "*Man frage nicht...*" [Kraus's last poem: 'Don't ask why all this time I never spoke. / Wordless am I, / and won't say why. / And silence reigns because the bedrock broke. / No word redeems; / one only speaks in dreams. / A smiling sun the sleeper's images evoke. / Time marches on; / the final difference is none. / The word expired when that world awoke.' Translated by Max Knight] is the concentrated result of the genesis of *The Third Walpurgis Night* and as such the climax of Kraus's satiric work. 3. In its intention and effect *The Third Walpurgis Night* is in the tradition of the philippics of German writers against their fatherland. 4. Karl Kraus uses key phrases of National Socialist propaganda to test the effects of his stylistic principle of satiric destruction on

this brutishness. 5. Kraus transfers the central problem of *The Third Walpurgis Night*, the separation of the cliché content from its linguistic form, into the structure of his work by crossing the boundary lines of artistic satire in the interest of political action. 6. Kraus's enforced concern with artistic works of other ages in the last numbers of the *Fackel* is only another form of satire. (Frühwald, 111–125)

It is obvious that Stremmel disagrees with Heinrich Fischer and agrees with Wilhelm Alff on a basic point: the way in which Kraus's writings should be edited and presented. A popular edition of *Die Dritte Walpurgisnacht* (Munich: Kösel, 1967) contains an afterword by Alff ("Karl Kraus und die Zeitgeschichte 1927–34") prefaced by Heinrich Fischer, who says, even as he praises Alff's competence, that he agreed to its inclusion only reluctantly because he felt that it reduced Kraus's symbolic, apocalyptic vision to mere *Stofflichkeit* (materiality, meaning concern with subject matter or information). Annotating Kraus's work and placing it in the context of his time reduces the satirist's apocalyptic vision to the material plane and takes it back to that topicality based on concrete subject matter that Kraus always strove to escape. Kraus felt that his work would increase in significance and relevance as the specific occasion, the political, historical, literary, and personal details receded into the background and that the symbolic, timeless, paradigmatic quality of his work would then come to the fore. Never interested in merely providing "information," Kraus felt that language would overcome the obstacle of a reader's unfamiliarity with circumstances and details. Fischer is convinced that the repeated close readings of Kraus's writings that the satirist called for would result in clarity and comprehension without background information and explanatory notes. He concedes that Alff's essay is good of its kind, but since the author writes from the viewpoint of a historian, his remarks are irrelevant in a work that is on the same prophetic level as *The Last Days of Mankind*. Fischer also admits that this approach is likely to be welcomed by younger readers, to whom names like Engelbert Dollfuß, Emil Fey, Ernst Rüdiger von Starhemberg, Johannes Schober, Otto Bauer, and Karl Renner, organizations like the Schutzbund and the Heimwehr, or the events of July 1927 are not very meaningful. Actually, Alff does not provide identifying lexical notes for Kraus's many allusions but gives an unimpassioned survey of Austrian history and politics during the half-dozen years preceding the genesis of Kraus's work. Believing that it should be read as a topical account of 1933 rather than a literary work, Alff places it in the context of German and Austrian politics. Kraus himself rejected the accusation that his support of the hapless Chancellor Dollfuß at the time he wrote the *Dritte Walpurgisnacht* placed him in the corner of "clerico-fascism," for he rejected all such facile political or ideological labels. Wilhelm Alff believes that *The Third*

Walpurgis Night is aimed more at Austria than at Germany and concludes that "it is the depiction of what the regime of Chancellor Dollfuß was saving Austria from" (365).

Michael Scharang's remarks on *The Third Walpurgis Night* (1987) sound like an angry young man's *"J'accuse"* uttered in Kurt Waldheim's Austria. Regarding this work as still unknown and suppressed, singularly unbearable for postwar society, Scharang believes it to be part of the general repression of Austria's role in the Nazi period. With this work, which described the unfathomable early horrors of the Nazi regime and mercilessly exposed the roots of Austro-Fascism and the connection between minor crooks and major criminals, the satirist dealt the Austrians and the Germans a blow from which they have yet to recover. He was wrong about the Austrian fascists, mistaking them for unselfish patriots who would never deliver their country to the bloodthirsty Germans. Up to that time the satirist had taken the world at its word, but fascism and Nazism did this by themselves, pulling the rug out from under satire. Scharang views "Mir fällt zu Hitler nichts ein . . . " as a sort of trap that unmasks those who do not bother to read the succeeding three hundred pages and therefore believe that this statement stamps Kraus, the self-righteous, voluble know-it-all, as a dumbstruck, craven failure — but Austrian postwar society, with its numerous old Nazis and fascists, likes the idea of a mute Karl Kraus. By dying two years before the Anschluß, Scharang concludes, the satirist was spared witnessing the Austrian contribution to the third Walpurgis Night.

Karl Kraus's sixtieth birthday was celebrated with a musical-literary matinee that included the showing of a new film, *Karl Kraus liest aus eigenen Schriften* (Karl Kraus Reading from His Works), several articles, and the publication (by Richard Lányi) of *Stimmen über Karl Kraus zum 60. Geburtstag* (1934) with tributes by Knut Hamsun, Henri Barbusse, Karel Čapek, Marcel Ray, Jan Münzer (his French and Czech translators), Alban Berg, Oskar Jellinek (poetic "Thanks of the German Language to Karl Kraus"), and others. Berthold Viertel's elegiac contribution sums up the feelings of those still loyal to Kraus:

> Karl Kraus has turned sixty. When we were boys of fourteen . . . we read his *Fackel* while hiding it under our school benches. We never stopped reading it — but now he has stopped writing it. After a lifetime of powerful speech this warner is now silent. For there no longer is anything to warn about. Everything happened the way he knew it beforehand, foresaw and foretold it. All horrors have come to pass — that war and this peace. He has had the harshest fate: to be proved right in such a frightful way. So he finally fell silent, like the prophet Samuel who went up on the mountain and did not look down upon the lost city. The harshest fate, the fate of the prophet who is confirmed by misfortune. They were all

writing feuilletons when Karl Kraus started writing his *mene tekel*. Today they continue to write their feuilletons, but Karl Kraus is silent. What?! He has turned sixty? So much the worse for all of us. He has lived to be sixty in vain. What good is it to eulogize him now? The future will eulogize him. Our downfall at least does one thing for him: it accredits his thought and his writing. The future will make use of it. (40)

7:   Panegyrics and Pans

Leopold Liegler's book *Karl Kraus und sein Werk* (1920) is an extended exercise in hagiography. Unrelievedly reverential and uncritical, it was published by a bookstore that served as a headquarters for Kraus's books and readings, and it was printed by the firm of Jahoda and Siegel, which produced *Die Fackel*. In Kraus's lifetime, Liegler's panegyric, which appeared in a second edition in 1933, was the standard reference on the satirist, and despite its turgid style and painfully evident anti-Semitic orientation, it is still essential reading for its background of an age and its perceptive presentation of salient features of Kraus's life and work.

Right at the outset the author wins the reader's sympathies by saying that work on his book made the war years easier for him to bear. He views Kraus, "the only living German satirist" (58), as a man who, like no one before him, was chosen to experience the problems of the age in himself. The anticorruptionism of the early *Fackel* proceeded from a critique of the press (which Liegler views as an expression of Jewish plutocratic materialism and pernicious capitalism) via a critique of society to a critique of culture; Kraus, the great protector of Austrian values, "is attached to this country with an ardor that he himself hardly acknowledges; he is and will remain an Austrian with all his characteristic traits" (61). Among these the author mentions a spiritual joie de vivre, a certain irrational quality of thought and action, an almost childlike cheerfulness and benevolence, and a love of *raisonnement*, but also a cruel fanaticism where corruption is evidenced. Pointing out that the satirist tends to view even the most trivial phenomena as exemplary and to expose their roots, the author believes the important thing is "the reflection of the occasion (*Anlaß*) that the satirist projects onto an artistic plane in accordance with his generalizing ethical perspective" (65). His uncompromising, inexorable approach is born not of an insatiable urge to judge and condemn but of an unconditional moral imperative that leads him to recognize only a responsibility toward his own self. Liegler presents a useful differentiation between humor and satire. A humorist is a great forgiver and conciliator who sympathetically and cheerfully integrates all dissonances into a serene philosophy, whereas a satirist is an uncompromising avenger. Like Juvenal and Aristophanes, who satirized the general dissolution of their cultures and used their wit to remove their opponents symbolically, Kraus cannot forgive his intellectual and spiritual adversaries. Liegler engages in some wishful thinking when he writes:

"Vienna made Karl Kraus necessary, but to the extent that it was receptive to intellectual qualities, it recognized, appreciated, and loved him" (93). However, the author seems to retract this statement near the end of his book, when he writes that the "usual ferment" (415) of the man who is the very antipode of the Viennese brand of *Gemütlichkeit*, emotional laxity, and political immaturity has had relatively little effectiveness, and for this Liegler blames the psyche of Austrian and Viennese intellectuals, who have talent but are charmingly slack and devoid of character.

Liegler really hits his stride in the section entitled "Weltgericht" (Last Judgment) in which he discusses *The Last Days of Mankind* and adduces items and examples that are not found in Kraus: newspaper ads that he describes as subhuman evidence of profiteers who traffic in human misery, people who offend with a tastelessness that borders on ghoulishness. "In this chaos," he writes, "Karl Kraus was one of the few who clearly and fearlessly stated the significance of all these horrors, this bestiality that had become a duty, sobering up those who had allowed themselves to be bedazzled by the rapture of the first months of the war and consoling and energizing those who had despaired" (239).

Valuable material is also contained in chapter 3, "Die Sprache," on Kraus's relationship to language, which to him was not merely a means of communication but a way of uncovering intellectual and spiritual connections. Liegler points to Kraus's models, the German Romanticists Novalis, Schlegel, and Brentano, who, like him, were dialecticians, fragmentists, aphorists, and wits, writers and thinkers who believed in the oracular quality of language; and the author traces this relationship by quoting their statements. In this leisurely exploration of Kraus's verbal art and "language mysticism" (323), which he defines as "the unfathomable experience . . . that in the chosen word, idea, formation, color, and mood come about in such a mysterious way that the outer world is not only designated but, by virtue of the associative potential supplied by this word, interpreted as well" (313), Liegler gives sensitive stylistic analyses of Kraus's seminal wartime essay (and address) "In These Great Times . . . ," in which Kraus linguistically deflates the "greatness" of wartime, and of several poems, epigrams, and aphorisms. The author ingeniously elucidates some of these with the aid of diagrams, charts, and graphs to show the architectonic construction of much of Kraus's prose and verse. In his puns the key is often supplied by some visual feature. For example, when Kraus writes that a man cannot be unappetizing enough for the satirist not to *angreifen* him, the dual sense of the verb ("touch" and "attack") is clearly conveyed. Meaningful artistic structures are also highlighted by diagramming the contents of a *Fackel* issue (474–83, May 23, 1918) and of a collection of verse (*Worte in Versen* iii). In Kraus's aphorisms Liegler discerns unparalleled linguistic precision and intensity, and he attempts to defend the satirist's poetry against the charge that it is conventional in diction and uses unimaginative, traditional rhymes.

Liegler also comments on *Die chinesische Mauer* (The Great Wall of China), a collection of essays whose theme is the entire complex of Judeo-Christian hostility toward nature. In contrast to this asceticism Kraus presents the Chinese standpoint as ideal; it sunders enjoyment and ethics and thus keeps both inviolate, enabling the Chinese to juggle and master life and love without encumbering the necessities of life with the freight of conscience.

The usefulness of Liegler's book is enhanced by photos and the facsimile of a proofsheet from Kraus's wartime play, with his handwritten corrections and marginalia.

Liegler, who is sometimes described as one of Kraus's secretaries or assistants, had a falling-out with Kraus over the proper way to present or edit the Austrian dialect in the plays of Johann Nepomuk Nestroy, but he did remain loyal to Kraus. In 1936 Richard Lányi printed Liegler's essay *In Memoriam Karl Kraus,* based on his obituary in the *Basler National-Zeitung* of June 16, 1936 and his memorial address over Radio Vienna the same day. Here Liegler is more balanced and less adulatory than in his book. Painfully aware that Kraus has often been misunderstood, the author states as the satirist's great theme "the unmasking of the liberal-capitalistic press as a tool of the banalization and mechanization of intellectual concerns" (6). In this quest Kraus, a mystic of language, believed that language was a magical key and an instrument for bringing order into chaos. He was "accursed to judge and condemn, to be inhuman out of humaneness," (6) but this mission made him such an absolutist that he no longer lived in the real world and did not accept relative standards. Only his stature as a satirist was the foundation of his spiritual superiority and the moral legitimation of his judgmental stance. He lived the paradox of an absolute existence in a kind of *coincidenta oppositorum,* a simultaneity of opposites, and this made him both a stumbling block and a touchstone for his contemporaries. He was forceful, severe, and hermetic, yet also childlike and open to genuine enjoyment, naive and sophisticated, kindly and inexorable, petty and magnanimous. When he erred, he did so as a Platonist who regarded ideas and laws as more important and more binding than the objects and practices of reality.

Berthold Viertel's book *Karl Kraus. Ein Charakter und die Zeit* (1921) is notable on several counts. This rapturous, occasionally rhapsodic evocation of the satirist as a guide and model represents the thanks of the younger generation, those who served in World War I and to whom Kraus represented "an importunate, ruthlessly admonishing creditor of our innermost salvation" (83). Viertel's essay was, in fact, written in Eastern Galicia during the war and published in Siegfried Jacobsohn's journal *Die Schaubühne* before Kämmerer of Dresden issued it in book form. Two years later Kraus dedicated his play *Wolkenkuckucksheim* (Cloudcuckooland) to Viertel, and the latter, who had a distinguished career in the theater as well as being a poet and an essayist, directed Kraus's dream plays *Traumstück* and *Traumtheater* in Berlin in 1925. While Viertel does not pretend to imitate Kraus's style, his language was clearly influenced by the satirist, whose new *Fackel* he began to read at the age of fourteen. "He refreshed and rejuvenated us, no matter how young we were, and he imbued us with creative warmth" (15). The author views Kraus's satire as a struggle of the satirist against creatures of his invention and as a play of the imagination. When he met persons satirized by Kraus, he was disappointed. "In reality they were not as exciting, stimulating, or controversial as in the writings of Karl Kraus" (13). Viertel views Kraus as first and last a satirist, and one who worked on the difficult soil of Vienna. "Vienna expected an enjoyable *chronique scandaleuse*," he writes; "he could have grown old as the ill-mannered darling of Viennese grace . . . and been permitted a wooden sword that left light scratches . . . but Kraus became a spoilsport" (19). Paradoxical though this may seem, Viertel believes that "Kraus's satiric effect was so purifying that he was able to praise again" (22). Describing satire as the art of praising, of an evaluating passion, the author argues that satire devalues so that there might be a proper valuation.

The dual occasion of Kraus's fiftieth birthday and the twenty-fifth anniversary of *Die Fackel* gave rise to *Karl Kraus*, a rapturous thirty-five-page booklet written by the Swiss critic Max Rychner (1924). The author attempts to integrate Kraus into the ranks of the eminent practitioners of a *littérature militante* who have adopted the Voltairean *Écrasez l'infâme!* as their watchword. Juvenal said that it is difficult not to write satire. "Every age," Rychner writes, "has its satiric spirit that grows out of it organically. . . . His linguistic creations ennoble the inadequacies that our age drags along" (10–11). By the red light of the *Fackel*, a declining culture has to learn what fear is, and its every issue is a linguistic masterpiece and a joust with a culture whose insignia Kraus long ago identified as marks of the decline of the West. In an effort to place Kraus in the tradition of such great critics of the press and journalists as Schopenhauer, Flaubert, and Gérard de Nerval and to link him with such great thinkers of the nineteenth century as Nietzsche and Kierkegaard, Rychner describes the satirist as the most untimely (*unzeitgemäßeste*) citizen of Vienna and Austria. With reference to Kraus's fight against the press, which is more than tilting at windmills, he quotes what the Danish philosopher wrote in 1846: "If Christ came into the world today, his target would not be high priests but journalists" (19).

Kraus's artistry is what saves him from despair over his dismal material; if he were stripped of his artistry, he would be no more than a sensible censurer. Not surprisingly, Rychner is on the satirist's side in his polemics against Franz Werfel and Albert Ehrenstein; the attack by the latter is likened to a glowworm that pretends to outshine or dim the light of the *Fackel* but only winds up singeing its wings. "Thus far no arrow directed at Kraus has escaped the fate of hitting, in boomerang fashion, the person who shot it off" (27). Those who see in Kraus only a grumbler (*Nörgler*) should read him on Nestroy or Altenberg, for he is a fighter with an angry but magnanimous heart. The truth he discerns may not be everyone's truth, but in serving it so enthusiastically he has turned it into a goddess that we need to venerate.

Was it Walter Benjamin's abstruse style that led Karl Kraus to characterize the German critic's major 1931 essay on him, one of the most insightful and suggestive appreciations of many aspects of the satirist's work, as wellintentioned but incomprehensible? Benjamin's "Karl Kraus" appeared in four installments in the *Frankfurter Zeitung*, and it is available in English in *Reflections*, a collection of Benjamin's essays, aphorisms, and autobiographical writings translated by Edmund Jephcott (1978). In his introduction Peter Demetz, the book's editor, characterizes Kraus as "a towering cult figure for a particular generation of Austrian and German writers . . . to many the Isaiah of decaying old Europe or at least the Jewish Swift of Vienna . . . [who] combined the interests and energies of H. L. Mencken, Sören Kierkegaard, and a demonic Woody Allen, all in one" (xxxv). In his essay Walter Benjamin displays an acquaintance with critical writing on Kraus from Robert Scheu to Leopold Liegler and Berthold Viertel. Commenting on Liegler, Benjamin says that his work springs from an apologetic posture and that he undertook the impossible task of certifying Kraus as an ethical personality. Far from standing at the frontier of a new age, Kraus stands at the threshold of the Last Judgment, a man to whom everything falls within the sphere of justice, which is to say, within the sphere of language. With reference to Kraus's attitude in the "great times" of World War I, Benjamin finds the image of "a silence turned inside out, a silence that catches the storm of events in its black folds, billows, its livid lining turned outward. . . . The trinity of silence, knowledge, and alertness constitutes the figure of Kraus the polemicist" (243). Identifying quotation as the basis of Kraus's polemical procedure, which is expressive of the satirist's passion to unmask his adversaries by imitating their language, Benjamin points to the peculiar interplay between reactionary theory and revolutionary practice. "Only in despair did he discover in quotation the power not to preserve but to purify, to tear from context, to destroy. . . . All the martial energies of this man are innate civic virtues, only in the melee did they take on their combative aspect. But already no one recognizes this any more, no one can grasp the necessity that compelled this great bourgeois character to become a comedian, this guardian of Goethean linguistic values a polemicist, or why this irreproachably honorable man went berserk. This, however, was bound to happen, since he thought fit to begin changing the world with his own class, in his own home, in Vienna" (271). Benjamin displays a becoming awareness of Kraus's interlacing of biblical pathos with a stubborn fixation on the offensive aspects of Viennese life, but a number of critics concerned with Kraus's attitude toward the social and political problems of his time have taken exception to Benjamin's statement that "the sociological area never becomes transparent to him" (259).

A few years before publishing his essay in the *Frankfurter Zeitung* Benjamin had commented on Kraus in a dramatically more evocative fashion in the section called *Kriegerdenkmal* (Monument of a Warrior) in his book *Einbahnstraße* (One-Way Street, 1928, quoted from Benjamin, *Schriften* i, 1955, 553–54).

Nothing more dreary than his adherents, nothing more God-forsaken than his adversaries. No name that would be honored more fittingly by silence. In ancient armor, grinning grimly, a Chinese idol, brandishing his drawn swords in both hands, he performs a war dance before the sepulchre of the German language. The man who is "only one of the epigones who live in the old house of language" has become the guardian of its crypt, keeping vigil day and night. No post has ever been guarded more faithfully, and none has ever been more lost. Here stands a man who draws from his world's ocean of tears like a Danaid, and the rock that is to bury his enemies rolls Sisyphus-like out of his hands. What is more helpless than his conversion? What more impotent than his humaneness? What more hopeless than his fight against the press? What does he know of the forces truly allied with him? Yet what prophetic vision of the new magicians can compare with the listening of this shaman, whose words are supplied by a dead language? . . . Murmurs from a chthonic depth of language prophesy for him — as helpless as only spirit voices can sound. Every sound is incomparably genuine, but they all leave one perplexed like the speech of specters. Blind as manes, obtuse as spirits that know only the voice of the blood and do not care what they perpetrate in the realm of the living, language calls upon him to wreak vengeance. But he cannot err, for its mandates are infallible. Whoever comes within reach of his arm is already judged; in his mouth a mere name becomes a judgment. When he opens his mouth, the colorless flame of wit licks his lips. No one who walks on the paths of life would ever encounter him. On an archaic field of honor, on an enormous battleground of bloody labor, he rages before a deserted sepulchre. The honors of his death will be immeasurable, the last that will be bestowed.

Karl F. Kocmata's twenty-four-page wartime pamphlet *Karl Kraus, der Krieg und die Helden der Feder* (Karl Kraus, the War, and the Heroes of the Pen, 1916) is a rather crude pastiche of *Fackel* themes and an obvious attempt to bask in the reflected glory of the satirist. The author claims to be the voice of youth hailing a crier for humaneness in the desert of wartime culture as well as the conscience of his time. "Karl Kraus has become the spokesman of those who lie in the trenches and are defenseless against the commercial speculations of our poets. . . . With few exceptions, our poets have gone mad in the terrible ravages of wartime" (8–9, 12). Kocmata gives a sort of dishonor roll of those who were quick to scale the ramparts of rhyme and jump on the bandwagon of bathos and banality: Gerhart Hauptmann, Richard Dehmel, Ludwig Ganghofer, Hans Müller, Richard Schaukal, Ludwig Thoma, Felix Salten, Alfons Petzold, and others. By contrast, it is the mission of Kraus, a bastion of decency and dignity, to sketch in his *Fackel* an indelible picture of the times for the present and the future, registering this century's lapse into barbarity.

The very title of Fritz Kreuzig's pamphlet *Ave Karl Kraus!* (1919) indicates its extravagant tone. It consists of five rapturous poems and five equally gushy, visionary, evocative pieces of poetic prose. As Kreuzig evokes a Viennese phantasmagoria of cultural decline and bewails the chaos produced by technology and newsprint, Kraus is seen as an apostate of life, a great scourge and prophet, a bacchant out of torment, an ascetic out of a creator's joy, and a torchbearer of Eros. It is, however, difficult to fault Kreuzig's conclusion that one's "attitude to the problem Karl Kraus is a fine sieve for cultural values" (7). Kreuzig borrows the last line of Goethe's drama *Götz von Berlichingen* when he writes, "Woe to the century that expelled you / pushed you away!" (7).

On October 25, 1925, the essayist and journalist Anton Kuh, a noted Viennese wit, delivered an extemporaneous address at the Konzerthaus that was shortly thereafter issued by J. Deibler, Vienna, on the basis of a stenographic protocol. In a supercharged, tumultuous atmosphere and with numerous interruptions by hecklers, Kuh engaged in verbal pyrotechnics in an effort to expose and eliminate the "pestilence of Kraus worship and the motif of having the last word" (17) and to excoriate "the satanic, talented scion of a Jewish house, the frothy, good- for-nothing product of decadence, ambition-crazed, self-righteous, full of the jiggling, squeaky-voiced, clownish talents that jump about the tables at a ritual wedding" (52). Kuh's title, *Der Affe Zarathustras*, derived from Friedrich Nietzsche's *Thus Spake Zarathustra*, specifically the episode "On Passing By" ("Where one can no longer love, one should pass by"), in which Zarathustra encounters a "foaming fool" called "Zarathustra's ape" because he imitates his speech and ideas.

Right at the outset Kuh acknowledges his unruly audience, fanatical on one side or the other, by expressing this chilling insight: "I see, unfortunately: Whether it's Hitler or Karl Kraus, it's all the same" (9). Not surprisingly, Kuh, who was working for the press czar Imre Békessy at the time, depicted Kraus as a demagogue, monomaniac, and paranoid (43), a malign influence generally. "The work of this man is a series of deprecations, uprootings, polemical attacks . . . an uninterrupted chain of polemics against Harden, Heine, Nietzsche, Békessy" (14). *Die Fackel* is characterized as an *"Anspielungstalmud"* (38) — a Talmud of allusions or insinuations. Just as Kraus held Heine responsible for the feuilletonists, Kraus must be held responsible for the Krausians (though Kuh claims that the satirist despises his adherents). In his view Kraus demolished Heine because "he somehow sensed a certain consanguinity of Jewish intellect in the poet and told himself: One of us will have to fall by the wayside" (48). Kuh, himself Jewish, depicts Kraus as being "nailed to the cross of the *mishpocha"* (22), a member of the plebeian intelligentsia who is burdened by disagreeable family complexes. The detective-like glance that he practiced in his own family enabled him to recognize what could be unmasked and apprehended in the outside world. Another Jewish quality discerned by Kuh is Kraus's lawyerlike (*advokatorisch*) mind. Kuh's diatribe caused Kraus to bring suit against him for defamation of character, but he did not prevail until a later occasion.

The tone of *Der Fackelreiter*, a pamphlet published by Emanuel Bin Gorion (actually Berdiczevsky) on the eve of the Nazis' accession to power (1932) is unrelievedly ironic and even snide. "How come," asks the author, "that the press, at which Kraus has been taking potshots for more than thirty years, has continued to expand in uncanny fashion?" (4). The villains of the press cannot be rooted out if they are fought with their own weapons; the system, not individuals, needs to be attacked. The wartime address "In These Great Times . . . " is essentially an attack on the press, but what should have been excoriated was the state and the warring powers. *The Last Days of Mankind* is not about (or against) war but lashes out at far less important concomitants and side issues of the carnage, such as war correspondents, "individual little heads of the war hydra. . . . No war correspondent ever drove anyone to death! The effect is perverse from someone who in wartime had nothing better to do than to write. He should have preached compassion and love instead of hate!" (14). Kraus's "unparalleled egomania" (14) leads him to relate everything that happens in the world to his person and to prove that he is always right. This professional moralist . . . prosecutor and judge in one" (14) lacks love and pain. In several hundred issues of the *Fackel*, the most boring journal in existence, there is not one positive idea or valuable suggestion. Kraus "looks at the world from the perspective of a dachshund," and "his writing style is similar to a pogrom" (14). To demonstrate the banality of Kraus's rhymes, Bin Gorion presents a persiflage of two of his love poems. "An meinen Drucker" elicits this comment: It is "a grotesque idea to sing the praises of a printer — not as a person but as a printer of this author's works" (8). In Kraus's readings the author sees only "declaimed issues of the *Fackel*" (9), and he makes fun of Kraus's austere Offenbach performances in programmatic opposition to the opulent productions of Max Reinhardt or Erwin Piscator. Not surprisingly, Bin Gorion is on Alfred Kerr's side in Kraus's postwar polemic against the author of notorious poetic wartime tirades against Romanians, averring that he much prefers a converted militarist to a person who never errs. It is unfair to judge wartime attitudes and actions born of patriotic rapture with the standards and feelings of the postwar period, and "it is unfair and a sign of a base mentality to rummage around in a person's past" (11).

In a one-page epilogue Bin Gorion deals with Kraus's relation to Judaism, characterizing his attitude as provocative, tactless, and unethical. He points out that all negative figures of Kraus's world theater — war profiteers and mendacious journalists — bear Jewish names and that Kraus displays an almost pathological indulgence in Yiddish expressions. "In contrast to the classical apostates of earlier times," he writes, "who became accusers and persecutors of the synagogue out of opposition against a rigidified theology or pain caused by an undeserved pariah's existence, Kraus appears as a simple, naked, shameless, cynical renegade" (16).

8: Shrunk by "Shrinks"

The psychoanalyst and writer Fritz Wittels published some essays in the early *Fackel* under the pseudonym Avicenna. In 1908 Kraus printed a series of aphorisms dealing with the disloyalty that he was experiencing in some cases and foreseeing in others. Wittels may have been offended by some veiled allusions to him, for in 1910 he published a novel entitled *Ezechiel der Zugereiste* (Ezechiel the Newcomer), in which there is a Kraus figure named Benjamin Eckelhaft (Nassty), editor of *Das Riesenmaul* (The Giant Maw). Another unflattering portrait of the satirist is given in the story of Ernesto, an exhibitionist with "hysterogenic complexes," which is included in Wittels's collection of essays. *Alles um Liebe* (All for Love), issued in 1912. On January 12, 1910, Wittels had presented a paper entitled "The Fackel Neurosis" at a meeting of the Vienna Psychoanalytic Society that was attended by such luminaries as Sigmund Freud, Alfred Adler, Eduard Hitschmann, Josef Friedjung, Otto Rank, and Wilhelm Stekel. At that meeting, whose protocol is included in *Minutes of the Vienna Psychoanalytic Society 1908–1910* (1967), Wittels identified three problems with regard to Kraus. He had become a journalist of his own inclination and then, when all paths to that goal had been smoothed out, "suddenly shifted gears, because of some personal motive, to become an 'anticorruptionist'" (383). Later he changed again: "Journalists interest him no longer; he throws himself into the problem of sexuality" (383), and later still he became a writer of aphorisms, contenting himself with a "form of expression that is the most unimpassioned of all and is not suitable to permit so volcanic and high-spirited a writer to give full vent to his feelings" (383). Wittels claims that Kraus's neurotic attitude toward one particular newspaper was the starting point for his hatred of journalists. (Kraus's father was named Jacob, the "blessed one" of the Bible, "Benedictus" in the Vulgate, and Wittels sees significance in Kraus's attacks on men whose names start with a B: Benedikt — but, curiously enough, not Bacher, for years the codirector of the *Neue Freie Presse* — Bahr, Bukowics, Bauer, and Buchbinder.) Wittels further claims that Kraus's relationships with his parents as well as his siblings are filled with enmity: "He hates them, a circumstance that may perhaps explain a motive that was always recurring throughout his life: He attaches himself to someone in passionate friendship which later turns into the bitterest enmity. . . . The continual repetition of this game in Kraus's life is the representation of the relationship of his brothers and him-

self to their father. . . . The capstone to this chain of evidence is the fact
that the senior Kraus was a manufacturer and produced pulp for newspapers" (385–86).

In the second period of the *Fackel*, Wittels continues, Kraus's private
neurosis became associated with the general neurosis of the time. "In this
phase Kraus has, in some respects, himself lived through much of what
Freud has found out by means of scientific work and has presented it in artistic form" (386). But there was "an involution back into neurosis;" in
fact, Wittels wishes to demonstrate "how out of neurosis art emerges, and
out of art once again neurosis" (388). "Kraus is a misshapen man," he goes
on, "as was Voltaire and as court jesters are described as having been.
Mockery seems to be linked with physical deformity, and in that way to be
suitable as a special domain of the Jews" (387).

In the discussion that followed Wittels's paper, Alfred Adler called
Kraus "a philistine run wild for whom the path to adequate self-indulgence
became cut off" (389); to Wilhelm Stekel, Kraus was "a paranoiac with
marked megalomania" (391); and Josef Friedjung delivered himself of the
opinion that Kraus's "pedantic sense of form is perhaps to be derived from
the fact that in his parental home German was not always spoken correctly
and purely" (392). Sigmund Freud said that he could evaluate Kraus "only
in a phenomenological and not in a moral sense" (392); he had originally
thought that Kraus might become an effective advocate of the cause of
psychoanalysis, but he had later recognized this to be an error in judgment:
"He lacks any trace of self-mastery and seems to be altogether at the mercy
of his instincts" (392). The *Minutes* also record that "Freud personally
finds Kraus's intellectual dependence on Peter Altenberg, who represents
the aestheticism of the impotent, distasteful" (392). Freud's early appreciation of Kraus is expressed in a letter he wrote the satirist on January
12, 1906, in which he speaks of "the partial conformity between your
views and endeavors and my own" (Freud, *Briefe 1873–1939*. Frankfurt:
S. Fischer, 1960, 248) and disavows any complicity in the accusation of
plagiarism leveled by Wilhelm Fliess against the late Otto Weininger and
another writer. Freud is careful to point out, however, that he does not
share the satirist's high regard for Weininger. Within the framework of
Kraus's rejection of psychoanalysis, the evidence indicates that he respected
Freud personally — Krausian ideas are paralleled in *Civilization and Its
Discontents* — but had little or no esteem for his disciples and imitators.

Among the participants at the Vienna "Krausfest" whom Arntzen discusses in unflattering terms in his book *Karl Kraus und die Presse* (1975) is
the German psychoanalyst Margarete Mitscherlich-Nielsen, whose remarks
on Kraus were printed under the title "Sittlichkeit und Kriminalität: Versuch einer Psychoanalyse" (An Attempt at a Psychoanalysis) in the Swiss

newspaper *Basler Nachrichten* (May 4, 11, 18, 1974). Arntzen briefly reports that Mitscherlich attempted to "punish" Kraus for his opposition to Freudian psychoanalysis, though not to destroy him, for she indicated that psychoanalysis could have helped the satirist to a better understanding of people — but would he then not have had to give up his satire? A more extensive critique of Mitscherlich's views may be found in *Karl Kraus and the Soul-Doctors: A Pioneer Critic and His Criticism of Psychiatry and Psychoanalysis* by the Hungarian-born American psychiatrist Thomas S. Szasz (1976). Szasz points out that Mitscherlich, "an unrepentant Freudian" (82), "proposed, in dead earnest, that there was a scientifically established connection between Kraus's spinal defect and his inclination to write satire . . . His spiritual uprightness was thus impugned by his bodily deformity" (86). On the face of it, Szasz is a vigorous champion of Kraus, whom he calls a "noble rhetorician" in contrast to Sigmund Freud, a "base rhetorician," but the stridency of his self-serving remarks soon makes it obvious that this prolific maverick is using Kraus only as a stick with which to beat (once again) the psychoanalytic-psychiatric establishment. The translations of Kraus's writings on the subject to which Szasz devotes a major portion of his book are nothing short of hair-raising and will be dealt with in another context.

Margarete Mitscherlich-Nielsen's psychoanalytical remarks on Karl Kraus, which were reprinted in the special 1975 Kraus issue of *text+kritik*, present the satirist as a lifelong melancholic and insomniac, as a vengeful manic depressive who managed to repress his feelings of guilt. Only his aggressiveness kept him from killing himself, and his attacks were his best defense mechanism, yet he felt persecuted by everyone. According to Mitscherlich, his accusations were masked self-accusations, and his anti-Semitism helped him deny his Jewish self-hatred. In analyzing Kraus's childhood experiences, Dr. Mitscherlich comes to the conclusion that his small stature and physical weakness caused him to become a model pupil in school. The curvature of his spine is seen as a constant psychic burden. Kraus had a loving, empathic, and vulnerable mother and an authoritarian, business-minded father, whom the son, according to Mitscherlich, equated with the *Neue Freie Presse*. Kraus's fight against such powerful institutions as Vienna's (and possibly Europe's) foremost daily is seen as an unfinished contest with Jacob Kraus. In the author's view, Kraus had a tendency to fly into a narcissistic rage and a hatred born of relatively trivial offenses. His relationship to his mother affected his love for the promiscuous Annie Kalmar and Sidonie Nádherný, who rejected his offer of marriage. Only from women did Kraus accept such hurts. After his mother's untimely death, a favorite teacher named Heinrich Sedlmayer became a substitute for her. A puppet theater is seen as an early transitional object that shaped

Kraus's desire to become an actor. Though he needed and wanted the applause of his readers and listeners, he despised them; Mitscherlich is not sure whether he despised his dependence on them or whether he tried to free himself from this dependence by despising them. Kraus himself had no guilt feelings, but he was prepared to bear the guilt of others. What tied him to "Sidi" was his "masochistic neurosis" and an "unconscious need to be punished" (34). He repeatedly chose women of whom he knew that he was neither their first nor their only lover. In general, Kraus turned his tendency toward self-laceration outward. His rage was originally directed at his mother, whom he regarded as unfaithful because she had borne her tenth child after him and then had left him when he was a teenager. "He coped with his jealousy by glorifying prostitution and presenting the combination of mother and whore as magnificent, unadulterated nature" (35). Expressing a commonly held belief about the nature of Kraus's obsession with language, Mitscherlich writes: "Both in an erotic sense and as an attempt to cope with profound separation anxieties, language had for him the unconscious symbolic significance of a transitional object" (36). In his supermorality and murderous aggressiveness, Kraus did not overlook any weakness of his adversaries, but often this was just a projection of his own feelings. In the satirist's postulate of absolute purity and perfection of language, Mitscherlich discerns a neurotic compulsion. She concludes that from Dreyfus to Dollfuß he was guilty of aggressive misjudgments and distorted half-truths.

Edwin Hartl, perhaps the foremost nonacademic Austrian critic of Kraus, attempts to set the record straight in a highly controversial matter in "Karl Kraus und die Psychoanalyse" (1977). He points out that many contemporaries attack Kraus and thereby defend themselves or the group with which they identify. Too often theory is equated with practice, but it should be borne in mind that Kraus attacked the psychoanalysts and not their doctrine, for which he had more respect. "Kraus has been misinterpreted," writes Hartl, "jubilantly by opponents and indignantly by adherents of Freud" (161). According to him, Kraus expressly exempted Freud from his satiric opposition until he had reason to suspect that Freud did not object to the practices of his disciples. What motivated him was a desire to defend creative people, both dead and alive, against patterns of psychoanalytic misinterpretation.

Hartl is careful to correct Ernest Jones, who wrote in his standard biography, *The Life and Work of Sigmund Freud* (1955), about Fritz Wittels's attack: "Somehow or other Kraus got to hear of Wittels's paper, and he responded by making several fierce attacks on psychoanalysis in . . . *Die Fackel*. Freud, however, did not take them seriously enough to be worth replying to" (118). Kraus did publish six aphorisms critical of psychoanalysis in 1910, but these concern psychoanalytic practice. His opposition dates from 1908, and at that time Kraus published numerous aphorisms directed against Wittels. However, Wittels' paper and the figure Benjamin Eckelhaft in his novel *Ezechiel der Zugereiste* show that it was Wittels who took revenge on Kraus, not the other way round. "In the early years of this century," writes Hartl, "Sigmund Freud and Karl Kraus were something like *dioscuri*, twin-like in their bearing and destiny, and far ahead of their time in their moral and other views" (161). Freud had as tough a time with the so-called Freudians as Kraus had with the so-called Krausians. While Kraus never attacked Freud, the father of psychoanalysis wrote Arnold Zweig in 1927 that Kraus was very low on his scale of esteem. In *Sigmund Freud: A Life for Our Time* (1988) Peter Gay points out that in a letter to Ferenczi dated February 1910 Freud spoke of the "unbridled vanity and lack of discipline of this talented beast, Karl Kraus" and shortly thereafter told the same associate that Kraus was "a mad half-wit with a great histrionic talent that enabled him to mime intelligence and indignation" (215).

Michael Worbs's study *Nervenkunst* (Art of the Nerves), the subtitle of which translates as *Literature and Psychoanalysis in Fin-de-Siècle Vienna* (1983), contains a chapter on Kraus's relationship with psychoanalysis and psychoanalysts. "It is not surprising," writes the author, "that those two outsiders and unsparing critics of fin-de-siècle Vienna [Kraus and Freud], who defined their position as a rejection of cultural hypocrisy, decadence, and aestheticism, should have been fellow travelers for a few years" (151). Kraus and Freud were originally allies in their struggle against Victorian repression and distortion of sexuality, but by 1907 or 1908 the satirist was criticizing the movement, the Freudians (whom he likened to "sorcerer's apprentices" in Goethe's sense), and psychoanalytic practice (for instance, neurosis-based interpretation of literature and art) rather than psychoanalytic theory. Wittels is seen as a sometime mediator who attempted to combine Freudian and Krausian ideas.

9: "Performer: Karl Kraus"

In the weekly *Sturm* (October 10, 1910, 94) Mirko Jelusich gave an evocative account of Kraus's first reading in Vienna (from his own works "Heine and the Consequences" and "The Great Wall of China"):

> To delineate the exceptional importance of the editor of *Die Fackel* here would be tantamount to carrying coals to Newcastle. . . . Kraus is the preeminent satirist of Austria, cheered by his fanatical adherents and feared by his adversaries, who have no weapon against his powerful attacks, his biting scorn and his crushing contempt but rigid, constant, impotent silence. That this silence is useless was shown by Kraus's reading, which was packed. . . . It was extraordinarily riveting to observe Kraus . . . how his face grew rigid and threatening and his shoulders were lifted like those of a beast of prey, how his right fist twitched across the table and seemed to choke an invisible throat, how he poured a verbal Niagara Falls over his breathless listeners. . . . All in all, an extraordinary evening that was marred only by the abashing thought that it had taken so long to enjoy the beauty of Kraus's linguistic skill . . . That this was his first reading in Vienna was not Kraus's fault, but Vienna's.

An even more graphic account of an early Kraus recital was given by the Danish writer Karin Michaelis in the newspaper *København* on November 14, 1911:

> All the lights have been extinguished. Only two candles shed their light up there on the green-covered table. They sparkle uncannily. Now comes Kraus. Young, with uncontrolled limbs, shy as a bat, he hurries to the table, anxiously barricades himself behind it, crosses his legs, strokes his forehead, wipes his nose, collects himself like a beast of prey ready to leap, waits, opens his mouth as if to bite, shuts it again, waits. An infinitely gentle, infinitely sad smile trembles on his face. A fleeting, stately, shy joy melts all severity in his young, intelligent, embittered-looking face. His nervous hands move over the manuscripts that he has brought along. He begins — sternly, thoughtfully, energetically, compelling through conviction. If he had spoken in Chinese or Persian, people would have followed him with equal suspense. His own inner fire has the same effect as the spark from a locomotive rushing by on a summer-parched prairie: everything flares up while he speaks. For an hour and a quarter he brandishes the blade of the word. Now his voice is hoarse with a quiet rage, now it sounds melodious, as if he were inserting a stanza from a folk song; now it rises to a roaring storm in which one can hardly distinguish a

word from a scream; at another moment it pierces the air like blows from gleaming weapons. . . . He pauses and rushes outside. He hurries, flees — his shadow appears in huge outline on the black wall — and disappears behind a curtain.

Kari Grimstad's study *Masks of the Prophet: The Theatrical World of Karl Kraus* (1982) is the most comprehensive and most ambitious treatment of the subject. The author has undertaken the arduous task of chronicling and evaluating Kraus's multifarious relationships with the theater and its practitioners. Using *Die Fackel* as her primary base, she proceeds chronologically and divides her study into five chapters that reflect the several masks worn by the role-playing Kraus; these are somewhat condescendingly entitled "The Gadfly," "The Knight-in-shining-armour," "The Prophet," "The Grand Inquisitor," and "The Defeated Idealist." It is all there — from Kraus's disastrous debut as an actor in 1893, complete with oversize costume and ill-fitting wig, to his late performances of Nestroy, Offenbach, and Shakespeare and his seven-hundredth public reading a few months before his death in 1936.

It is not clear whether Grimstad intended her book as a contribution to theatrical history and the history of drama criticism or to a better understanding of Karl Kraus, the man, the satirist, and the performer. While she succeeds in the former endeavor, albeit in a minor way, she fails to illuminate Kraus, for her generally unsympathetic attitude keeps her from seeing that Kraus's life and work were all of a piece and makes her reduce Kraus to small dimensions. Since she does not acknowledge that Kraus was first and foremost a satirist, she is unwilling to accept him on his own terms and thus tends to read him against the grain, as it were. Being preoccupied with the trees of specificity, all those fads and feuds, she does not see the forest of universality. Furthermore, she displays little appreciation of the special nature of satire, its needs, purposes, techniques, and privileges, its absoluteness and rigorousness; and she seems to expect of a satirist, even one sui generis like Kraus, tact and taste, modesty and moderation, balance and fairness, logic and specificity, erudition and consistency.

On her guided tour through the theatrical museum of *Die Fackel* Grimstad properly emphasizes the fact that ethics and aesthetics were invariably linked in Kraus's criticism and showmanship, that his theatricality was both an ethical and an aesthetic tool. She gives a useful overview of Kraus's evolving and often contradictory views on the theater and his relationship with actors and directors. Kraus's feuds with Bahr, Bukowics, Buchbinder, and Bauer are clearly set forth. So are his assessments of the Burgtheater directors Burckhard, Schlenther, and von Berger; the actors Girardi, Sonnenthal, Wolter, Matkowsky, Lewinsky, and Kalmar (all positive), Tressler, Reimers, Kainz, Odilon and Moissi (all negative); the critics Kalbeck,

Goldmann, and Salten; and the playwrights Schnitzler, Hauptmann, Ibsen, Wedekind, and Wilde. Oddly enough, Grimstad devotes only a few pages to Kraus's own plays, ostensibly because Hans Heinz Hahnl has already produced a thorough study of them, but surely few readers will have access to an unpublished Vienna dissertation of 1947.

In her sober assessment of Kraus, the author second-guesses the satirist at every turn, impugns his motives, and does not tire of pointing out paradoxes, contradictions, and absurdities. While Kraus is grudgingly granted greatness in certain areas, such as ethics and language, Grimstad voices disapproval over the facts that Kraus sometimes criticized plays and actors he had not seen, failed to recognize the greatness of Grillparzer and Hofmannsthal, and in the parlous mid-1930s brought himself to devote many pages to his personal trivia. Although she admits that some of Kraus's polemics were morally justified, she sees little in his struggle against police chief Schober after the events of July 19, 1927, but long-winded theatricality. After a thoughtful discussion of Kraus's versions of Shakespeare she concludes that Elizabethan theatergoers would probably not have recognized their dramatist. As for his spellbinding public performances, she regards them as the "prototype of a demagogic situation. . . . The lecturer who relies on the magical, theatrical power of the word rather than on the cogency of his arguments is too closely akin to the political agitator, and the perfect audiences that Kraus tried to create seem uncomfortably like those that were enthralled by Hitler in the 1930s" (133–34).

Despite the faint praise with which Grimstad damns him in her concluding paragraphs, Karl Kraus emerges from these pages as an utterly unattractive person: an insufferable egocentric, would-be prophet, and failed magician who indulged in one *argumentum ad hominem* after another, a power-hungry man who criticized by insinuation and made mountains out of molehills as he conducted smear campaigns, a man whose prejudices and political blindness amounted to self-deception.

Georg Knepler's copiously illustrated book *Karl Kraus liest Offenbach: Erinnerungen, Kommentare, Dokumentation* (Karl Kraus Reads Offenbach: Memoirs, Commentaries, Documentation, 1984) is important on several counts. The author, a pianist and musicologist, met Kraus in the fall of 1928 and on thirty-nine occasions, between 1929 and 1931, served as his accompanist in performances of operettas by Jacques Offenbach. The author says that he wrote his book not only for oldtimers of his own generation but also for young people who have begun to discover Kraus for themselves, and that it was his intention to illuminate the life and work of the satirist, particularly in his last decade, from a hitherto neglected perspective. Kraus presented a total of fourteen Offenbach operettas. The socially critical, sometime utopian works of the German-born French composer provided an important counterpoise to the satirist's surroundings, and it is significant that Kraus, who discerned a great fellow satirist in Offenbach and used him for his depiction of an antibourgeois world, created almost 350 *Zeitstrophen* (topical stanzas inspired by his various campaigns and polemics) for those operettas, as compared to only 178 for Nestroy plays. Knepler points out that "what Offenbach meant to Kraus can be understood only if one has some knowledge of Kraus, his life and work. Conversely, no one can understand Kraus fully who does not appreciate his enthusiasm for Offenbach" (7). It is well known that Kraus could not read music and did not have a trained voice, but he refused to take solfège or voice lessons, presumably because greater musical knowledge might have interfered with his concentration on the word. Why, then, did he need music at all? Knepler suggests that Kraus was bent on achieving the intonation of a sentence (*Satzmelodie*) and felt that music would enhance and underline the language. The Offenbach performances were made possible by Kraus's "natural musicality, his instinctive grasp of the mimetic and gestic qualities of the music, and his phenomenal memory" (17).

Knepler discerns three phases in Kraus's occupation with Offenbach. The first began on February 20, 1926, with a performance of *Bluebeard*, and Kraus quickly integrated his Offenbach evenings into his "Theater der Dichtung" (Literary Theater, or Theater of Poetry), which also included plays by Shakespeare, Nestroy, Hauptmann, and Wedekind with the designation "Performer: Karl Kraus." For these he preferred smaller halls that seated fewer than a thousand, one of which he renamed the Offenbachsaal. This first phase included his futile polemic against Schober after the events of July 1927, the subject of thirty-three topical stanzas, as well as his victory over Békessy. The second phase, from 1928–29 to January 30, 1933, brought a new tension between Kraus and his audience as Kraus discontinued his readings for workers under the auspices of the Social Democrats and returned to his *Sprachlehre* (language study) and other "little" subjects. His performances of Offenbach were not affected, however, and on the occasion of the composer's 110th birthday in 1929 he performed seven operettas on eight days. *The Voyage to the Moon* was not performed until 1932 and only five times. What attracted Kraus to this minor work were the satiric possibilities inherent in viewing the earthly present from the perspective of the lunar past. A few lines in one of the topical stanzas seem to equate the Jewish press with the swastika and a Jewish quack (Zeileis) and Jewish editor (Benedikt) with Hitler. Knepler's commentary on this is bound to be controversial: "I plead for the recognition of the acuity and incorruptibility of a writer who, himself Jewish, regards Jewish hucksterism (*Händlergeist*) as just as damnable as the spirit behind the swastika" (166). The author, for many years a resident of the German Democratic Republic, believes that Kraus's ability to abstract into a common denominator (capitalism) a corrupt Jewish doctor, a mouthpiece of the Jewish bourgeoisie, and Hitler was unique before Bertolt Brecht came on the scene. Knepler's third phase extends from January 1933 to 1936, a period marked by Kraus's gradual silence. In 1932 there had been twenty-nine Offenbach performances, but in 1935 there were only eight.

Knepler's stimulating study far transcends musical matters as he comments, from first-hand experience, on Kraus's personality, describing him, despite all his contradictions, as courteous, understanding, sensitive, delicate, and lovable. He also comments on such key Krausian concepts as *Ursprung* (origin), which he believes to be a religious concept, the ancient idea of a golden age in which people lived without fear, greed, conflicts, and restrictive legislation. Referring to Kraus's poems "Operette" and "Offenbach," Knepler discerns a realm close to the *Ursprung*, a pure counterworld in which art can ideally flourish and singing is an accredited means of communication, an expression of joyous irresponsibility and zany illogic: "Only when poets, actors, and singers have abandoned any semblance of naturalness will they attain the desired naturalness of great art which, for Kraus, derives from the ideal realm of *Ursprung*" (94). What differentiates Offenbach from the harsher and more bitter satire of Shakespeare, Gogol, Nestroy, Wedekind, and Kraus himself are the grace and charm of his music. Knepler points out that Kraus's own "magical operetta" *Literatur* is far removed from this grace but that *Wolkenkuckucksheim* (Cloudcuckooland) fairly cries out for Offenbach's music. In the program of an Offenbach performance on December 9, 1928, Knepler's first service as a piano accompanist, Kraus described the latter play as a sublimated *Last Days of Mankind*, one transposed to an airier region.

Knepler also points to the largely unexplored and underrated visual element in Kraus. He was probably the first author who unmasked unworthy elements by pictorial means; photomontages appeared in the prewar *Fackel* long before John Heartfield, the widely recognized master of the genre. In a section titled "Karl Kraus and the Idea of Socialism," Knepler argues that Kraus was concerned with ideas derived from language rather than ephemeral journalistic opinions, with language rather than politics. Disagreeing with Alfred Pfabigan, who believes that Kraus never concerned himself with the replacement of capitalism by another system and thus helped to prevent a real revolution, Knepler denies that Kraus was apolitical, for he did call for a revolution against the bourgeois world. At the end of the monarchy, Kraus regarded the end of that world as possible, desirable, and necessary. He broke with the Social Democrats because they had acted halfheartedly or not at all, and after 1918 they seemed content to divide the spoils with the existing power structure. Knepler even claims that a disillusioned Kraus moved closer to the theoretical position of communism. If Kraus believed that compared with Social Democracy, communism had a more moral foundation, a wider horizon, and a more grandiose concept, why did he not become a communist or a Marxist? Knepler opines that in the 1930s the embittered Kraus, a latter-day Timon, regarded anything political as suspect and despicable, that the past was deemed superior to the present, and that all political and societal panaceas now seemed less humane to him than Offenbach's operettas. According to Knepler, Kraus was unable to accept a central idea of Marxism: that the human *Geist* (intellect or spirit) is a product of society. Instead, he thought that this *Geist* was above the stupidity and meanness born of political, social, and economic forces, and he doubted that the revolution desired by communism was based on *Geist*. Long tormented by the thought that a societal revolution might not be accomplished without violence and bloodshed, Kraus arrived at intuitive conservative judgments even as he admired revolutionaries like Rosa Luxemburg, Karl Liebknecht, and (for a time) Bertolt Brecht. Closing with the Krausian thought that he would leave all his erring behind as a guide, Knepler concludes: "It is part of Kraus's greatness that he does not require us to say that he was always right, but instead always compels us to join him in being thoughtful" (243).

10: Kraus and . . .

. . . the Concept of *Ursprung*

John Pizer's article "'Ursprung ist das Ziel': Karl Kraus's Concept of Origin" (1994) is the most comprehensive and most cogent investigation to date of one of the principal themes in Kraus's thought and oeuvre, one that is as compelling as it is ambiguous. The author shows that beyond its significance for an understanding of the satirist, the dichotomy *Ursprung* (origin) and *Ziel* (goal) influenced the thought of the noted critics Walter Benjamin and Theodor Adorno. The line "Ursprung ist das Ziel," ostensibly spoken by God to the poet, is contained in Kraus's poem "Der sterbende Mensch," which the satirist first read on November 19, 1914, at a gathering designed to benefit wounded soldiers. Pizer believes that this poem, with its evocation of a pure poetic realm, could have been intended as a counterpoise to the frequently jingoistic poetry of wartime. "Origin" may be a religiously tinged paradigm for creative authenticity and genuineness, a true source of humility, aesthetic rigor, and linguistic purity. Language may be seen as a means of returning to this origin. In analyzing this poem, Pizer asks whether the line "du bliebst am Ursprung" (you remained at the origin) is static or dynamic. "If origin is an immanent quality and everywhere present, what imbues it with a dynamic efficaciousness in the external world?" (5). He concludes that the answer may be found in the etymological root of the term *Ursprung*. The prefix *Ur* denotes something primary or original, and *Sprung* means "leap" — which adds up to a "primal leap" in analogy to *Urschrei*, the "primal scream" used in psychotherapy. In his book *Ursprung des deutschen Trauerspiels* (Origin of the German Tragic Drama), Walter Benjamin, who used "Ursprung ist das Ziel" as the motto of one of his "Theses on the Philosophy of History," attempts to define the concept and term in dynamic fashion. Pizer connects *Ursprung* with the technique of quotation, the "compilation of disparate but unglossed citations" (7), which Kraus and Benjamin shared: "Origin is the goal for Benjamin and Kraus, but on both a linguistic and epistemological level its approximation is not to be achieved through stasis but through a disruptive dialectic. Only when a citation is wrested from its original context and is made to stand unadorned by the rhetoric which had previously surrounded it . . . will its true ideological content be revealed"

(7–8). In this view, stripping citations from their larger semantic contexts returns them to their political and psychological origin.

Another poem analyzed in this context is the parabolic "Zwei Läufer" (Two Runners, 1910), a sort of orphic epigram about two runners sprinting along the track of time. The bold one from "nowhere" reaches his goal but makes way for his worried competitor from the "origin," who falls by the wayside but nevertheless always arrives at the origin. Can this paradox or dichotomy be explained only in religious or mystical terms? Can one runner symbolize the hegemony and progress of technology in our time and the other represent the frequently embattled and stifled spiritual element in our civilization? Do the two runners perhaps represent the two halves of a divided self, or does the parable contain a latter-day race between a tortoise and a hare? Pizer suggests that the concept of *Ursprung* also has implications for Kraus's attitude toward the Jewish bourgeoisie, which, having strayed far from the *Ursprung*, purveyed an impure language:

> Though Kraus was not a religious man in a traditional sense, he clearly felt a religious reverence for "origin" as an ideal aesthetic and epistemological *telos*. Remaining at the origin for Kraus meant attaining the goal of wisdom, of an extraordinary insight into and understanding of human affairs. Kraus's mediation between *Ursprung* and *Ziel* was alluring and complex, inspiring Walter Benjamin to conceptualize a dynamic mode of historical plenitude and Theodor Adorno to evoke the apparently antithetical ideal of history as ephemeral and radically other. (18)

A different religious interpretation of *Ursprung* is given by Emil Schönauer in his introductory essay to Jenaczek's *Zeittafeln zur Fackel* (1965). Defending Kraus against the charge that he was contradictory, subjective, and unfair, Schönauer points out that a time of disintegrating culture can be reformed only by the kind of satire that points to an ideal, Kraus's concept of *Ursprung*. He makes the interesting point that Kraus believed mankind to be guilty of betraying God's words and thus lost in a metaphysical sense. The satirist was aware of sharing in this guilt and tried to atone for it with his oeuvre. "In the face of mankind's sins in World War I," Schönauer writes, "the awareness of this guilt culminated in the realization that this work could also mean an exculpation of mankind before the intellect" (xviii). The author regards Kraus as a passionate existential thinker who lived his beliefs: "Karl Kraus lived his faith, which was so close to the Christian faith, more truthfully than most Christians lived theirs" (1). Theodor Haecker was the first to point to an intellectual relationship between Kierkegaard and Kraus. Both despaired of their ages, but each based his work on faith: Kierkegaard's was the Christian belief in an eternal life in the spirit, whereas Kraus was sustained by his belief in the lost *Ursprung* (which Schönauer interprets in this same Christian sense).

. . . the *Grubenhund*

Every Kraus aficionado smiles at the very mention of the word *Gruben-hund*, which designates a type of intellectual hoax and Krausian satire that is pure humor. The appearance of Hans E. Goldschmidt's book *Von Gru-benhunden und aufgebundenen Bären im Blätterwald* (1981) was and is ample reason for such smiles. The title of this compilation, which is copi-ously illustrated with facsimiles and cartoons and looks like an April Fool's issue of *Die Fackel* (except, of course, that truth is stranger than fiction, or fooling), is utterly untranslatable. *Grubenhund* means, literally, "pit dog" and *Blätterwald* "leafy forest." However, since *Blätter* also means "news-papers," *Blätterwald* is a common reference to the press, or the world of journalism. "Jemandem einen Bären aufbinden," literally "to tie a bear on someone," is an idiom meaning to make someone the butt of an April Fool's joke. The *Grubenhund* was the product of a coffeehouse bet made by a Viennese industrial engineer named Arthur Schütz in 1911, three years after Karl Kraus had managed to get the *Neue Freie Presse*, which had given him the silent treatment as a satirist, to publish him as a "geologist" in the guise of a fictitious engineer named Berdach. Early in 1908 there was a minor earthquake in Vienna, and this was an opportunity for people to get their names in the paper, for every night table that shook was duly reported and registered. Even though Kraus's letter to the editor contained obvious pseudoscientific nonsense, it was promptly printed. The whole thing seemed to Kraus like a foretaste of how the Viennese would behave when the end of the world came. In his amusing book Goldschmidt gives pride of place to Kraus as the *Urheber,* the originator or copyright owner, of this type of put-on, but Schütz is presented as the *Züchter,* or breeder, of the "dog." In his fanciful letter to the *Neue Freie Presse* a fictitious mining engineer reported that during an earthquake his *Grubenhund* had shown marked signs of unrest. A *Grubenhund* is a small miner's cart attached to a crane; only an ignorant or careless reader would suppose it to be a "pit dog." In 1916 the satirical zoo created by Kraus and his circle was enlarged by the addition of the *Laufkatze,* ostensibly a kind of cat, but in reality a crane carriage or traveling trolley used in a mine. (An approximate English equivalent of the gist of such letters would be a statement like "The me-owing of a cat o'nine tails keeps me awake at night.") Kraus gleefully reg-istered the implications of such monumental put-ons, and the *Grubenhund* became a widely appreciated symbol for the ignorance, cupidity, presump-tion, and philistinism of the press. Schütz, that master of mystification, continued to ply his trade in the groves of the *Grubenhund* for decades to come, and Goldschmidt's dishonor roll of the journals bitten by this "dog" is a long one. In 1931 Schütz's book *Der Grubenhund: Eine Kultursatire* was issued by Kraus's own printers (and publishers) Jahoda and Siegel, and a new edition appeared in 1953 in Vienna under the imprint of Wilhelm Frick. However, in the 1950s Schütz sadly realized that the postwar world was manufacturing its own *Grubenhunde*. Surely this says something about the parlous state of satire itself, for where is the bedrock of sanity from which barbs can be launched and satirical sallies can be undertaken?

. . . Mark Twain

In "Diogenes in Vienna," a chapter in *"Our Famous Guest": Mark Twain in Vienna* (1992) the American scholar Carl Dolmetsch undertakes to explore and illuminate the somewhat enigmatic relationship between Kraus, who "occupied a place in Austrian literary history roughly analogous to that of H. L. Mencken in the U. S. at the same period" (245), and Mark Twain, who was in Vienna when *Die Fackel* was founded. Both of these "iconoclastic pundits" and "gadflies to the bourgeoisie" (247) were household names in their countries "despite significant political and philosophical differences between 'The Sage of Baltimore' and 'The Scourge of Vienna'" (247). The author calls Kraus's journal "the most eagerly awaited, most widely read, most instantly discussed periodical in the Habsburg Capital, if not, indeed, in the entire Germanic world. For two generations any Viennese burgher not conversant with the contents of the latest *Fackel* risked being branded an ignoramus or a hopeless reactionary" (245). In the third issue, dated late April 1899, Mark Twain, with whose writings Kraus was not yet acquainted, is mentioned as a busybody who attended everything and whom the *Neue Freie Presse* fawned over. It is uncertain whether the two men met, but Kraus is known to have attended a speech by the American. Kraus's satire on Mark Twain's press-manufactured celebrity was "one of the most caustic as well as perhaps most widely read lambastings the American author received at any point in his career" (247–48). Mark Twain did not react in any way. The author believes that the two writers would have had many common interests and traits to discuss and savor. Both were idiosyncratic, self-centered literary mavericks, personas skilled at imagemaking, giving public readings and producing striking aphorisms, and they also shared such "dark" themes as death, suicide, and oblivion. Viewing Kraus as "a prime example of the uprooted, assimilated, but also alienated artist and intellectual endemic to *fin-de-siècle* Vienna of the type one sees in Sigmund Freud, Gustav Mahler, and Ludwig Wittgenstein, among others," Dolmetsch advances the somewhat far-fetched notion that anti-Semitism was a covert factor in Kraus's *Fackel* assault on Mark Twain; his real name, Samuel Clemens, might have led the Austrian to suspect that the American was a Jew! In any case, "Mark Twain served as a handy club for Kraus to bash the *Neue Freie Presse* and the liberal Jewish press with" (252). He was, at any rate, prejudiced against what he regarded as upstart Americans and inferior literature. Dolmetsch gives a reasoned assessment of these and other points, but surely he errs when he says that Kraus was "literate, indeed well-read, in English, as his excellent translations of Shakespeare's plays and sonnets clearly indicate" (253).

. . . Verbal Play

In his book *Das Wortspiel bei Karl Kraus* (Verbal Play in Karl Kraus, 1965), based on his Göttingen dissertation, Christian Johannes Wagenknecht concerns himself with what he regards as the most revealing stylistic feature in Kraus's writings. To the satirist, verbal play was never an end in itself but always served his artistic intentions. It was a divining rod that identified sources of thought, laid bare hitherto hidden verbal and Ideational connections, and often served as a touchstone for the truthfulness or untruthfulness of a statement or a mentality. Wagenknecht displays a becoming sense of the difficulties inherent in arriving at a satisfactory definition of verbal play, especially if one differentiates between *verbales Spiel* and *Wortspiel*. (The latter word is usually translated as "pun," a term that is not often associated with artistry). The author speaks of "vertical" and "horizontal" verbal play. As a subdivision of the former kind he discusses a type particularly favored by Kraus: amphiboly, an ambiguity of discourse that stems from the uncertainty of grammatical construction rather than the meaning of words, with a phrase or sentence capable of being construed in more than one way. Basing himself on about one-tenth of the 922 numbers of the *Fackel*, Wagenknecht provides useful tables to illustrate the incidence of verbal play at various stages of the satirist's career. The very first issue of Kraus's periodical has thirty puns on twenty-six pages. In the war years and the last years of the *Fackel* (1929–35), a great increase in verbal play may be noted, and the very last *Fackel* article has more than seventy instances of verbal play on nineteen pages — an indication that in times of frustration, anger, and despair the satirist felt impelled to wield the weapon of wordplay to a greater extent. In his searching examination of Kraus's metaphors and wit as well as the credibility of his verbal play, Wagenknecht concerns himself with the methods used by Kraus to expose the subjects or objects of his satire to ridicule and opprobrium, giving a particularly detailed account of Kraus's feud with Moriz Benedikt, the editor of the *Neue Freie Presse*.

In a related study, *Mordshetz und Pahöl: Austriazismen als Stilmittel bei Karl Kraus* (1992), originally an Innsbruck dissertation, Ulrike Lang concerns herself with Austrianisms as stylistic devices in Kraus's writings, pointing out that such uniquely expressive locutions were used by Kraus in linguistic montages or other forms of verbal play with ironic, deprecatory intent as an enhancement of his polemics and satires. The author gives a useful history of Austrian German and discusses its style, syntax, morphology, pronunciation, bureaucratese, allegorical language, and stylistic levels. She notes that Kraus regarded as an Austrianism anything not found in the classic or normative German literary language and did not differentiate between Austrianisms and the Viennese dialect. Paradoxical though it may sound, Kraus, the Austrian, was not always able to recognize Austrianisms as such: Cases in point are *Advokat* (lawyer), *Partezettel* (death notice sent through the mail), *Tramwaykondukteur* (streetcar conductor), and *Matura* (comprehensive examination required for graduation from a secondary school); but most other Austrianisms, such as *pumperlgesund* (healthy as a horse), *Rotzbub* (snotnose), *Gschaftlhuber* (busybody), or words ending with the diminutive suffixes *-erl* (*Mascherl,* little bow, bow tie) and *-el* (*Büchel,* little book), Kraus used consciously and deliberately. Concentrating on Kraus's collections *Sittlichkeit und Kriminalität* (Morality and Criminal Justice), *Literatur und Lüge* (Literature and Lies), and *Untergang der Welt durch schwarze Magie* (Destruction of the World by Black Magic — that is, printer's ink), Lang points out that Kraus wrote for himself the role of a "satiric persona" that, like the *Nörgler* (Grumbler or Carper) in *The Last Days of Mankind,* was not always identical with himself but a highly stylized and therefore fictional figure. The satirist was concerned with laying bare the Viennese mentality and using local color to achieve ironic detachment, a reduction of pathos, derision, and other satiric effects. Sometimes a juxtaposition of terms belonging to a higher stylistic level and those pertaining to a lower one has the contrastive effect of destroying clichés, uncovering concealed conflicts, or exposing mendacious attitudes and activities. Kraus is bent on satirizing typical Viennese by highlighting their linguistic particularities and peculiarities. For instance, by describing a German writer with Austrian locutions, he integrates him into an Austrian milieu (which Kraus rejected) and thereby deprecates him.

One of the most valuable features of Lang's book is a dictionary of words, from *der Advokat* to *zuständig nach,* contained in the writings she covers. The readability of this study, which features numerous little paragraphs, is not enhanced by what may be described as the author's spurning of the Ph factor. Some English equivalents of her German spellings would be fase, morfologic, fonetic, lexicografy, geografic, fenomenon, frases, and atmosfere.

In "Der Wiener jüdische Jargon im Werke von Karl Kraus" (Viennese Yiddish in the Work of Karl Kraus, 1975), Caroline Kohn provides for the first time a lexicon of Viennese Yiddish expressions used by Kraus with ironic or imitative intent for his polemics and satires. While Kraus, who did not know Yiddish, disliked its intonation and abhorred a mixture of Yiddish and the Viennese dialect, this patois once again served him as an acoustical mirror that he used to show how far people could stray from linguistic purity in what he termed a language-forsaken age. Caroline Kohn's twenty-page lexicon includes a brief history, characterization, and phonology of Yiddish that conveys the insight that the Yiddish heard in Vienna was a mixture of western and southeastern Yiddish as spoken in Galicia, Bukovina, and northeastern Hungary, with the eastern values predominating. The author, who is not Jewish, is aware that she would have to know Hebrew to engage in a more scholarly etymological study. She points out that many words that are regarded as quintessentially Viennese (for example, *meschugge, koscher, Chutzpe, Masel, Dalles, Emmes, Schmus, Schtuß, Mischpoche, Taam, Ponem, Tachles, Zores*) are actually Yiddish and in some cases have become part of thieves' argot. Despite Kraus's dislike of what he regarded as an impure language, he acknowledged J. Solotwinski's appreciative Yiddish article about him in the Viennese Yiddish journal *Jüdische Morgenpost* (*Fackel* 649–56, June 1924, 104). Of equal interest and usefulness is Caroline Kohn's "Lexique viennois dans l'oeuvre de Karl Kraus" (1975), an even more comprehensive compilation of Viennese dialect words and expressions used by Kraus with satiric intent. As in the Yiddish lexicon, the author often provides specific references to writings in which the satirist used a certain term or phrase.

In an article entitled "Der Stilbruch als Stilmittel bei Karl Kraus" (1986), Sigurd Paul Scheichl deals with stylistic incongruity as a feature of Kraus's style and attempts to show that such stylistic devices as an alternation of German-Jewish jargon with the language of German classicism appear as vehicles of parody, irony, and satire that serve to deflate pathos and highlight contrasts, the social milieu, and the like.

The Swiss scholar Rolf Max Kully concerns himself with Kraus's use of names in his article "Die erotische, die polemische und die poetische Verwendung der Eigennamen in den Werken von Karl Kraus" (1990). Kully shows that Kraus played poetically or erotically with the name of his beloved Sidonie/Sidi and with polemical intent with names like Schlenther (Schlender, Schlenter, Schlemmter) and Emanuel/Mendl. When he refers to "Benedikt's dictation" and "Benedikt's prayer" in *The Last Days of Mankind*, it is clear that he is juxtaposing the editor of the *Neue Freie Presse* and the pope. Kraus held the literary historian Albert Soergel up to ridicule by juxtaposing his name with such near homonyms as *Sorge* (worry) and *Töl-*

pel (oaf). He also points out that Jews named Moses sometimes became in turn Moriz and Maurice and that a Herschel metamorphosed himself into a Horace or Horaz.

. . . Modernism/Modernity

Two recent studies concern themselves with Kraus's ambivalent attitude toward and position in modernism and modernity.

According to António Ribeiro in "Karl Kraus and Modernism: A Reassessment" (1995), Kraus is usually portrayed as a "cultural conservative, indulging in dubious 'language mysticism' and cultivating an inflexible allegiance to classical conception of language and literature, hostile to modernity in all its forms" (145). Ribeiro sets out to show that Kraus's "fierce and uncompromising critique of modernity is carried out . . . with aesthetic means that are characteristically modern" (145) — in other words, from within the paradigm of modernity. The author points out that "the notion of 'progress' runs through [Kraus's] entire oeuvre as a metaphor for the dark side of modernity that tailed to fulfill what it had promised" (145). Yet, he argues, Kraus's work does not reflect nostalgia for a purer world, a civilization not yet transformed and corrupted by technology, or a primitive desire to return to nature. Rather, Kraus opposed a modernity that was unable to cope with the tremendous powers it had unleashed. In Kraus's view, the dark side of modernity was typified by the "black magic" of printer's ink. Ribeiro does not regard Kraus's notion of *Ursprung* as reactionary but views it as the conscious aesthetic construct of an epigone: "It is the realm of the non-instrumental and of the non-identical whose ultimate model is language and the art of language" (146) — a latent utopian possibility that forever beckons as a corrective to a world that threatens to be engulfed by meaninglessness and chaos. The author characterizes the satirist's technique of copious quotation as a "method of subversive intertextuality" that became his "response to the crisis of communication and to the modern experience of fragmentation" (150). With reference to Kraus's montages and collages, Ribeiro points out that he "discovered the satirical potential of photography well before the Dadaists and John Heartfield" and that "the satirical gloss represents perhaps the most thoroughly 'modernist' aspect of Kraus's writing" (152). In line with the diversity and plurality within modernism, the author pleads for a breadth of definition, and he concludes that Kraus combined an "ascetic thrust with a vivid and close awareness of the condition of modernity" (154).

In "Karl Kraus und die Moderne" (1994), Gilbert Carr points to Kraus's positive view of such modern creative spirits as Strindberg, Wedekind, Brecht, Altenberg, Trakl, Lasker-Schüler, Schönberg, and Kokoschka. He also reminds us that Kraus gladly availed himself of such innovations as the motor car, the airplane, and the radio. What needs to be investigated, he argues, is the connection between Kraus's critique of modernism and his linguistic art, the interaction between traditionalism and modernism. "The espousal of tradition does not preclude a modern intertextuality," he writes (506). In *The Last Days of Mankind* Carr discerns a "fruitful tension between archetypal satire and expressionistic montage" (512). The author regards Kraus's unsystematic use of glosses and aphorisms as particularly revealing of the tension between tradition and modernism. In the 1920s Kraus's "Theater of Poetry" was reflective of cultural conservatism, but his readings generally were an effective forum for topical public protest. This and other evidence seem to prove the paradox discerned by Walter Benjamin, the strange alternation between reactionary theory and revolutionary practice in Kraus's life and work.

11: Bound Bouquets and Brickbats

Martina Bilke's book *Zeitgenossen der Fackel* (Contemporaries of the *Fackel*, 1981, originally a Mainz dissertation, 1979) concerns itself with the satirist's relationship with his readers. Being based on Karl Kraus's unpublished correspondence in the municipal archives of the City of Vienna, it has great documentary value and offers many new insights. It is, among other things, a companion volume to and welcome continuation of Jenaczek's *Zeittafeln zur Fackel*.

Sophie Schick's foreword attempts to define Kraus's work and function. "What differentiates a satirist from humorists," she writes, "is the ethical basis of his production. . . . The main theme of any satire is the threat to human existence" (9). Satire is ahistorical, but the satirist lives in an age from which his occasions are derived, that gives rise to his insights as well as his misjudgments. Karl Kraus was trying to illustrate the logical consequences of a mindless and ruthless business mentality that fostered a belief in change and progress. Schick highlights Kraus's prophetic quality and the disturbing timeliness of his work as she points out that in "The Discovery of the North Pole" (1909) he wrote that "progress makes purses out of human skin," that we find a reference to Germany as a concentration camp in his notebook for March 1915, and that in 1933 he discerned the simultaneousness of electrotechnology and myths, atomic fission and funeral pyres.

In her comments on the genesis of the *Fackel* and Kraus's dialogue with his readership via their letters and his answers, Martina Bilke takes us behind the scenes, as it were, and supplies valuable "backstage" insights. The very first letter received, dated April 1, 1899, was by a jurist named Gustav Morgenstern who thought that *Die Fackel* should be called *Der Blitz* (The Lightning). Despite regular notices that manuscripts were not welcome, there were numerous submissions, even after November 1911, when Kraus began to limit his journal to his own writings, by those who were attracted to the *Fackel*'s stature as an outsider publication. Following a discussion of some of Kraus's prewar polemics (Maximilian Harden, Heinrich Heine) as reflected in the *Fackel*, the author shows that the letters received during World War I reflect Kraus's extraordinary moral stature in wartime. "The *Fackel* was regarded as a liberating counterpoise to the reports of war correspondents who romantically transfigured the trenches" (66), and "Kraus's struggle against cultural decline received such a high moral evaluation that no one at the front ever reproached him with not having been called up for military service himself" (69). Commenting on Kraus's public readings, beginning with one in Berlin on January 13, 1910, Bilke points out that the often ecstatic or hysteric reactions in letters were mostly to the reciter's style rather than to the contents of the readings. The Vereinigung Karl Kraus (Karl Kraus Society), which existed from 1930 to 1932, is seen as a quixotic attempt to combine an adherence to the Social Democratic Party with loyalty to the satirist.

Bilke makes a somewhat dubious attempt to give a typology of *Fackel* readers, dividing them into those with primarily linguistic interests, educated, aesthetically oriented people who attended the "Theater of Poetry" and cared less for topical writings, and workers and others with political interests for which the Social Democratic Party was the focus after 1920. The second group, which primarily belonged to the middle class, was disappointed by Kraus's attitude in 1933 and 1934, reducing the readership of the *Fackel* largely to the first group. She is on firmer documentary ground in her useful compilation of *Fackel* imitations and counterpublications, for the most part short-lived and issued in Vienna, which in several instances copied the journal's appearance. These include *Die Geissel* (The Scourge), originally named *Die Secession* (1899, Heinrich Skofitsch, Eugen Markus); *Sturm!* (Storm!, Munich 1900, F. Schmid, R. Loewendahl); *Im Fackelschein/Im Feuerschein* (By Torchlight/Fireglow, 1901, Justinian Frisch, the son of Moriz Frisch, the first printer of Kraus's journal); *Don Quixote* (1902, Ludwig Bauer); *Freie Blätter für alle* (Free Journal for All, 1902, Wilhelm Gunther); *Der Skandal/Die Glossen* (1907, Benno George, that is, B. Georg Meisels); *Neue Freie Worte* (1911, Karl F. Kocmata, pro-Kraus); *Die Laterne* (Robert Peiper, Josef Engelhart, pro-Kraus); *Torpedo* (Robert Müller, 1914, only one issue); *Der Knockabout* (1914, Karl Adler, Albert Paris von Gütersloh, 1914); *Der Querulant* (The Bellyacher, 1920, Karl Adler, only two issues); *Der Pinsel* (The Brush, Erwin Rosenberger, only two issues).

Bilke's comments on Kraus's relationship with editors of other journals are also of considerable interest. Kraus met Siegfried Jacobsohn, the editor of *Die Schaubühne* (The Stage), later given a more topical and political orientation and renamed *Die Weltbühne* (The World Stage), and the two editors exchanged journals; but later Erich Mühsam, Karl Adler, and Fritz Wittels polemicized against Kraus in the Berlin journal. Kraus's exemplary attitude in the war caused Jacobsohn to favor Kraus again in many ways — for example, by publishing a worshipful study of Kraus by Berthold Viertel, which appeared in book form in 1921, and organizing and promoting Kraus's readings in Berlin.

Bilke also concerns herself with the attitudes of contemporaneous writers toward Kraus. In the anti-Kraus comedy *Der neue Simson* by C. Karlweis (Karl Weiss, 1902) there is a Kraus figure named Alfred Ackermann. The critic Rapp, a minor figure in Arthur Schnitzler's novel *Der Weg ins Freie* (The Road into the Open, written between 1905 and 1907), has some traits of Kraus. In *Café Klößchen* (Café Meatball), a satiric prose play about the Berlin literary scene (1912), the expressionistic author Alfred Lichtenstein has a figure named Lutz Laus (Louse), the editor of *Der Dackel* (The Dachshund), who is known as Dackellaus in analogy to Fackelkraus. The author also attempts to illuminate Kraus's public position in his time by commenting on Kraus's relationships with Franz Werfel, Hugo von Hofmannsthal, Arthur Schnitzler, Max Brod, Ludwig von Ficker, Theodor Haecker, Joseph Roth, Franz Kafka, and Bertolt Brecht.

In an epilogue Bilke concludes that the fact that individual aspects of Kraus were noticed, but not his life work as a whole, sheds light on the problematic existence of his satire and on the problems associated with its reception.

Franz Schuh and Juliane Vogel have provided a valuable complement to Martina Bilke's *Zeitgenossen der Fackel* with their book *Die Belagerung der Urteilsmauer: Karl Kraus im Zerrspiegel seiner Feinde* (Besieging the Wall of Judgment: Karl Kraus in the Distorting Mirror of His Enemies, 1986). The title of this typology of opposition to Kraus derives from Elias Canetti's essay "Schule des Widerstands" (School of Resistance), in which Canetti says that Kraus fashioned a Great Wall of China for himself piece by piece and sentence by sentence — but no one knew what was behind it. It was an end in itself, and its components were the satirist's judgments. Kraus kept adding to that wall, but it was guarded only by one legendary, solitary, and unapproachable watchman. The compilation by Schuh and Vogel contains German-language texts that undertook to beleaguer and attack this seemingly unbreachable and indestructible wall. In his afterword Schuh attempts to get to the bottom of critical enmity toward Kraus. "What is distinctive about Kraus," he writes, "is that his solitude cannot be touched by approbation any more than by rejection. . . . Speaking about Kraus is always bound to remain risky, because it is impossible to express what is essential: his nonidentity and uniqueness" (207, 208). However, Schuh adds, it is equally impossible, or hopeless, *not* to speak about him. Displaying a becoming sense of the fact that Kraus's works are all of a piece, the editor points out that individual essays have value only in the aggregate, as stones in the wall of judgment.

The editors follow each of their selections (complete essays or excerpts from larger works) with a biography of the writer, the circumstances of the work's genesis and publication, and a bibliography. Among the hostile

critics included are Robert Müller, Richard Flatter, Fritz Wittels, C. Karlweis, Franz Werfel, Albert Ehrenstein, Anton Kuh, Franz Leschnitzer,
Oskar Pollak, Egon Erwin Kisch, Willy Haas, Hans Habe, Marcel Reich-
Ranicki, Fritz Raddatz, Mechthild Borries, and Hermann Kesten. The
editors quote from Kesten's crude article in the *Frankfurter Allgemeine
Zeitung* of April 4, 1974, in which Kraus is called "a waster of great talents . . . a humorist without humor . . . a dictator at his own desk . . . a
contradictor who tolerated no contradiction . . . who wept when the little
dictator Dollfuß died but not when Dollfuß had workers mowed down . . .
a pacifist who defended the French general staff against Dreyfus and supported the court martial . . . a writer who always quoted himself and made
himself the measure of the world, but usually of a microscopic world"
(147). Kesten depicts Kraus as a man who wasted his wit, esprit, linguistic
power, and moral enthusiasm; and he even takes a negative view of the
generally admired drama *The Last Days of Mankind*, which he characterizes
as a dreary cabaret sketch of 635 pages, and the no less striking aphorisms,
which Kesten likens to a swarm of locusts. As for Willy Haas, the editors
regard him, like Max Brod, as part of the "Prague Revenge" on Kraus for
his persiflage of the Czech-born German-Jewish expressionists. In the
Rundfrage of 1913 Haas had written, "I admire Kraus, for I regard him as
pure and truthful," but in his autobiography *Die literarische Welt* (the title
of the influential periodical that he once edited) he called Kraus "a deliber-
ate seducer and poisoner" and "a born sadist" (Munich: List, 1957, 22).

   Schuh and Vogel also include an excerpt from Hans Habe's autobiography *Ich stelle mich* (1954). To his credit, the son of Imre Békessy did not
uncritically side with his father, who never confided in his son about his
long-drawn-out polemical affair with Kraus. While Habe does not regard
Kraus as a great writer, he does assess him as a first-rate polemicist and a fanatic in the tradition of the legendary moral *Haudegen* (old warriors) of
the Middle Ages. Interestingly enough, Habe believes that Kraus opposed
Békessy because he saw in him a caricature of himself. Commenting on
Borries's defense of Heine against Kraus, a work that the editors regard as
simplistic platitudinous, and more journalistic than scholarly, they agree
with Helmut Arntzen in pointing out that the author granted Heine the
historical context that she denied to Kraus. Finally, Schuh and Vogel concern themselves with Kraus's hatred and his love in "Karl Kraus. Sein Haß,
seine Liebe," an essay included in the contemporary critic Reich-Ranicki's
book *Nachprüfung: Aufsätze über deutsche Schriftsteller von gestern* (Re-
examination: Essays About German Writers of Yesteryear, 1977). Reich-
Ranicki describes Kraus as vain, self-righteous, and self-important, an auto-
crat who needed fans and disciples, for just as he could not live without
hating, he could not hate without being constantly admired. A man of

much wit and little humor and devoid of self-irony, he never revised or corrected his views, never admitted errors or injustices. His critique of language was always tantamount to a critique of society and vice versa. According to Reich-Ranicki, the satirist applied equal rigorism to an improperly placed comma and the outbreak of a world war. His fight against the press was really a fight by a self-hating Jew against Judaism, or what he took as such. Reich-Ranicki believes that the major part of Kraus's work is shopworn, dusty, and forgotten today. And what has remained? Several cabaret scenes, a few polemics, and a number of aphorisms. In the critic's view, it is frightening that many of his fans still regard Kraus as infallible. Is this a longing for the absolute, the need of many intellectuals for a spiritual leader?

In an article published in the Kraus issue of *text+kritik* (1975) and entitled "Affe oder Dalai Lama?" (Ape or Dalai Lama) with "Kraus-Gegner gestern und heute" (Anti-Krausians Yesterday and Today) as a subtitle, Jens Malte Fischer deals with much the same material and many of the same authors that may be found in *Die Belagerung der Urteilsmauer*. Fischer begins by reminding his readers that as early as May 1899 Kraus was attacked and beaten up in a café (at the behest of Hermann Bahr and Julius Bauer), and he quotes what a pleased journalist wrote about this incident: "It takes quite a robust constitution to be a satirist and polemicist. If Herr Kraus cares about surviving the first quarter of the *Fackel*, he will have to change the way he writes" (*Fackel* 9, 1899, 27). After briefly commenting on the anti-Kraus writings of C. Karlweis, Fritz Wittels, and Albert Ehrenstein, he presents Robert Müller's pamphlet as still worth reading today because the author saw in Kraus a mixture of two enduring psychopathological types: the *Weltverbesserer* (do-gooder) and the *Gehetzter* (driven man). Fischer characterizes *Der Affe Zarathustras*, an impromptu speech delivered by Anton Kuh in a stormy atmosphere in Kraus's "own" Konzerthaussaal on October 25, 1925, and printed, on the basis of the stenographic protocol, by J. Deibler (Vienna) later that year, as the shallow, self-serving work of one of Békessy's wittier and more charismatic journalists, an address full of clever formulations, demagogic half-truths, Jewish self-hatred, and oversimplifications whose theme is "Kraus and the Krausians" or "Kraus and the Consequences." Kraus's performance of twelve Shakespeare plays in his adaptation (a *Nachdichtung* or *Nachschöpfung* rather than an *Übersetzung*) drew this comment from Richard Flatter, an established translator: "Someone who wishes to translate Shakespeare into German without knowing English is a culpable dilettante working on another man's intellectual property and must not escape punishment" (152). In such contemporary negative critics as Fritz Raddatz, Hans Hennecke, Marcel Reich-Ranicki, and Hermann Kesten Fischer discerns factual errors and distortions. Commenting on Mechthild Borries's book on the relationship between Kraus and Heine, Fischer believes that the author wants to use Kraus's essay on Heine as the Archimedean point with which Kraus's entire oeuvre can be lifted off its hinges. Concerning Walter Benjamin's recognition of a peculiar alternation of reactionary theory and revolutionary practice in Kraus, Fischer writes, "Kraus was no conservative revolutionary but a conservative with progressive features" (156). He concludes his survey of anti-Krausian critics, particularly his contemporary opponents, by quoting the satirist: "Größerer Gegner gesucht" (Wanted: a greater adversary).

Karl Kraus und seine Nachwelt: Ein Buch des Gedenkens (Karl Kraus and His Posterity: A Memorial Volume, edited by Michael Horowitz, 1986) reprints, in facsimile form, page proofs corrected by Leopold Liegler and Helene Kann for a volume that had been typeset by the house of Richard Lányi in Vienna as the first publication of the Karl Kraus Archive but could not be issued in March 1938. Right after the satirist's death, Liegler collected obituaries, documents, and photos. In his foreword to this compilation, dated Christmas 1937, he wrote, "This book has a dual content: Kraus as he was and as we ought to preserve him, and an extract from the world the way it has been since his demise" (6).

Several contributions by Ernst Křenek include an excerpt from his address at a memorial in the Konzerthaus on November 30, 1936. "His speech was free, yet he never spoke freely, always read from a manuscript . . . In keeping a protocol of delusion and deterioration he was indefatigable and yet powerless in the face of all that rushed in upon him. . . . The *liber scriptus* . . . that will be presented on Judgment Day will contain many pages in the tiny hieroglyphs from his hand" (22). Calling Kraus "perhaps the most, and most frequently, misunderstood figure of the entire epoch" (26), Edwin Rollett writes, "Karl Kraus was never influenced or constricted by time periods and their currents; his activity unfolded outside and above what we call the *Zeitgeist*" (24). Robert Scheu, one of the earliest commentators on the satirist, believes that only once in his life, in his final years, did Kraus exchange the function of an observer for that of an activist. He did not change his mind about politics, but by way of an exception, practiced (for once) practical rather than pure reason. "Karl Kraus was an event — primarily an Austrian but also a German and European one, an unparalleled hallmark of an epoch. . . . He had the bravery of his profession as well as the courage to be lonely and to defy the contempt that a philistine probity tried to impose upon him" (35). Peter Kuranda wrote in the *Neues Wiener Tagblatt*: "The passionate polemicist could communicate only where there was an outward occasion. He needed a counterposition to take up a position: pro-Nestroy and anti-Grillparzer, pro-Offenbach

and anti-Johann Strauß, pro-Altenberg and against all of contemporary literature. All in vain. . . . He shrank back from the great disenchantment of
the world that began in the 19th century. His thought could not grasp
modern science and its imperturbable progression to new syntheses" (49).
It is hardly surprising that the assessments of Kraus in the *Neue Freie Presse*
("a literary Dalai Lama," said Stefan Großmann, [52]) and in such Nazi
journals as *Die Bewegung* and the *Frankfurter Zeitung* were negative, but
Das Wort (Moscow) also saw Kraus as a supporter of Austro-Fascism and
therefore a traitor. *Der Kampf* (Prague, June 1936) carried this comment
by Oskar Pollak: "A fighter who went over to the enemy when the artistic
and intellectual struggle turned into a class struggle. A proclaimer of the
downfall of the middle class who himself perished shamefully with it" (57).
Writing in the *Ost-Kurier* (Budapest), Emmerich (Imre) Békessy uncom-
prehendingly but magnanimously viewed Kraus as a man who got jealous
when someone played on his turf and thought that he should perhaps have
invited Kraus to join his staff: "He was, take him for all in all, a great journalist" (59). T. N. Hudes (Warsaw) characterized Kraus as "Till Eulenspiegel on the Danube shore" (66), and in the *Selbstwehr* (Prague) Z. F.
Finkelstein compared Kraus with Moriz Benedikt, both of whom he
viewed as false prophets. "In his journal Benedikt gave the burgeoning new
Judaism the silent treatment, and Kraus besmirched it in *Die Fackel*. One
was a parvenu, the other a dazzling Harlequin. Together they harmonized
in the hymn of hate of apostates" (68). In a later issue of *Selbstwehr* Victor
Kellner, once one of Theodor Herzl's associates, responded to Finkelstein's
"unfair characterization" by pointing out that Kraus never denied his Jewish origin. "The Jewish self-hatred he is charged with can only be interpreted as perverted love for the deep and pure wellsprings of his Jewish essence" (68–69). Kraus did attack Jewish reality inexorably and mercilessly,
but it gave us a purer and more beautiful image of the Judaism that we felt
called upon to realize. In language, too, Kellner saw something basically
Jewish: "the paradoxical union of pathos and wit, passion and clarity" (70).
Other Jewish commentators took a similarly benign view of the departed
satirist. Thus Meier Teich (*Ostjüdische Zeitung*, Czernowitz) quoted
Kraus's statement of July 1934 that he loved a primal, unspoiled Judaism;
the *Jüdische Rundschau* of Berlin viewed Kraus as a prodigal son whose
talent was wasted on a world not germane to it; *Der Jude* saw the satirist's
concerns as Jewish-inspired and called Kraus "one of the most important
representatives of Judaism within the German people" (76); and Pavel
Eisner, writing in the *Prager Presse*, called Kraus "the last heir of the great
prophets" (79). Heinrich Fischer (*Wiener Zeitung*) reminisced about
Kraus's last years, when the satirist's strength was waning and he hoped
that his mind would overcome his physical infirmities. The book closes

with Oskar Samek's speech at Kraus's grave in the Zentralfriedhof at the unveiling of a stone on June 12, 1937, the first anniversary of the satirist's death.

12: *Traduttore Traditore?*

This pithy pun, which even makes do without a verb, represents an important contribution of the Italian language to the ongoing discussion of the perennial problems of translation and the troubled figure of the translator. One would have to think long and hard to come up with an equally mordant and memorable equivalent in another language to express the egregious idea that translation is treason and the translator a traitor. "Renderer render" might do in English, though a person who renders a text from another language is not commonly referred to as a "renderer," and "rending" or tearing such a text can hardly be considered a treasonable activity.

Did Karl Kraus, who had little or no English, "betray" Shakespeare when he undertook to "render" several of his plays as well as the *Sonnets* on the basis of existing translations and his empathic appreciation of the Bard? Kraus would probably have subscribed to Walter Benjamin's conception of the task of the translator: "A translation, instead of resembling the meaning of the original, must lovingly and in detail incorporate the original's mode of signification. . . . It is the task of the translator to release in his own language that pure language which is under the spell of another, to liberate the language imprisoned in a work in his recreation of that work" ("The Task of the Translator," in *Illuminations*. New York: Harcourt, Brace & World, 1968, 78, 80). One person who disagreed with this statement was Richard Flatter, a Viennese attorney with an excellent knowledge of English who had achieved prominence as a translator of Shakespeare. In *Karl Kraus als Nachdichter Shakespeares*, a pamphlet published in 1934, Flatter took issue with Kraus for saying that no nonpoet could render Shakespeare, while a poet need not know the language of the original to create a true *Dichtung*, a work of literature. Flatter states that with Kraus's new versions of the first two witches' scenes from *Macbeth*, printed in the *Fackel* of April 1926, the satirist had inspired him to become a Shakespeare translator, and he calls the man who thinks he can be more Shakespearean than Shakespeare a "presumptuous dilettante" (86). However, commenting on Kraus's editions of the *Sonnets* (1933), Albert Bloch (1937) argues that if Kraus had known English, his versions would not have been so beautiful. "Perhaps the result is not always immediately identifiable as Shakespeare, certainly it is always undeniably Karl Kraus. . . . Stimulated by the very hopelessness of [Stefan] George's bungling preciosity on the one hand and his equally bungling but obvious efforts, on the other, to follow the original as nearly as possible with literal exactness, Kraus laid hold of this botchwork version and, with the occasional aid of a few of the other existing translations . . . he took the *Sonnets*. . . and simply rebuilt them, restored them . . . to a figure, firm and final, worthy at last to appear under the name of Shakespeare" (22).

Georg Kranner's study *Kraus Contra George: Kommentare zu den Übertragungen der Sonette Shakespeares* (Kraus vs. George: Commentaries on their Translations of Shakespeare's Sonnets, 1994) is doubly useful as the most comprehensive study of the relationship between Kraus and George and as a searching exploration of the philosophy underlying the two men's translations of Shakespeare's poetry. In assessing the two literary antipodes' relationship to the Bard, the author concerns himself with Kraus's view of Stefan George and his circle and with Kraus's renditions of the sonnets as they differ from George's. Is the fact that Kraus did not express himself on the German poet until the 1920s to be interpreted as tacit approval or even esteem? The author discusses three phases in Kraus's attitude toward the austere George: apparent silent respect from the fin de siècle to the early 1920s, presumably because George, discerned as a seeker of beauty and high priest inhabiting a higher sphere, eschewed the literary hustle and bustle and also wrote some beautiful poems; a complex and cryptic critique of George and his circle up to 1927; and polemics against George and Friedrich Gundolf, his preeminent literary and academic spokesman, from the late 1920s to the early 1930s, including a rejection of George's aestheticism and lapses from normative grammar and syntax as well as a critique of George's esoteric stance in Kraus's poem "Nach 30 Jahren" (After Thirty Years — i.e., of the *Fackel*).

A section headed "Aspects of Literary Translation in Karl Kraus" provides a transition from the theoretical to the practical part of Kranner's study. Musing about how the German word for translating, *übersetzen*, could be broken down or varied to yield *über-setzen* (carrying across) or *üb' Ersetzen* (practice substitution, or replacement), Kraus was opposed to literal translation and alien linguistic elements, believing that the empathic conveyance of thoughts and feelings was more important than words. The intention of Kraus's renditions, which he called *Nachdichtungen* (literary creations, or recreations, after the original, or free translations) rather than *Übersetzungen* (translations), was to create in his own language the *Wortgestalt* (verbal shape, or structure) of the original. Kraus's view that the proof of literary work is its untranslatability is close to Walter Benjamin's in his seminal essay "Die Aufgabe des Übersetzers" (The Task of the Translator). The satirist believed that it was permissible to shakespearize Shakespeare and nestroyize Nestroy, so to speak, and that fealty was owed to the spirit of the target language rather than to the meaning of the source language. Since Kraus knew little or no English, his translations were inspired (and accredited) by extant translations. His *Nachdichtungen* of the sonnets were prompted by his correspondence with Richard Flatter, a Viennese attorney whose considerable knowledge of English was, in Kraus's view, not matched by his faithful but pedestrian translations from the Bard. Kraus, on the other hand, felt that a close comparison of existing German versions of Shakespeare, coupled with an instinctive appreciation of his work, provided him with superior understanding of an *Urtext* to which he had no access.

In comparing Kraus's *Nachdichtungen* of the sonnets with what Stefan George called his own *Umdichtungen* (with this prefix indicating a poetic reworking or reformulation), which appeared twenty-four years before Kraus's versions, Kranner offers copious examples to show that George's versions are much closer to the sense and vocabulary of the original, whereas Kraus did not attempt to reproduce Shakespeare's complexities. Because he wished to use and preserve "old words" and aimed at a kind of generalized simplicity and sentimentality, his style was more declamatory than George's. Unlike the more philologically and etymologically oriented George, Kraus had no interest in reproducing quotations and allusions, allegories and images, ornamentations and compounds, archaisms and neologisms. In an effort to achieve *Innigkeit* or *Innerlichkeit*, the strong feelings or inwardness that have often been regarded as characteristic of the German mind or heart, Kraus tended to replace "feuilletonistic" or "sensual" adjectives with nouns, thus glossing over many complexities that George's modernistic language attempted to capture. Generally speaking, Kraus regarded his translations of Shakespeare's plays and poetry as part of his great ongoing project, *Sprachlehre*, a critical concern with the fascinating structure, resources, and optimal usage of the German language. In the early 1930s Kraus presumably intended his *Nachdichtungen* of Shakespeare, within the framework of *Sprachlehre*, to provide a linguistic, aesthetic, logical, and poetic counterpoise or antidote to the worsening political situation, his increasing isolation, and his mounting despair. In this respect Kranner speaks of a "debaroquization of Shakespeare" (112).

An author who avers, as did Karl Kraus (and in all likelihood uniquely), that even three decades after his death he would care more about a comma's being in its proper place than about the dissemination of his entire oeuvre, imposes a tremendous responsibility (and visions of treason) upon his or her translators. Limiting myself to problems of translating Kraus into English, I must note that the satirist's essential untranslatability has long been axiomatic and repeatedly stated by noted critics, though the "wall of untranslatability" has been breached in several instances. On May

27, 1977, George Steiner wrote in a review of my two volumes *In These Great Times* and *Half-Truths and One-and-a-Half Truths.* "There is . . . a very real case for saying that Karl Kraus ought not to be translated. Those who grapple with the great theme of the relations between language and political crisis, those who concern themselves with the tortured genius and destruction of European Judaism, or those who try to get into distinct focus the seminal, explosive role of Vienna as intellectual-ideological capital of modernism will have to tackle Kraus in the original." As the main difficulties of translation, Steiner sees the "lapidary brilliance and stringency" of the satirist's prose, the critic's belief that "the entire dense fabric of Karl Kraus's writings is local . . . deliberately rooted in and circumscribed by local terrain" — Vienna as the milieu of the satirist's sensibility, as Dublin was James Joyce's — and his feeling that there is "no niche in British discourse at all like that shaped and filled by Kraus's lyric, erudite, histrionic barrage" (647). On the occasion of a new (British) edition of my Kraus reader, Steiner reiterated his misgivings: "Would Karl Kraus have wanted to be translated? . . . Kraus had so maniacally appropriative a sense of language, so strident an obsession with linguistic purity, that translation into the world pidgin of current Anglo-American might have made him flinch" ("Karl Kraus: Fear and Loathing in Vienna," 1984). By "world pidgin" Steiner presumably means the intellectual discourse in English-speaking countries; Kraus in English should not read or sound like Anthony Burgess, Susan Sontag, or Steiner himself. But the critic goes on to answer his own question: "He [Kraus] might indeed have been flattered by the idea that some of the most local rhetoric and fantasy produced in modern literature should now be brought to the attention of an international public."

The distinction of having been the first English translator of Karl Kraus belongs to the German-American artist Albert Bloch (1882–1961). In 1908 the young painter went to Europe, where he became a member of the artistic group The Blue Rider in Munich and came under the spell of Karl Kraus, who became his literary mentor. Bloch, who attended many of Kraus's readings, is repeatedly mentioned in *Die Fackel.* Thus the journal of March 1925 (679–85, 107–8) carries a letter from Bloch in which he avers that his native English benefited from the German he read in the *Fackel.* After his return to the United States, Bloch joined the faculty of the University of Kansas, where he taught until his retirement in 1947.

In 1930 Bloch published a little volume modestly entitled *Karl Kraus: Poems,* containing his very competent though slightly old-fashioned translations of eighty-nine poems and excerpts from *Die letzten Tage der Menschheit.* The book appeared under the imprint The Four Seas Company, owned by the Boston subsidy publisher Bruce Humphries, Inc. Karl Kraus had asked Theodor Haecker, of the Brenner Circle, to testify to the accuracy of the translations, and the book was advertised and sold in Vienna by the firm of Richard Lányi. The great rarity of this publication is due to the fact that Bloch, evidently a perfectionist, soon bought up the remaining copies and had them pulped. However, in the year of his retirement he included ten poems with the designation "After the German of Karl Kraus" in a collection of his own poetry (*Ventures in Verse.* New York: Frederick Ungar, 1947), which is introduced by "To Karl Kraus," a rapturous poem that Bloch had written for Kraus's birthday in 1928 and that exists in several versions. Many of Bloch's translations of Kraus, Georg Trakl, and other German-language poets have been restored to print in *Albert Bloch: German Poetry in War and Peace*, a dual-language anthology edited by Frank Baron and published by the University of Kansas in 1995. "Rapturous" is also the word for the translator's foreword to the 1930 publication, and no denigration of Bloch's excellent and meritorious pioneer work is intended if I quote one passage from it to indicate to what extent Bloch was influenced by Leopold Liegler's book as well as by Kraus's own discourse at the time. "He [Kraus] disdains nothing: no scrap of street-slang, or proletarian argot or peasant dialect, no filthy tatter of newspaper patois or of the all-too familiar Jew Jargon, which during the past several decades has permeated not only the daily conversation, but even sometimes the seriously intended writing of the most anti-Semitic Viennese bourgeoisie — everything whirls madly into the ruthlessly receptive maelstrom of his word, to rise purified again as organic essence of his wondrous creation" (20).

My own efforts as a translator of Kraus reflect disagreement with George Steiner's statements about the "local" limitation of Kraus's satire and the risk of rendering him into today's "world pidgin." It was, on the contrary, belief in the universality of many of Kraus's satiric insights that encouraged me, and presumably other translators as well, to render careful (and, alas, minimal) selections from his writings not into British, Australian, Canadian, or American English but into a language that could integrate Kraus into the great satiric heritage of the English-speaking world. The prose gems called aphorisms, which Kraus produced in such abundance in the tradition or heritage of Georg Christoph Lichtenberg or Johann Nepomuk Nestroy, seemed like a good starting point. My distinguished forerunner in this regard was W. H. Auden, who, as a sometime resident of a small Austrian town, Kirchstetten, spoke a fluent Austrian German and in 1962 included twenty Kraus aphorisms in the *Viking* (in England *Faber*) *Book of Aphorisms* that he coedited with Louis Kronenberger. Apart from misunderstanding two of these aphorisms, Auden did fine pioneer work, and only the press of other duties kept him from translating all the aphorisms contained in *Beim Wort genommen*, a postwar collection that incorporates the three volumes published in Kraus's lifetime. In my introduction to *Half-Truths and One-and-a-Half Truths* I expressed my regret at the fact that many of the most brilliant and characteristic of Kraus's thousands of aphorisms, particularly those dealing with language, imagination, the artistic process, and verbal creativity, had to be excluded because of their essential untranslatability and that in other cases too many explanatory notes would have been needed to clarify the allusiveness and complexity of Kraus's insights. In some cases, to be sure, Kraus's verbal play transfers easily to the new language. "Ja, es ist ein chlorreicher Krieg!" — "Yes, it is a chlorious war!" "Es handelt sich in diesem Krieg . . . " "Jawohl, es handelt sich in diesem Krieg!" — "In this war we are dealing . . . " "Yessiree, in this war we are dealing!" But I also gave a few examples of the difficulties inherent in transferring Kraus's imaginative response to language to another language. I rendered the aphorism "Man lebt nicht einmal einmal" as "You don't even live once"; the trite German saying "Man lebt nur einmal," which has an equivalent in the equally trite hedonistic saying "You only live once" (or, more correctly, "You live only once"), has been turned around by Kraus. My translation seems to reflect a pessimistic Weltanschauung, a mere opinion. Yet Kraus has utilized the resources of the German language to express an idea directly derived from this language: *einmal*, stressed on the first syllable and meaning "once," is preceded by *einmal*, stressed on the second syllable and meaning, in conjunction with *nicht*, "not even." To reproduce this grammatical or syntactical feature of German and still convey Kraus's basically life-affirming thought, one would have to explore the possibilities of the English language and come up with something like this: "Your chances of living a happy, fulfilled life are not even even." But surely such a relatively verbose and labored version could not match the concision of Kraus's aphorism. Another case in point, in which an English rendition, however ingenious, represents only a compromise, is this aphorism: "Je größer der Stiefel, desto größer der Absatz." On the face of it, this is a shoemaker's truism: "The bigger the boot, the bigger the heel." However, each noun has multiple meanings; *Stiefel* can also denote "blather" or "nonsense," and *Absatz* can also mean "sale" or "paragraph." My rendition, "The bigger the bull, the bigger the bull market," reproduces only part of the satirist's thought and verbal wit. In view of Kraus's interminable paragraphs, his detractors might well use this aphorism against him. One of Kraus's most insightful American critics, Jay F. Bodine, has also commented on this aphorism:

> It has become exemplary for his achieving polysemous ramifications: "*Stiefel*" has the meanings of "boot," "a large measure of alcoholic drink" and "routine nonsense" — while "*Absatz*" can be translated with "heel," "paragraph" and "sale or disposal of goods." Thus the topic concerns not

only the mercantile disposal of big boots with large crushing heels but
also the marketing of extensive prose replete with drunken and/or ever-
repeated inanities. . . . Kraus the artist brought forth perhaps tens of
thousands of such formulations — cross sections of his circa 22,000-page
oeuvre have been analyzed to show such samples of word play at the rate
of five to twelve per page. . . . The word play was often part of his critique
of language use and of language users — always calling attention to the
mentality, motivations, intentions, and value systems behind particular
uses of language use. (1989, 146–47)

Alas, such considerations are largely lost on certain translators of Kraus,
who, in the words of the old popular song, must be called fools who rush
in where angels fear to tread. For example, in an otherwise meritorious
collection, *No Compromise* (1977), edited by Frederick Ungar, a New York
publisher who became a "Krausian" in his youth in Vienna, we find this
meaningless aphorism: "The words 'family ties' have a flavor of truth"
(232). The key is the word *Familienbande*. *Bande* (plural) does mean
"ties," but *Bande* (singular) means "gang," and Kraus clearly meant dubious relatives whose behavior justifies thoughts of the second meaning.
"How is it that I have all the time not to read so much?" from the same
collection (230) is awkward and does not clearly express Kraus's thought:
"Where shall I find the time to do all this nonreading?" The competent
translations of *Fackel* essays, letters, and court documents in *No Compromise* (by Sheema Buehne and others) and in Ungar's other volume, *The
Last Days of Mankind*, which contains about one-third of Kraus's play, ef-
fectively complement my two volumes, the above-mentioned selection of
aphorisms, and the Kraus reader, which contains prose, poetry, and a hun-
dred-page reading version of *Die letzten Tage der Menschheit*, with translations by Max Knight, Joseph Fabry, Karl F. Ross, and myself.

The strident tone of Thomas S. Szasz's book *Karl Kraus and the Soul-
Doctors: A Pioneer Critic and His Criticism of Psychiatry and Psychoanalysis*
(1976) and the author's statements that "Iggers and Zohn . . . have tried
to achieve literal fidelity to the original text and succeeded in doing so by
sacrificing all the esthetic and linguistic values for which Kraus lived" (4)
and that "because Iggers and Zohn have aimed at fidelity rather than form
in their English rendering of Kraus, their translations are execrable" (95)
were reason enough for me to subject Szasz's own renditions of Kraus's
writings on psychoanalysis and analysts, which cover more than one-third
of his book, to close scrutiny. The transgressions against both fidelity and
form as well as against Kraus's esthetic and linguistic values, not to mention
sound common sense, that I uncovered led me to wonder how such a distorted and skewed view of what Kraus actually wrote could serve as a basis
for informed criticism. My polemic with Szasz, a Hungarian-born Ameri-

can psychiatrist and prolific author, beginning with an open letter to him and his editor Beverly Jarrett entitled "A Case of 'Translation Envy' or Shrinking a Shrink," was carried on in the pages of the *ATA Chronicle*, the journal of the American Translators Association (6, 1, January-February and April-May 1977).

Giving numerous specific examples, I showed that the foe of fidelity and liberator from literalness cuts, expands, combines, interprets, transposes, editorializes, and even completely rewrites at will. Szasz occasionally does convey the gist of what Kraus wrote, but because he feels free to leave out words, phrases, sentences, qualifiers, elaborations, and connecting statements, a most peculiar kind of distortion results. Often Szasz is verbose where Kraus is laconic, or a *terrible simplificateur* where Kraus is complex or ambiguous. Here is one of Kraus's most striking aphorisms about war (in my translation): "War is, at first, the hope that one will be better off; next, the expectation that the other fellow will be worse off; then, the satisfaction that he isn't any better off; and, finally, the surprise at everyone's being worse off." This is how Szasz renders (rends?) it: "War: first, one hopes to win, then one expects the enemy to lose, then one is satisfied that he too is suffering, in the end one is surprised that everyone has lost." One does not have to know much German to understand that Szasz has played Kraus false here. The doctor views war as a win-or-lose situation, yet Kraus is not concerned with battles at all, but with the effect of war on people, with their everyday discomfort and suffering. Does anyone need to be told that armies can win at the front while it is a case of *schlechter gehen* or *besser gehen*, people being worse off or better off, at home? The whole tragedy of war is reduced by an incompetent and insensitive translator to "I win, you lose." One of Kraus's wittiest aphorisms deals with the psychoanalytic interpretation of literature. "Psychoanalysis unmasks the poet at a glance," Kraus says, and now it is time to return the favor and think of poetry and art when someone speaks of sex. "Für diese Retourkutsche der Symbolik biete ich mich als Lenker an!" *Retourkutsche* is a colloquialism meaning a smart repartee, a clever comeback, or a return in kind, and Kraus is saying that he would like to get in on the fun and start symbol-hunting, wordtwisting, and manipulating the materials of psychoanalysis the way the psychologists have been interpreting the symbolism of poetry and art. But this is what Szasz, whose knowledge of idiomatic German is nowhere in evidence, has come up with: "For this return trip of the coach of symbolism from the depths of the unconscious I volunteer as coachman." Perhaps there is loony logic in this amusing image of a coach of symbolism rattling along the peaks and valleys of the subconscious, but when one remembers that on page xiv of the foreword Szasz promised "an authentic and attractive English version . . . in a style that displays, as does

Kraus's own, the spirit no less than the sense of his message," one has been taught an object lesson in presumptuousness and hypocrisy.

One of Kraus's most frequently quoted (or misquoted) aphorisms is this one: "Psychoanalyse ist jene Geisteskrankheit, für deren Therapie sie sich hält." For some mysterious reason even such careful scholars as Rollo May and Peter Gay render *Geisteskrankheit* as "disease" or "illness," when it clearly means "*mental* illness" (rather than "spiritual disease," as a few translators would have it). Kraus himself got into the act and compounded the felony, so to speak, when he reprinted, in the very last issue of *Die Fackel* (917–22, February 1936, 93), the following excerpt from "The Twilight of Psychoanalysis," *American Mercury*, August 1935, 387: "The words of the brilliant Viennese editor Karl Kraus, who wrote that 'Psychoanalysis is the disease whose symptoms it purports to cure,' are the best epitaph that can be found for a dying science." Perhaps Thomas Szasz may be forgiven for his mistranslation, which finds him in such good company; after all, to him mental illness is merely a myth. But he really indulges himself by "opening up" Kraus's pithy thought and offering this elaboration as well: "Before Freud, doctors cautioned that the cure may be worse than the disease; now they ought to caution that there is a cure which is a disease — namely psychoanalysis."

Is there a Gresham's Law of translation by which bad translations drive out the good ones? Richard Kostelanetz, a prolific writer and filmmaker, is, like Szasz, an advocate of Kraus; but with such supporters, who needs detractors? In "Another Father for Us All," a generally favorable review of *In These Great Times* (1991), Kostelanetz writes, "I find in Kraus an intellectual father I'd known about but had not recognized before" (215). He wonders about the quality of the translations, however: "Whereas the most famous Kraus aphorism is known to me (and to Thomas Szasz, whose *Anti-Freud* was published by Syracuse University Press in 1990) as 'Psychoanalysis is the disease of which it claims to be the cure,' here the rendering is 'Psychoanalysis is that mental illness for which it regards itself as therapy.' This is so inferior it gives reason to question everything else. Indeed, given Kraus's commitment to clear expression as a moral imperative, inept translations are doubly sinful." The "fresh" translations by Szasz "are superior enough to suggest that, more than a half-century after Kraus's death, we are still waiting for a definitive English translation of his rich and terribly sympathetic intelligence" (216).

Surely this final insight cannot be faulted. Kostelanetz's earlier reference is to the paperback reprint of Szasz's 1976 publication (following British and French editions), which sports a new title and a new preface but is otherwise completely unchanged. Having been unwilling to be taught a lesson, Szasz, who has a large readership, deserves to be pilloried. He and

Kostelanetz, who thoughtlessly damns the efforts of several competent Viennese-born translators because he cannot tell a bogus product from the genuine article, must be the despair of every *traduttore*, and each man is a *traditore* if ever there was one.

13: The Postwar "Kraus Renaissance"

In his wide-ranging study *Der Abbau einer verkehrten Welt: Satire und politische Wirklichkeit im Werk von Karl Kraus* (The Demontage of a Topsy-Turvy World: Satire and Political Reality in the Work of Karl Kraus, 1969), Michael Naumann attempts to place Kraus in the context of world satire and to examine the justness of the work of Kraus, whom he calls the only genuine German-language satirist in the twentieth century. Kraus occupied a unique position in the agony of the Danubian monarchy, but his satire far transcended Vienna and Austria-Hungary and extended into other German-speaking realms and into the world of ideologies. "Kraus's *Fackel*," writes Naumann, "constitutes a phenomenology of the advanced pathogenesis of the ideologies of his age and ours" (12). In six major chapters and numerous short sections the author analyzes the nature and resources of Krausian satire — its occasions, citations, wit, and apocalyptic dimensions. In a section entitled "Vienna and Its Waltzes" Naumann examines Kraus's attitude toward Vienna and views the Ringstraße as "the petrified waltz motif of an epoch" (111), undoubtedly the most impressive camouflage of the vacuum of values that Kraus discerned.

Considerable human interest attaches to the critical writings of Paul Hatvani (pseudonym of Paul Hirsch), whose life began in Austria and ended in Australia. A talented essayist and poet in his youth, which coincided with what has been described as "the expressionistic decade," Hatvani resumed his literary activities in his old age and after his "rediscovery" in the 1960s gave pride of place to Karl Kraus, an idol of his earlier years, whom he considered to be of undiminished relevance. In "Versuch über Karl Kraus" (1967) Hatvani emphasizes that what was new in the satirist's work was his recognition of the fateful and indissoluble connection between the word and morality, language and ethics. Even though the author describes Kraus as a socialist outside of socialism and an intellectual champion of the idea who was outside the party, he feels that those who attempt to claim the satirist for a certain party or ideology confuse a moral-artistic conscience with a political orientation and mentality. Hatvani presents Kraus as an exemplar of "total satire" who is above the ideologies and tergiversations of political parties. He defines this as a system of interrelationships and interconnectedness in which utterances and situations can be measured (and judged in an ultimately constructive way) by the most rigorous, absolute standards and value systems, with every symptom becoming a symbol.

Hatvani develops the idea of total satire at greater length in "Karl Kraus und die totale Satire" (1975). He appreciatively remembers an article that listed Kraus among those who created the emotional and conceptual landscape of the twentieth century, placing the satirist in the company of Freud, Klimt, Kokoschka, Wittgenstein, Weininger, Mach, Schönberg, Berg, and Webern — all Austrians! Kraus, however, must be regarded as sui generis; it is pointless to search for forerunners, groups, or rubrics to whom or which the satirist belongs, and in this connection (or lack of it) a new definition of "outsider" is needed. Even though Kraus's writings are never theoretical or parabolic and are always based on a confrontation with reality, his satire seldom concerns itself with occasions but always with the resonance or echo of what has transpired — ostensibly a reality of the second order, but one essential for his satiric quest. Kraus places the world before a tribunal that consists of his three selves: writer, judge, and moralist. "His verdicts cannot be appealed, for the total satirist makes demands in accordance with his own value system which, in contrast to the rest of the world, remains absolute" (69). Hatvani concludes that satire is not a *Beruf* (vocation) but a *Berufung* (calling).

"Karl Kraus did not write 'in a language,' but through him the beauty, profundity, and accumulated moral experience of the German language assumed personal shape and became the crucial witness in the case this inspired prosecutor brought against his time," wrote Erich Heller in *The Disinherited Mind* (1957, 239). This statement by a veteran Kraus scholar may be one of the most widely cited insights into a salient feature of Kraus's satire. However, presumably playing more than the role of an *advocata diaboli*, Wilma Abeles Iggers has commented as follows: "What moral experience can there be in a language? If language has any relation to morality, other than in the way in which it is used, would it then not rather reflect first of all the character of the users? How could it be evaluated by anyone other than the users, i.e., heirs of narrower or wider human experience? How can one juxtapose moral experience of language with time, and how can the German language assume personal shape? Why the German language? How can Heller assume that with Kraus, who knew no other language well?" (1975, 35). Most readers will understand, however, that Heller, who also makes the apodictic statement "His work is untranslatable" (235), is referring to Kraus's conception of language (and in his case, the German language) as a great touchstone. "The tirades of rhetoricians, the pamphlets of politicians, the feuilletons of renowned authors are passed through the filter of language, leaving behind these dregs of folly and residues of false pretense" (239). Decades before Hannah Arendt, in her assessment of Adolf Eichmann, coined the phrase "the banality of evil," Erich Heller expressed a disturbing insight when he wrote that "we have not yet grasped the demonic possibilities of mediocrity. . . . It was Karl Kraus who discovered to what satanic heights inferiority may rise. He anticipated Hitler long before anyone knew his name" (249). The "heroes" of the play *The Last Days of Mankind* are seen as "troglodytes living in the skyscrapers of history, barbarians having at their disposal all the amenities and high explosives of technical progress, fishmongers acting the role of Nelsons, ammunition salesmen crossing Rubicons and hired scribblers tapping out on their machines the heroic phrases of the bards" (249). Concerning himself with the nature of satire, a genre that he considers too vaguely defined, Heller believes that Kraus, whom he calls the first European satirist, is in a different class from Heinrich Heine and George Bernard Shaw, who are by comparison merely earnest jesters. With reference to Friedrich Schiller's insight (in his essay "Über naive und sentimentalische Dichtung," On Naive and Reflective Poetry) that the true satirist would have been a great poet if the moral perversity of his age had not embittered him, Heller presents Kraus's poems as a confirmation of the authenticity of Kraus's satire: "They set in relief the works of hate against a background of light. As the scope of his satirical work widened and the darkness of its world deepened, so his poetic genius gained in simplicity and spontaneity, his lyrical work in tenderness and affection. It shows his satire to be the imploring gesture of a lover who seeks to guard what he loves against the evil of the world closing in upon it" (255).

Erich Heller's essay "Dark Laughter," which appeared on the eve of the Kraus centennial year (1973), is ostensibly a review of the Kösel Verlag's fourteen-volume edition of Kraus's writings as well as of the books by Iggers and Zohn, but Heller has only a few words of praise for the two monographs, and it is clear that the Kösel edition only provided an occasion for the publication of another magisterial Heller essay about Kraus. As the satirist's "great and inexhaustible theme" Heller sees the "casting of a perverse stage director who allowed the tragedy of mankind to be enacted by characters from an operetta" (21). In an effort to highlight the diversity of Kraus's themes, Heller points out that Kraus was not a mystic. "For Karl Kraus everything that truly was was sayable: war, killing, money, hunger, journalists, lies, machines, infamy; but also trees, fountains, dogs, love, and the peace above the mountain tops on a summer evening" (22). Yet the special quality of his satire must be viewed in the context of his contemporaries in the dying decades of an old empire:

> Karl Kraus was one of the remarkable generation of men who, despite all their differences, unmistakably belonged to the last days of the Austrian monarchy. They were prophets of its end, or messengers of a radically

new beginning, or subtle analysts of its decadence. . . . The men of the
Austrian "apocalypse" were mostly Jews or at least not quite un-Jewish:
Karl Kraus, Otto Weininger, Franz Kafka, Gustav Mahler, Arnold Schönberg, Hugo von Hofmannsthal, Sigmund Freud, Arthur Schnitzler, Joseph Roth, Ludwig Wittgenstein, Hermann Broch, and it comes almost
as a surprise, or strikes one as an act of wilful "racial" discrimination, that
the names of Adolf Loos, Alban Berg, and Robert Musil cannot be added
to this list. (24)

Heller's article elicited a response from another noted European-born
critic, Walter Kaufmann (1973). Calling Kraus "a very questionable figure"
(36), Kaufmann accuses Heller of coasting on the remembrance of things
past, writing as he did twenty years ago without taking cognizance of more
critical views of the satirist, and contributing to the myth of Kraus in the
English-speaking world. Kraus's "megalomania often becomes tedious"
(36), and his literary judgment was warped by prejudice and therefore un-
distinguished. After all, he ignored Kafka and Rilke, denigrated George and
Hofmannsthal, failed to recognize Freud's genius, was irresponsible in his
treatment of Heine, and overvalued Altenberg and Lasker-Schüler. In
Kaufmann's view, Kraus was "not a shining example of intellectual integrity. . . . In the end he remained a pedant whose flashes of wit did not
compensate sufficiently for his consuming resentment, his appalling lack of
judgment, his bigotry and his unscrupulous methods" (37). In his reply, in
the same issue of the *New York Review of Books*, Erich Heller points out
that insofar as Kraus had a share in Jewish anti-Semitism, he was a fellow
anti-Semite of Karl Marx, Heine, Weininger, and Kafka. Since he was not a
literary critic, he did not feel obliged to render just verdicts, and this explains his occasional inconsistencies and injustices. As for Kraus's polemic
against Heine, Heller calls it "luminously biased and distinguished" (37),
and Kraus was primarily concerned with Heine's "consequences": feuilletonism and journalese.

Kraus always emphasized the connection between language and morality; for him language was the moral criterion for a writer or speaker. Yet J.
P. Stern sees fallacies and pitfalls in what he calls Kraus's "moral-linguistic
imperative":

We cannot, on the social scene, identify linguistics, insensitivity and ob-
tuseness and even downright abuse of language with moral torpor or de-
generacy — though we may see in them signs of ignorance, or of a poor
education, or thoughtlessness in verbal matters. . . . On the other hand,
the use of language as an indicator of positive values is, if anything, even
more problematic; there is at least one occasion when Kraus's insistence
on the sublime literary value of a political manifesto landed him in an attitude one would like to call absurd were it not irresponsible. (1966, 80)

The reference is to Kraus's evaluation of Emperor Franz Joseph's manifesto "An meine Völker" (To My Peoples) of August 1914 as an "exalted . . . most humane proclamation . . . a poem" ["erhabenster . . . menschlichster Anschlag . . . Gedicht"]. Stern expresses a basic objection to Kraus's absolute equation between word and world when he writes:

> To say that the imagination, or the sensibility, of a man is coextensive with his morality is very much like saying that his language is coextensive with his experience. These two assertions encompass Kraus's entire work, and both are open to the same logical and existential objections. One finally wonders whether, in basing his entire work on these two equations, Kraus was not, after all, succumbing to the curse of Vienna, the city in which the experiment of replacing morality and politics by the life of the imagination was carried to the point of moral paralysis and political disintegration. (83)

In the 1960s some younger German critics and editors touched off a series of polemics in Austria and Germany by producing negative assessments of Karl Kraus. One might have expected Fritz J. Raddatz, the editor of the Berlin-born satirist Kurt Tucholsky, to appreciate the other great satirist of the German-speaking realm as well, but the opposite was the case. In his essay "Der blinde Seher: Überlegungen zu Karl Kraus" (The Blind Seer: Reflections on Karl Kraus, 1968, later included in his book *Verwerfungen* [Rejections]. Frankfurt: Suhrkamp, 1972). Raddatz describes Kraus as an irrationalist who personalized every problem by always asking "who" rather than "what," presided over a reductive process from a great linguistic hoard via aphoristic small change to speechlessness, and, caught up in his own solar system, fought *Zeitung* (newspapers) rather than *Zeit* (the age), ignored the great social, political, and technical currents and issues of his time, and was never interested in uncovering origins or connections. "Kraus's critique of Heine is a 23-page aphorism, a Viennese capriccio" (523), his *ad personam* polemics are trivial and ineffective, and his verbal cataracts are overwrought and full of foam. Calling Kraus's prose destructive, Raddatz "translates" or deconstructs Kraus's wartime essay "In These Great Times . . . " in the manner of Kraus's own "translations" from Maximilian Harden's overblown prose. Raddatz even rejects *The Last Days of Mankind* as linguistically and dramatically monotonous, "an Austrian illustrated broadsheet of horrors" (528) that is not as good as the art of George Grosz. Monologues and dialogues, he claims, are not Kraus's forte — with one exception: the monologue of the Nörgler (Grumbler) in Act 5, Scene 54, "one of Kraus's great political texts" (528). Raddatz takes an altogether negative view of *The Third Walpurgis Night*, "an intellectual declaration of bankruptcy" (528), a frightening book of verbose emptiness and banal polemics that failed to examine Hitler's language and political program. One of Raddatz's more egregious and easily refutable statements is this one: "In the entire book there is not the slightest hint of LTI" (532). (The term *Lingua Tertii Imperii*, the language of the Third Reich, was coined by Viktor Klemperer, a scholar who had survived the Holocaust, for his examination of the dehumanizing abuse of the German language during the Nazi period.)

In its issue of January 1970 the Viennese journal *Literatur und Kritik* dealt with polemics on the subject of Karl Kraus, and there and elsewhere Kraus's detractors (Raddatz as well as the like-minded German critics Joachim Kaiser, Curt Hohoff, and Ivo Frenzel) clashed with such pro-Kraus critics as Friedrich Jenaczek, Helmut Arntzen, Hilde Spiel, Edwin Hartl, and Werner Kraft.

In his book of essays entitled *Karl Kraus, Arthur Schnitzler, Otto Weininger* (1962), the Prague-born historian Hans Kohn presents a small typology of intellectuals from a cosmopolitan city in which Jews have played an important role. These three men are viewed as loners who did not belong to any clique, ideology, or combative group. Kraus and Weininger were in opposition to the prosperous educated Viennese bourgeoisie that was Schnitzler's home. Only the last-named remained in the Jewish fold, though he, like Kraus, was really an agnostic. Kraus and Weininger rejected both Vienna and their Jewishness, but Kraus, like Freud, remained tied to the city and what to him were its numerous satiric occasions. "Weininger proceeded from generally valid hypotheses," writes Kohn, "and applied them to concrete life, often doing violence to it, whereas Kraus based himself on a concrete moment and individual case to which he attempted to give validity" (47). Like Weininger, Kraus was a fanatical absolutist and a moralist, but on a more apocalyptic plane, and both men had a basic disregard for history and politics. Heinrich Heine was not such a fanatic, and thus he appeared to Kraus as his own antithesis: "The satirist Heine, who was not a great and upright character, often displayed surprising insight into broad historical and political connections. In his constant, exhausting struggle against the evils of the press and linguistic deterioration, Kraus, who far surpassed Heine in strength of character and ethical devotion to his work, frequently saw the great outlines of the political and intellectual development less clearly" (53). Kohn seems to contradict his statement, however, when he discusses *The Third Walpurgis Night* (which was not published in its entirety until 1952) as a work of undiminished timeliness in which the author showed that the demonism of the new Germany openly and unmistakably manifested itself in its own proclamations and announcements — not only to the enraptured masses but also among scholars and intellectuals.

In Kraus's polemical writings small problems are sometimes accorded the significance of catastrophes, and his pathos often seems out of place. . . . With moral pathos and great bitterness Kraus fought against the priggishness of the Jewish press of Vienna, its power to destroy culture, and its capitalistic venality; in World War I he displayed in exemplary fashion his profound shock at all the suffering and stupidity of the war; but he devoted less attention to the even greater forces that threatened German culture after 1918 and were rooted in Germanophilia and the overvaluation of national characteristics. (56, 60)

Kohn feels that Kraus was insufficiently aware of the decline of parliamentarianism and party structures, of the general predilection for rootedness and blood lines, for leaders and aristocratic types, to the detriment of the common man and common sense.

In his uncommonly comprehensive and perceptive two-part essay "Reflections on Karl Kraus" (1973), the American sociologist and critic Robert Lilienfeld, commenting on all the important aspects of Kraus's work, concerns himself with Kraus's relevance to our own time and place. Now that the wall of silence around Kraus has begun to crumble, Lilienfeld points out, Kraus would hardly have appreciated his new vogue as the hero of the European establishment, but he was right in one respect:

As his work goes out of date, its timeliness emerges. . . . Many features of American life would be strange to Karl Kraus, but there are things he would recognize. The unconquerables are back, and he would recognize them. In his time he could track them down and uncover their lies, for they had only the press, but now they have not only the press but radio, television, films, and the universities. . . . America, it is to be hoped, may prove to have moral reserves which Austria did not. . . . Kraus himself was a journalist; how does it happen that he denounced his own profession? It was not the institution itself he attacked but rather the attitudes it tended to generate: the use of thought, language, and imagery for some other purpose than the expression of truth. It was this against which he warred. We have multitudes of literati who misuse their minds in that way. But we have no Karl Kraus." (572)

Another insightful essay on Kraus appeared in the literary supplement of the New York newspaper *Village Voice* in September 1985, Michael Feingold's "A Kraus Divided: German Literature's Best-Kept Secret." Feingold, a theater critic and translator, invites readers to follow him into the intricate palace of German literature,

built by someone with M. C. Escher's perversely tricky sense of space; to get from any one hall to any other, you must pass through an asymmetrical, weirdly decorated Viennese rotunda of the late Imperial period. Though no one inside the palace can avoid this bizarre spot . . . no one

outside knows it exists, as the building is obstinately constructed to conceal it from external view on all sides, even though — or maybe because — it contains some of the palace's most fantastic treasures. We will
call this centrally located curiosity Karl Kraus. (1)

Commenting on such recent publications as the Kraus reader *In These
Great Times* and Kraus's correspondence with Sidonie Nádherný ("a thousand love letters full of doting, badgering, blarneying, sulking, self-pitying
affections,"11) Feingold points out that "like H. L. Mencken, whose view
of America was as oddly skewed as Kraus's angle on Vienna, he channeled
his alienation from other humans into a fixation on their language" (10).
The author sees Kraus as an important linking figure who connects Brecht
and Heine, Kafka and E. T. A. Hoffmann, the expressionist playwrights
and Goethe and Kleist: "The many doors in his magical upside-down room
in the palace of German literature open out in all directions, back to the
troubadours and onward to the newscasters" (11). In Feingold's view,
Kraus was, in a sense, the first modern writer even though he had no use
for modernism and "hated the technological advances and social upheavals
that combined to produce it" (11). As the spirit that drove Kraus's work
the author sees "a humanistic daimon of mockery, skepticism, passion and
anger which our own society sorely needs" (11).

That the critic, librarian, and essayist Werner Kraft (1896–1991), who
lived in Jerusalem from 1933 to his death, was an early advocate of Kraus is
indicated by his correspondence with Martin Buber in March 1917 (*The
Letters of Martin Buber*, edited by Nahum Glatzer and Paul Mendes-Flohr,
1991). On March 11 of that year Kraft wrote to Buber: "I should like to
call your attention to the fact that the name of Karl Kraus — a prodigious
figure, at once a Jew and a man of the highest aims — has to this day been
mentioned but once in your journal [*Der Jude*, The Jew]. . . . I love Kraus
because he suffers the world conflict of the spirit as a man who with glori-
ous wholeness is rooted in the Word. I love him also because he is the only
Jew I know who is organically bound to the German heart, because he
himself possesses one." (209). Martin Buber responded on March 15: "I
commissioned an essay on Kraus from a contributor months ago . . . but I
have done so only because I esteem Kraus, not because I regard him as 'a
prodigious figure, at once a Jew and a man of the highest aims'; having the
highest aims is no prodigy in a Jew, but is his nature" (210). On March 17
Kraft wrote to Buber about "the tremendously true polemic" that Kraus
had "in all his purity" been waging against Franz Werfel (212).

The Prague-born poet, novelist, and dramatist Werfel, one of the leading figures among the early literary expressionists, was a youthful admirer
of Kraus, who, in turn, had printed and recited several of Werfel's poems
and announced his first collections in *Die Fackel*. Werfel, who had contrib-

uted a dithyrambic essay to Ficker's *Rundfrage über Karl Kraus* (1917), in which he described his encounter with the satirist as "a mystical experience" and spoke of "the hour which binds my planet to his" (37–38), had turned away from Kraus, who rejected and lampooned expressionism before his essay appeared in pamphlet form. The two men shared the same publisher, Kurt Wolff of Leipzig, for a few years, but in 1916 Wolff was persuaded by the satirist to publish his writings under a separate imprint. The dissension between Werfel and Kraus having been expressed in several of their poems and essays, Kraus lampooned Werfel for his pathos-filled stance of cosmic empathy with all mankind, and Werfel retaliated with a poem that reflected his new view of Kraus as a crafty and self-righteous judge. In the third part of Werfel's "magical trilogy," *Spiegelmensch* (Mirror Man), the title character delivers the following vulgar prose soliloquy:

> What shall I do in the coming days of idleness? I've got it! I will join the prophets — the major prophets, of course. To begin with, I shall found . . . a periodical and call it — *The Lamp?* No. *The Candle Stump?* No! *The Torch?* Yes! Ah! My fingers are itching with all the great writers of world literature! People shall think that Goethe plus Shakespeare's genius has been reincarnated in the form of a shyster lawyer from the East. I will turn city gossip into a cosmic event and cosmic events into city gossip. I will juggle puns and pathos so skillfully that everyone who feels, after reading the first line, that I am a comical informer and fartcatcher will have to admit, upon reading the next line, that I am Isaiah incarnate. But, above all, I will appear as the cabaret performer of my apocalyptic pronouncements, for I am a good actor, and that is what I am recognized by, to say nothing of my ability as an imitator of animal voices and . . . an acoustic mirror. (188–89)

Since the above-mentioned publisher did not succeed in eliminating this from the book edition (Munich: Kurt Wolff, 1920), Kraus had his later writings published in Vienna by the *Fackel* publishing house. Kraus struck back with his "magical operetta" *Literatur oder Man wird doch da sehn* (Literature or We'll See About That), which he first read in Vienna on March 6, 1921, a month before *Spiegelmensch* had its premiere at the Burgtheater. In this play there is a Werfel figure named Johann Wolfgang. The feud between Kraus and Werfel was renewed in the latter's play *Paul Among the Jews* (1926), in which Paul, an advocate of Christian love (and presumably a self-portrait of Werfel), prevails over the cold and heartless Rabbi Beschwörer, a Kraus figure, who has hitherto held sway via the vanity of the word. However, Kurt Wolff reports a poignant and rather revealing statement made by Werfel to a mutual friend in his last years: "If Kraus had lived long enough to be forced to emigrate, as I was, I would have gone to him and made my peace with him" (Wolff, *Autoren, Bücher, Abenteuer*. Berlin: Klaus Wagenbach, n.d., 97).

In 1952 Werner Kraft edited a little Kraus reader that appeared in the series *Verschollene und Vergessene*, devoted to writers who had dropped out of sight and were largely forgotten. An introductory essay is followed by a selection of short prose and poetry as well as some photos and facsimiles. "Karl Kraus knew about the transitoriness of a satirist whose subject matter dies," writes Kraft. "However, the evanescent material of this linguistic work was born of the spirit, and this makes it essentially imperishable. A future age will recognize who Karl Kraus was. It will take the road from the dead subject matter back to the living spirit and truly appropriate the fiery thought of a thinker fighting for a lost cause" (15).

Twenty years after the satirist's death Kraft published his book *Karl Kraus* (1956). This is not a "life and works," for the author has little to say about Kraus's biography, but a collection of seven searching essays in which an erudite critic attempts to place Kraus in the intellectual and cultural context of his time, to present him from within, as it were. Pointing out that "to a rare extent, his work is his biography" (14), Kraft is aware that his approach "could not give an exhaustive presentation of the intellectual and moral substance of an enormous oeuvre" (9). The man who "brought to his task an outraged heart, a keen intelligence, and the commitment of his person" (14) in countless variations made himself the measure of his era's moral bankruptcy. Throughout his book Kraft displays a becoming awareness of the multifarious contradictions in Kraus's life and work that have caused confusion among readers and critics alike. In line with his conviction that a lyrical undercurrent runs through Kraus's entire oeuvre, that his prose is "*lyrisch unterströmt*" (180), the author includes in virtually every essay cogent and illuminating interpretations of Kraus poems that tend to refute and counteract some other critics' judgment that this poetry is too intellectual and not elemental enough. In Kraft's view, poetry is just a special coinage of Kraus's language and has the same function as language itself — to be a criterion of worth and unworth.

In a chapter on Kraus's childhood and youth, for example, Kraft analyzes such poems as "Memoiren" and "An einen alten Lehrer" and discusses the influence of the puppet theater and the old Burgtheater to show that Kraus's mother "may have bequeathed him the emotive power of compassion and his penchant for dreaming" (39), that "the marionette is the quintessence of womanhood, spiritualized and disembodied" (46), and that "everything that Kraus thought about theater and acting, and about art in general, springs from the great theatrical impressions of his youth" (53). Commenting on Kraus's early anti-Zionist (or really anti-Herzl, anti-*Neue Freie Presse*) satire *Eine Krone für Zion*, Kraft points out that despite its scintillating wit, it does not do justice to its subject. He discerns two important motifs in this work: the satirist's belief that complete assimilation of the Jews is necessary, and faith in socialism, which would alleviate the misery of the Jewish masses in Eastern Europe with socialist measures, not with bourgeois Western Zionist activities. Later Kraus abandoned the latter faith and replaced it with a messianic belief in the curative power of *Untergang* (decline, dissolution) in the name of linguistic ideas that he equated with goodness and integrity.

In his discussion of *The Last Days of Mankind*, Kraft points out that all German political thesis plays of the 1920s and 1930s are directly or indirectly indebted to it, though neither their authors nor the critics have felt impelled to cite this source. In his view Bertolt Brecht was influenced by it and continued Kraus's satiric method in his drama *Furcht und Elend des Dritten Reiches* (published in English as *The Private Life of the Master Race*). All the satiric themes in Kraus's play had already been covered in the prewar *Fackel*: "The press as the mouthpiece of the bourgeoisie, the destruction of culture by politics, bourgeois morality and its consequences and the devaluation of language by clichés" (138). Kraus now abandoned his Austrian conservative stance and became the great accuser of the German-Austrian war effort. Poetry became a resuscitating force for him in wartime.

Commenting on *Heine and the Consequences*, Kraft believes that "doing an injustice to Heine is not as important as the fact that Kraus was seeking a new kind of justice in search of the person responsible for the 'consequences,' namely, Heine himself" (163). The author seems pained in his discussion of the complex relationship between Kraus and Heine, to whom Kraus conceded talent but not character, and he believes that "Kraus was an unsystematic thinker who never worked inductively but always deductively, on the basis of shifting historical constellations; therefore the truths he found were always relative in nature" (171). Curiously enough, Kraft does not discuss "feuilletonism," which may be regarded as Heine's chief "consequence," the facile, linguistically deceitful, and ultimately deleterious blending of substance with form, a heritage on which journalists have drawn to this day.

Kraft's discussion of the relationship between Kraus's linguistic thought and the music of the Second Viennese School is indebted to the writings of Ernst Křenek and belongs in another context. However, considerable interest attaches to the author's analysis of such important poems as "Bekenntnis," "Fernes Licht mit nahem Schein," "Flieder," "Der Tag," "Fahrt ins Fextal," "Schnellzug," "Nächtliche Stunde," "Erlebnis," and "Vor dem Einschlafen," the last-named being one of Kraus's dream poems. "For Karl Kraus," writes Kraft, "dreams are the strongest weapons against the psychoanalysts, who want to interpret them. . . . No personal guilt feelings connect this strong dreamer with the weak world that has produced Sigmund Freud . . . so that he might cure its sickness. Where there are guilt feelings in Karl Kraus, it is the guilt of others that he is prepared to expiate" (265). Kraft also comments cogently on Kraus's aphorisms — for example, this suggestive one: "An aphorism cannot be dictated to a typist. It would take too long." According to Kraft, this can be interpreted in two ways: 1) An aphorism is the product of a flash of insight, and having been born with lightning speed, it cannot be captured by a typewriter. 2) The thought process that gave rise to an aphorism goes on and is endless.

"If his struggle was futile," concludes Kraft, "it was his epoch that failed, not he" (361). He closes his study with the Kierkegaard statement (of 1849) that Kraus used as a motto for his play *Die Unüberwindlichen*: "An individual cannot help his epoch or save it, he can only express that it is going to ruin."

Karl Kraus: A Viennese Critic of the Twentieth Century (1967) by Wilma Abeles Iggers represents the virtually unchanged text of the author's doctoral dissertation written at the University of Chicago in 1952. The book has many of the earmarks of an academic study, such as a tendency to overstate the author's case and an overly "busy" organization that defines or summarizes virtually every paragraph in advance. The book's admirable comprehensiveness is indicated by such chapter headings as "The Pernicious Press," "War as a Symptom of the Contemporary Crisis," and "Reactions to Political Events," but in her zeal to present Kraus in bite-sized portions, as it were, the author often concentrates on trees to the detriment of the forest. Her demystification and analytical evaluation of Kraus are clearly intended to provide a critical counterpoise to the adulatory "would-be scholarly articles by authors who write out of the fog of their fondness for the Kraus of decades ago" (xvi). However, the rather bilious tone of this study early on conveys the impression that while Iggers does offer a close reading of Kraus, the satirist is often read against the grain here. "One would entirely misunderstand Kraus's significance," writes Iggers toward the end of her book, "if one were to try to analyze his views in a purely intellectual manner, to try to define his concepts, and to arrive at theories" (192). Yet this is precisely what she does for the most part. "If I say that Kraus was often unfair to those whom he satirized," she writes, "I do not mean that a satirist must not exaggerate or caricature; such methods are essential to satire" (36). It is hard to square this insight with such ingenuous statements as these:

> Satire, this very tool of Kraus's passion for justice, was frequently transformed into a tool of injustice when he used it to apply strong moral stigma [*sic*] to people or works where he believed to see evidence of

moral laxity, while they may basically merely have been counter to his taste. . . . His satire was often large-scale slander, applicable to almost all the notables of his time. . . . If there was very often no reply to Kraus's attacks, it did not necessarily mean that he was entirely right and his opponent wrong. Very often the victim was simply afraid of Kraus's sharp tongue and therefore preferred to drop the matter rather than engage in further discussion. . . . In order to clarify a small point of doubtful significance, Kraus was willing to destroy the most cordial relationships or even human beings." (15, 68, 19, 36)

Some of Iggers's keenest insights are contained in the chapters entitled "The Social Role of Woman" and "The Jewish Problem." "Kraus's revolt against convention," she writes, "concentrated on the destruction of the barriers to the full sensual expression of women," yet "it denied woman any participation in the intellectual and artistic realms. . . . Kraus's formula of the equilibrium of man's mind and woman's sensuality might sound like a plea for equality, except for the fact that he placed his main emphasis on the view that woman's main function was that of inspiring man" (170). In the fullest discussion of Kraus's convoluted Jewishness that had appeared up to that time, Iggers tries to provide evidence that Kraus's writings about Jews are particularly subjective and that the label "Jewish self-hatred" might properly be attached to the satirist. For one thing, "in all the 37 years of *Die Fackel* there was hardly an issue which did not contain a gloss poking fun at a Jewish journalist's language" (174). For another, "what makes the claims that Kraus was an antisemite seem more justified . . . are his own statements which condemn not this or that Jewish group, but the Jews, or the Jewish spirit, in general" (188). Even at the time of the Nazis Kraus could not bring himself to side with the liberal Jewish press against the common foe. A more conciliatory insight is expressed in this statement: "If he was not willing to recognize as much good in Jews as did the average non-antisemitic Viennese, this was, no doubt, partly due to his feeling of greater responsibility for those who actually were his own people" (176). "Heine's peripheral position as a Jew," writes Iggers, "was not unlike Kraus's own. However, if both were critical of the Jews, it seems that Heine arrived at a more cosmopolitan standpoint than Kraus, thus being able to satirize his Jewish and gentile fellows more equally, without being emotionally much more involved with one group than with the other" (70).

Iggers takes a negative view of Kraus's poetry: "It is hardly possible . . . to be deeply moved by Kraus's poetry. It leaves no images behind, and strong feelings are rarely transmitted by it. . . . Instead of seeing, as he did, his usual satire as the reverse of lyric poetry, one is likely to consider his lyric poetry merely the reverse side of his usual coin: one senses that the usually pessimistic and mistrustful Kraus only momentarily pretended to be full of the milk of human kindness" (14).

It would be difficult to fault the author's insight that "Kraus's work must be understood as a critique of contemporary civilization from a particularly Austrian point of view" (208). But surely restlessness was not Kraus's basic motivation ("Kraus's work . . . gives no evidence that he was ever truly at peace with himself," 198). There is no merit to her claim that Kraus "considered himself to be one of the greatest humorists of all time" (44), and the satirist would certainly not have appreciated being called a "publicist" (19). (The German word *Publizist* means "journalist," but the English term is associated with advertising or public relations). Iggers's copious footnotes include many helpful translations from the German, but these are not always reliable; for example, on page 26 *bestreiten* means "dispute," not "supply," and *Sperrgeld* (32) is not an "admission fee" but the fee charged by a building superintendent for unlocking the front door after hours.

My own monograph on Karl Kraus appeared in 1971 in the Twayne World Authors Series. While series requirements imposed a certain limitation on the format and the style, it also posed the welcome challenge to provide an introduction to Kraus, his life and times, as well as to set forth the salient features of his satire. The book was intended for an English-speaking readership, but it was gratifying to note that two decades later a virtually unchanged German translation found appreciative readers on the continent as well. At the time of writing, next to nothing by Kraus had appeared in English translation, and the Kösel Verlag had just begun to issue its reprint edition of the complete *Fackel*. Sustained by Karl Kraus's own epigrammatic or ahistoric insights that "only those distant in time or space / can know my satire's true face" (*Worte in Versen* iii, 133) and that "I have to wait till my writings are obsolete; then they may acquire timeliness" (*Beim Wort genommen*, 1955, 164), I was less concerned with contributing original facets to Kraus scholarship than with making this unique phenomenon more accessible to the (perhaps mythical) general reader. My book is divided into the following chapters: "A Life Between Love and Hate," "The Torch," "K. K. versus Kakania," "The Prostitute Turned into a Virgin," "The Last Days of Mankind," "The Unconquerable," "The Theater of Poetry," and "The Word Passed Away. . . . " The numerous quotations from Kraus's writings in the text are supplemented by an Aphoristic Sampler that was later expanded into a collection of some 450 aphorisms bearing the Krausian title *Half-Truths and One-and-a-Half Truths* (1976).

Hans Weigel's book *Karl Kraus oder Die Macht der Ohnmacht* (Karl Kraus or The Power of Powerlessness, 1968), is the work of a noted storyteller, critic, dramatist, translator, and cabaret wit. It has no footnotes, endnotes, bibliography, index, or other features of a scholarly study, but it is not uncritical, and the empathic author is fully aware of his subject's contradictions and paradoxes. Its title derives from a statement by Kraus that he was aware of his powerlessness and that his pride in this awareness was integrated into his ineffectiveness. Weigel's three dozen vivid, short chapters, from "The Apocalyptic Humorist," "The Flight to the Theater," and "After the Deluge" to "His Homeland's Loyal Hater," "To Whom Have I Ever Done an Injustice?" and "He Was Ours," convey a lively sense of discovery. Weigel writes,

> No one mocked, vilified, and devastatingly attacked Vienna and Austria all his life as much as [Kraus] did, because no one loved Vienna and Austria more deeply and consequently suffered so much because of Vienna and Austria. . . . No one was a greater journalist than the man who regarded journalists as devils and held them responsible for the destruction of the world. . . . No one was as full of contradictions and so completely resists classification and comprehensive presentation. (11)

For example, he despised the audiences at his readings and hated the readers of his journal, proscribing any approval on their part, and yet he would not miss the applause, which he gratefully and proudly acknowledged, and reprinted at length favorable newspaper reviews. According to Weigel, anyone who attempted to do full justice to this phenomenon would have to be what Kraus regarded as repugnant and hateful: a psychologist or psychoanalyst, literary critic, historian, politician, an Austrian, a Viennese of Jewish descent — in other words, all of the latent personas within himself that Kraus negated and strove to overcome, and that he nevertheless lived all his life and seemed to rehabilitate through his work even as he seemed to destroy them. It is the Austrian, Viennese, and Jewish elements in Kraus that Weigel emphasizes in his study. "Karl Kraus's isolation in the dubious and corrupt Viennese world of journalists and artistic, political, and commercial profiteers of all kinds," he writes, "contrasts excitingly with his connections to the great people of his age" (71). (The author means Weininger, Strindberg, Liliencron, Wedekind, Oscar Wilde, and Peter Altenberg). Weigel also draws attention to Kraus's relationship with a kindred spirit, Josef Schöffel, who saved the Vienna Woods from deforestation in 1870 and to whom Kraus devoted an appreciative obituary in the *Fackel* in 1910. "It is a profoundly Austrian element of his nature and work to recognize negatives and to accept a turn for the worse with the phrase 'Nothing can be done about it' and to reiterate Nestroy's refrain 'The world will definitely not last much longer' like a *leitmotif* — even if something could still be done about it . . . even if only a feeble attempt could be made to stave off the catastrophe" (172).

Weigel is alive to the satiric importance of seemingly trivial occasions and jokes when he writes: "He set out against Moriz Benedikt — St. George, Till Eulenspiegel, and Don Quixote in one" (121). As a possible corrective to the rosy picture of "the world of yesterday" (the title of Stefan Zweig's poignantly nostalgic autobiography), Weigel writes:

> Whether out of ignorance or out of sentimentality, people . . . see prewar Vienna as an entity consisting of an eternal Vienna and much greatness that dominated the era: Freud, Schnitzler, Loos, Klimt, Schiele, Kokoschka, Otto Wagner, Josef Hoffmann, Schönberg. This transfiguration includes a regime that perceived greatness — if at all — only as a disturbance. . . . Karl Kraus was the voice of powerless reason in the infernal turmoil of destruction." (179–80)

The author views *The Last Days of Mankind* as "the only successful work of Karl Kraus, apart from his pure poetry, in which he transcends journalism as an object of observation as well as his own journalistic-critical point of view" (199).

Weigel quotes Robert Musil's characterization of Kraus on the occasion of Viennese performances of the satirist's plays *Traumstück* and *Traumtheater* in 1924: "A nasty man whom one would like to kill with silence, but he long ago interred himself, splendidly embalmed, in the royal tomb of a pyramid of his adherents' skulls" (263). Musil was willing to concede that Kraus wrote valuable prose in the field of satire, but his poetry and poetic prose, being allusive rather than fraught with meaning, are less expressive.

Referring to an obituary of Kraus written by Alfred Polgar (*Prager Tagblatt*, June 16, 1936), which in turn contains an allusion to a line by Friedrich Schiller, Weigel makes this excellent pun: "Karl Kraus hat den Besten seiner Zeit genuggetan und den andern genug getan" (264). Possible English versions might be that Kraus lived up to the best (of his time) and never lived down the others, or that Kraus was a match for the best and lit a match under the others.

Weigel points out that with the celebration of his fiftieth birthday and the twenty-fifth anniversary of the *Fackel*, 1924 was an exceptionally good year for Kraus. It also marked the beginning of his fight against the corrupt press czar Imre (Emmerich) Békessy (the "Buda pest"), which Weigel calls "the classic example of an admirable fight against evil, fought with intellectual weapons and linguistic perfection, comparable to the greatest polemical-literary documents of our time" (277). The author considers what might be called Kraus's "Bekessiad" as his greatest achievement after *The Last Days of Mankind*, and he regards Kraus, who finally succeeded in "kicking the crook out of Vienna," as the only Austrian of the century to have won two world wars (though he lost the third, against Johannes Schober). According to Weigel, Kraus made a mistake by including in his polemic against Schober not only the police riot of July 1927 but also Schober's earlier shielding of Békessy. "The break with the Austrian Republic and its Social Democratic Party," he writes, "broke him. His powerlessness, hitherto his constitutional strength, now became his weakness" (294).

In a chapter entitled "The Prodigal Son" Weigel clearly sets forth the satirist's shifting political views and allegiances. On the basis of his background and intellectual stance, the man who stated in the very first *Fackel* that he was not castrated along party lines has to be considered a liberal, as witness his attitude on the sexual question. For this very reason he had to distance himself as a prodigal son from liberalism as from all other groups and political orientations. Weigel calls Kraus's last political turn, his espousal of Dollfuß, "seemingly enigmatic, and yet only consistent" (305). "Karl Kraus leaves his desk and enters the political arena, having opted for Austria. This alienates his Socialist friends and does not win over his Christian-Social adversaries. The arena is empty" (321). When the October 1933 issue of *Die Fackel* appeared after a long hiatus, Kraus had several options: "To continue to be silent; to explain his silence; to collect himself and take a stand on what has happened; to keep issuing the *Fackel* with comments and polemics about seemingly 'small subjects' that continue to be topical, to retreat into language and Shakespeare and to serve his art; to write his often-announced memoirs" (323). Weigel believes that Kraus chose all of these and that this is what makes his last years so difficult to understand:

> The events of 1933 and 1934 in Germany and Austria proved Kraus wrong, rendering fanatical absolutism ineffective and calling for relativism. They immobilized the genre of satire and led him from a negation of politics to the heart of politics, making a patriot of the man . . . who had repeatedly regarded patriotism as suspect. . . . He had attributed all the evils of his age to the press, but surely this greatest of all evils had not come from the press . . . He had rejected all forms of war and militarism, but now he knew that the world could be saved only by a war. Above all — and this, I believe, was the cause of his death — all his life he had attacked "Jewishness" and occasionally used the term "Aryan" in all seriousness, and now he had to look on as an anti-Semitism of a very different kind was doing its bloody work. (328)

Now a Nazi commentator named Kraus among Hitler's spiritual ancestors, for had Hitler not fulfilled the satirist's boldest dreams by eliminating the Jewish press? "He seemed to achieve nothing," Weigel concludes, "and yet he achieved everything. Because God is *deus caritatis*, he has given the greatest power to powerlessness. Karl Kraus's failure was an achievement, and in his great negation we now discern only his greatness, for he hated out of love" (342).

In a review of Weigel's book (1968), Edwin Hartl disagrees with Weigel's thesis that in trying to shed or combat his Jewishness, Kraus hurtfully warred against himself. In Hartl's view, Kraus fought against corruption and nationalism no matter who represented it. In his great attempt to unmask his contemporaries, the mask must be regarded as a theatrical symbol. The paradoxical and contradictory elements in Kraus's life and work were provided by the satirist and his environment; he simply discerned and presented them. Hartl also tells this revealing anecdote: Karl Jaray spent years on the compilation of a complete register or index of the *Fackel*. When he proposed publication to Kraus, the satirist laughingly demurred, pointing out that this would only make it easier for readers to locate his contradictions!

Caroline Kohn's comprehensive 1966 study of Kraus is the revised German version, made by the Austrian-born French scholar, of her dissertation published as *Karl Kraus, le polemiste et l'écrivain, defenseur des droits de l'individu* (1962). Kohn, who has also written widely on Kraus under the name Lotte Sternbach-Gärtner, has produced a loosely organized, free-wheeling, uncritical life and works that is in a sense a continuation of Leopold Liegler's book. Kohn gives pride of place to Kraus's literary and political polemics (with Werfel, Ehrenstein, Kerr, Békessy, Schober, and the Social Democrats) and also attempts to integrate the satirist into the continuum of German literature. However, even if one makes allowance for the fact that a dissertation tends to overstate its case, and applauds the author for the zeal with which she handles a mass of material, including an extensive bibliography, her rhapsodic, cliché-ridden style and numerous factual errors have elicited negative appraisals from such critics as Christian Wagenknecht. One of the few positive assessments may be found in Wilma Iggers's article "Karl Kraus and His Critics" (1975), in which Kohn's book is described as "extremely well informed, broad in scope, aware of cultural currents going far back in time and far afield geographically . . . the only one containing an extensive chapter analyzing Kraus's character" (37). Caroline Kohn is also the author of *Karl Kraus als Lyriker* (1968), a book in which Kraus's poems are discussed as the positive side of the satirist's art. Kohn provides this useful classification of Kraus's poetic output: Women, Desire, Love; Nature; Personal, Philosophical; Artist, Language; Dream; Society; Justice; Clichés, Ink, Press; Technology, War; Vienna, Austria; Berlin, Germany.

14: At the Centennial and Beyond

Published on the eve of the Kraus centennial, *Wittgenstein's Vienna* (1973) by the philosophers Allan Janik and Stephen Toulmin attracted a large international readership. In this wide-ranging and stimulating cultural history of Habsburg Vienna many readers probably encountered the name of Karl Kraus for the first time. Chapter 3 is entitled "Language and Society: Karl Kraus and the Last Days of Vienna," but the spirit of the satirist hovers over virtually every page, for the authors assign to Kraus, whom they characterize as unclassifiable, a central place as a "representative ethical spokesman for his milieu" (10). This study attempts to place him in the context of fin-de-siècle Vienna, reveal the philosophical underpinnings of his life and work, and offer a new philosophical and ethical interpretation of his writings. Pointing out that Kraus was not a philosopher (and still less a scientist), the authors write, "If Kraus's views have a philosophical ancestry, this comes most assuredly from Schopenhauer . . . a kindred spirit . . . with a strong talent for polemic and aphorism" (74).

Janik and Toulmin make an occasional apodictic statement such as "Kraus was an implacable enemy of women's rights" (75) that will raise some eyebrows. They also offer an original interpretation of a central Krausian notion, the *Ursprung.* "For Kraus, the encounter between man and woman was the 'origin' by which reason was fecundated from the wellspring of fantasy. The product of this encounter was an artistic creativity and a moral integrity" (75). Another (and possibly related) "central notion that unifies the life and work of Karl Kraus is the 'creative separation' of the two spheres of factual discourse and literary activities" (57–58). This explains Kraus's opposition to the form of the feuilleton. Commenting on Kraus's attitude toward psychoanalysis, the authors write that "for Kraus, Freud and his circle were simply replacing the traditional Judaeo-Christian bourgeois myths about sexuality with another in the form of psychoanalysis" (75). In their discussion of "Krausians," Janik and Toulmin argue that "a whole range of intellectual and artistic creations, ranging from the music of Arnold Schönberg to the architecture of Adolf Loos — and including even, in its own way, Ludwig Wittgenstein's *Tractatus Logico-Philosophicus* — were intimately and consciously related to, and even extensions of, the critique of language and society conducted by Karl Kraus" (93). In fact, the authors regard the *Tractatus* as basically reflecting Kraus's worldview. "Wittgenstein's conception of philosophy is also Krausian" (199), and the philosopher's aphoristic propositions are a "Krausian medium for a Krausian message" (200).

The title of Helmut Arntzen's *Karl Kraus und die Presse* (1975), a little book written with Krausian verve and *saeva indignatio*, has a dual sense: the satirist's attitude toward the press and today's journalism in relation to Kraus. This polemical book by a German scholar noted for his writings on satire is based on his lecture "Karl Kraus Today" at the Vienna centennial "Krausfest" of 1974 and appeared as the first volume in a projected series of Kraus studies entitled Literatur und Presse.

In the first part, Arntzen gives a useful overview of Kraus's criticism of the press of his time and shows that this criticism is still relevant and, indeed, necessary. He points out that the self-serving censorship of the press and the radio, the *Totschweigetaktik* (silent treatment) that bedeviled the satirist in his lifetime and has persisted long after his death, is itself a source of information about the press. Through the press, he writes, "Kraus learned to understand the significance of language by viewing the reasons for and effects of its destruction as a destruction of thought and imagination by the discourse of the press" (39), a discourse that was perverted by clichés. Kraus always regarded the editorial part of a newspaper as an appendix to its advertising section, with clichés abounding in both. "Nothing has kept its identity to the same extent as the cliché . . . It is contagious and epidemic; it has made advertising possible and has reached the revolution" (56). After giving examples of such clichés and other horrors of journalism, the author points out that "all this was invented by Karl Kraus, and yet it was written in 1973" (53).

Arntzen devotes the second part of his book to his observations in Vienna, the symposium itself and its "fallout," the way it was covered by the press, and he polemicizes against some of its participants and critics a well as their antecedents. He finds such prominent commentators on Kraus as Hilde Spiel, Hans Heinz Hahnl, Marcel Reich-Ranicki, Margarete Mitscherlich-Nielsen, and Hermann Kesten, who described Kraus as a "forerunner of American gossip columnists" (71), seriously wanting in their knowledge of Kraus and their judgment. In general he believes that such people feel attacked by Kraus in their social role as critics and journalists and therefore attempt to destroy such a dangerous adversary without really bothering to get to know him. "Without any self-control," he writes, "today's intellectual mediocrities repeat the slanderous twaddle of their predecessors" (98). For example, Fritz Raddatz, the editor of the Berlin satirist Kurt Tucholsky and author of the anti-Kraus essay "Der blinde Seher," is described as a shallow, uninformed charlatan who works with distortions and "a few years ago knew nothing about Kraus except what was written in a *Fackel* about Tucholsky and about Kraus in a Tucholsky letter" (79).

Arntzen regards Mechthild Borries's defense of Heinrich Heine (1971) as methodologically dubious and journalistic rather than scholarly.

Another publication prompted by the Kraus centennial is Volker Bohn's collection of three essays entitled *Satire und Kritik: Über Karl Kraus* (1974). "The Strange Interplay: The Connection Between Kraus's Critique of the Press, Language and Literature" concerns itself mostly with Walter Benjamin's essay on Kraus of March 1931, Fritz J. Raddatz's anti-Kraus essays of 1966 and 1968, and Friedrich Jenaczek's refutations of them as well as Mechthild Borries's defense of Heine. In the second essay, "The Blind Mirror of the Age: Karl Kraus and the Theater," the author expresses surprise at the fact that Kraus venerated the old Burgtheater and yet championed Bert Brecht in the 1920s and 1930s. He follows Hans Mayer in identifying the two theatrical poles of Kraus's childhood and youth: the operettas he enjoyed in summer resorts and the old Burgtheater. His experiences of Nestroy, Offenbach, Shakespeare, Schiller, and Goethe represented *Ursprung* to him and became standards by which he measured his contemporaries. According to Bohn, Kraus's "*gesprochene Schauspielkunst*" (spoken acting) was similar to Brecht's epic theater; what attracted Kraus to Brecht was not the German playwright's theory but his poetic and dramatic practice, which to him seemed close to *Ursprung*. Bohn's third essay, "In the Legal Sphere: Juridic Practice, Satiric Process," makes the point that in his polemics of the 1920s (on Békessy, Schober, and Alfred Kerr) Kraus appeared in the role of a judge, possibly even a grand inquisitor. The author believes that Kraus's experiences with legal controversy permit certain conclusions about the theory of modern satire, and he identifies a basic motive of the satirist: to produce a generation that will not destroy culture.

The literary and linguistic elements in Kraus are cogently analyzed by J. P. Stern in his article "Karl Kraus and the Idea of Literature" (1975). In a daydream the author envisages readers of modern German literature divided into two groups. One of these believes that Kraus was "one of those typical querulous coffeehouse literati," a man who was said to have "waged a peculiarly quixotic linguistic campaign lasting more than 40 years against his fellow journalists" (37). The other group consists of "purblind enthusiasts" who read Kraus almost exclusively and venerate him as their supreme authority. To Kraus, literature was language at a high level of intensity and concentration, and intensity may be defined as "a density of internal and external references which inheres in a given text" (40) and also includes a concern for moral values. However, being anything but a systematic thinker, Kraus never fashioned a consistent theory embodying this view. Even though he "abhorred all systems, in politics as well as in ethics and aesthetics, and in his reflections on the grammar and prosody of German" (40), he consistently adhered to the idea of literature as heightened language. Stern compares Kraus to Henry James. "Though their reasons are very different, each develops a style which offers an ever more radical challenge to our habitual linguistic expectations" (40). Kraus spurned novels and other "entertainment literature," even on the high level of a Thomas Mann, ostensibly because they derive their inspiration from the *Stoff,* their material or subject matter, rather than the *Satz,* the sentence, the key unit of Kraus's *Sprachlehre,* or language study. Stern discerns in Kraus the use of ever briefer literary genres, essays, glosses, reflections, aphorisms, lyrical rather than narrative poems. Language-consciousness is what governed Kraus's decisions as to whom, or what, to admit to, or bar from, his literary pantheon. Those admitted include Goethe (with his poetry and *Faust,* part two), Jean Paul, Lichtenberg, Schopenhauer, Nietzsche, Matthias Claudius, and Peter Altenberg — none of whom subordinated the sentence to the subject matter. Not pretending to separate the historical situation from personal considerations, Kraus took an existential view of literature for his time, which he viewed as an age of decline whose language was the language of the press. As a counterpoise Kraus created his *Theater der Dichtung,* which the author views as "a sustained attack on the whole business of modern stage productions dominated by technological gimmicks, star actors, and overproducing producers" (4). Commenting on *Die Dritte Walpurgisnacht,* a typology of cacophonous voices born of a defective imagination, Stern writes, "Here politics is defined as the defeat of the imagination by its own self-generated lies." In a "complex interplay of allusions, puns, quotations" (47) figurative phrases and metaphors have become reality. The perpetrators of the horrors of the Third Reich must be viewed as the "heirs of those journalists and intellectuals (by no means always Gentile) who had made clichés out of reality and whose impoverished imagination Kraus had attacked and shown up 50 years before" (47). Kraus was among the first to recognize the perverted literary aspect of Nazism, which captured certain intellectuals with a heady brew of ethnic history, literary symbols, and stereotypes.

In his 1956 book on Kraus, Werner Kraft concluded that while the Austrian's satire is not *"tradierbar"* — that is, cannot be duplicated or continued — the intellect or spirit that produced it can be passed on. In an effort to help our age produce such a spirit, Kraft traces Kraus's intellectual tradition and the background that produced him in his book *Das Ja des Neinsagers: Karl Kraus und seine geistige Welt* (The Yea of the Naysayer: Karl Kraus and His Intellectual World, 1974). As he highlights Kraus's conservative thinking, Kraft points out that Kraus had a positive relationship to an important literary and cultural tradition, that "the satirist and polemicist was an admirer, the doubter a believer" (6). In five chapters that include copious quotations, he deals with "Precursors" (G. C. Lichtenberg, Henri Rochefort, Daniel Spitzer, Ludwig Speidel), "The Old Masters" (Shakespeare, Schiller, Goethe, Jean Paul, Hölderlin, Matthias Claudius), "The Heine Case," "The Later Ones" (Oscar Wilde, Ibsen, Strindberg, Detlev von Liliencron, Gerhart Hauptmann), and "Contemporaries" (Peter Altenberg, Adolf Loos ["Friends and diametrically opposed personalities," 166]), Frank Wedekind, Franz Werfel, Georg Trakl, Arthur Schnitzler, Else Lasker-Schüler, Sigismund von Radecki, Bertolt Brecht, and Walter Benjamin). To be sure, at least three of the last-named — Schnitzler, Werfel, and Brecht — are somewhat dubious entries in this context, for Schnitzler, whose attitude in World War I Kraus respected, never liked Kraus, and Werfel and Brecht must be regarded as erstwhile apostles who later became apostates. Kraft tries to show that Kraus's satiric style was indebted to the feuilletonists David Spitzer (of the *Neue Freie Presse*) and Ludwig Speidel, and he points to an interesting similarity between the first sentence of the first issue of Henri Rochefort's journal *La Lanterne*, which became a model for *Die Fackel*, and a later statement by Kraus. Rochefort: "*La France contient, dit l'Almanach Impérial, trente-six millions de sujets, sans compter les sujets de mécontement* (May 31, 1868: According to the imperial almanac, France has thirty-six million subjects — and this without counting the discontented subjects. Note the dual sense of "subjects.") Kraus wrote in the *Fackel* for January 1911, 315–316, p. 13: "Die Volkszählung hat ergeben, daß Wien 2,030,834 Einwohner hat. Nämlich 2,030,833 Seelen und mich" (According to the census, Vienna has 2,030,834 inhabitants — that is, 2,030,833 souls and me). The satiric scheme of the two statements is the same, but Rochefort deals with political man, whereas Kraus's is that of a man who does not wish to share his soul with all those other "souls."

In 1978 I made a survey, for presentation at a colloquium, of the attitudes of contemporary Austrian writers and critics toward Karl Kraus, basing myself on both published articles and replies to a brief questionnaire that I had devised. It was published in 1980 as "Karl Kraus im Bewußtsein österreichischer Schriftsteller der Gegenwart" (Karl Kraus in the Mind of Contemporary Austrian Writers).

Elias Canetti, a future winner of the Nobel Prize for literature, wrote an article entitled "Warum ich nicht wie Karl Kraus schreibe" (Why I Don't Write Like Karl Kraus, 1966), which was later widely reprinted under the title "Karl Kraus: Schule des Widerstands" (School of Resistance). Kraus was the young Canetti's idol in Vienna for five years and particularly excited him as a dynamic reciter. While he was under the satirist's spell, Canetti unquestioningly adopted his rejections and shared his feuds and enmities, but ultimately it became necessary for him to regain his own judgment and individuality, to break through the impregnable wall with which Kraus buttressed himself and his arguments. Kraus's permanent legacy to Canetti was, in addition to his pacifism, a sense that a man of mind must assume absolute responsibility for what goes on in the culture of his time. That Canetti continued to be influenced by the "school of hearing," the acoustically received word, which he owed to Kraus is indicated by the very title of the second volume of his autobiography, *Die Fackel im Ohr* (1980, *The Torch in My Ear*).

Considering that Hans Müller was a prime target of Kraus's satire in World War I, what the man later known, after his Swiss exile, as Hans Müller-Einigen has to say about Kraus in his autobiography *Jugend in Wien* (Youth in Vienna. Berne: Francke, 1945) is surprisingly conciliatory and magnanimous. "He bestowed upon me the distinction of his bitter enmity," he writes, speaks of Kraus's "pure, immaculate character," and calls him "an offended, disappointed, betrayed dreamer. . . . His oeuvre belongs among the few imperishable literary expressions of compassionate love" (167–68).

The critic Hans Heinz Hahnl, the author of a 1947 dissertation on Kraus and the theater, argues that "anyone who writes about Kraus today must know about which Kraus and for which public he is writing: about the historical Kraus, the social, moral, and cultural critic of a declining Austria and its bourgeois society . . . or about the great satirist and poet, the judge of language, the dramatist, and dramaturge" ("Der Satiriker zwischen Vision und Wirklichkeit," 1961, 6). Hahnl also makes the convincing argument that what is needed is a synthesis between the topical, time-bound Kraus and the eternal, timeless Kraus.

Negative notes are sounded by Paul Kruntorad and Erich Fitzbauer. Writing in *Die zeitgenössische Literatur Österreichs* (Contemporary Austrian Literature, 1976), Kruntorad rejects Kraus's "cannon fire on sparrows" and deplores the "Krausitis," the satirist's negative influence in contemporary cultural life. "It is as if Sherlock Holmes had left, as a golden rule for all detectives, an instruction to look for the missing comma to solve a murder" (147). Fitzbauer (in a letter to me dated January 27, 1978) is bothered by Kraus's almost psychopathically narrow threshold of linguistic tolerance, which tends to stifle creativity — but even this critic wishes there were a Karl Kraus to combat today's cultural and political outrages. In a letter dated February 17, 1978, György Sebestyén writes that while he admires Kraus as a great fighter and linguistic giant, he feels that one must have experienced him in person to be enchanted by him. Sebestyén regards *The Last Days of Mankind* as a gigantic work but an enormous oversimplification. Christian Wallner (in a letter of February 10, 1978) points out that "*Der Herr Karl*," a figure typifying the banality of evil that was created for the cabaret stage in 1962 by Carl Merz and Helmut Qualtinger, is a readily discernible descendant of Vincenz Chramosta, the demonically cruel grocer in Kraus's wartime play.

Wolfgang Kudrnofsky (letter of January 23, 1978) notes that Kraus is less quoted by literati and journalists than he was ten years previously because, "following a German trend, all criticism is immediately absorbed by the giant sponge of the firm Marx & Sons and then poured on the heads of the public as a gray, insipid Polit-sauce." Along with a letter dated February 23, 1978, Herbert Eisenreich sent me a rather harsh article about Kraus that he had intended for — of all places! — Friedrich Torberg's journal *Forum* but that had been published neither there nor anywhere else. Eisenreich changed his mind, however: "When one looks at today's journalists and writers, including Nobelists, one cannot have the slightest objection to Kraus." Writing in *Forum* (1961) Manès Sperber, who does not describe himself as a "Krausian," registers his reservations about polemics and satire that reduce persons to their errors, misjudgments, and weaknesses. Sperber, a novelist as well as a critic, also critiques Kraus's willful disregard of fiction. However, he appreciates the prophetic fighter and moralist with an attractive pathos and an intellectual and spiritual courage that has become rare today. "Sometimes I try to imagine," he writes, "what it means to be young in present-day Vienna, and then I am impelled to exclaim: Oh you poor kids, you have no Karl Kraus!" (230).

Reflexionen der Fackel, subtitled "New Studies About Karl Kraus" (1994), is a collection of a dozen essays by the Prague Germanist Kurt Krolop, most of which originated as previously published lectures. The word "Reflections" is deliberately ambiguous, and the author also intends to correct and modify the notion of a "Prague Circle" as enunciated by Max Brod, a harsh critic of Kraus.

"At the end of this century," writes Krolop in "Karl Kraus Today," "which witnessed in its first half two world wars with masses of victims, there is reason to recall to mind with undiminished urgency the warning message contained in *The Last Days of Mankind*" (18). Krolop reminds us of Elias Canetti's characterization of Kraus as a master of horror and says that in those poems that do not expressly reflect the *saeva indignatio* of the satirist, namely the nature poems, the foil of horror and thus the protest against the horrendous is always implicitly present. "La Trahison des Clercs" (The Treason of the Intellectuals) relates Kraus to the meaning of the phrase coined in the 1920s by the French thinker Julien Benda: the use of words to justify often anti-intellectual violence. *Clercs* is also related to clerics — thus encompassing *geistig* (intellectual) as well as *geistlich* (spiritual or clerical). Krolop notes that Kraus extended Benda's idea to include treason against nature. In another essay Krolop deals with foreign words habitually used in *Die Fackel*, and in connection with one of them, *Troglo-*

dyt (cave-dweller, Neanderthal), he points out that in the face of troglodytism, language to Kraus was no longer a bulwark but merely a refuge or asylum. "Prague Authors in the Light of the *Fackel*" contains an authentic list ranging from Bruno Adler to Paul Zifferer. In 1910 Kraus gave the first of his fifty-seven readings in Prague. "From the Prague German Theater," writes Krolop, "with its director Angelo Neumann and the liberal newspapers *Bohemia* and *Prager Tagblatt* to the German-language University of Prague . . . there was hardly a liberal institution in Prague that did not soon become an object of the *Fackel*'s satire" (125). Yet every German-speaking, literate inhabitant of Prague was bound to take cognizance of Kraus's journal. Franz Kafka was probably familiar with "Heine and the Consequences" before he heard Kraus read it in March 1911, and he remained an interested reader of the *Fackel*. Foremost among the Prague readers who collaborated with Kraus was the young philosopher Max Steiner, to whom Krolop devotes a separate essay. Steiner, characterized as "the first Prague author who unreservedly identified with the outlook and contents of *Die Fackel*" (128), converted to Catholicism and committed suicide in 1910 at the age of twenty-six.

Two of Krolop's essays deal with Kraus's relationship with Franz Werfel and his publisher Kurt Wolff. The author adduces evidence that despite a controversy, estrangement, and polemic extending over two decades, the fundamental sympathy between Kraus and Werfel remained. What they shared was an intellectual and moral quest for a practical, effective humanitarianism or panhumanism — not just a nostalgic vision of a lost paradise but something to be practiced by a socially conscious and ethically motivated intellectual. Other essays deal with Jaroslav Hašek, a fellow satirist of World War I, and Karel Čapek, who regarded Kraus as his teacher.

An "Eastern" view of Kraus more in keeping with the "party line" is contained in Franz Leschnitzer's article "Der Fall Karl Kraus" (The Karl Kraus Case) in the East Berlin journal *NDL* (1956). One gains the impression that the author really admires Kraus but wishes he had been a communist. After describing what he terms the "*Fackel* fever" and the unique atmosphere of Kraus's readings, he echoes what Kraus said about Heinrich Heine: The "love of our youth" is in need of revision (62). Leschnitzer believes that as yet no one has looked at Kraus from a Marxist-Leninist point of view. He has, to be sure, been written about by Austromarxists like Friedrich Austerlitz, bourgeois feuilletonists like Robert Scheu, aestheticists like Leopold Liegler, mysticists like Theodor Haecker, and irrationalists like Heinrich Fischer, Max Rychner, and Walter Benjamin — but surely all of these were idealists! Among the thirty people who participated in the Brenner *Rundfrage* there was not one Marxist. Even after World War I Marxist critics like Georg Lukács commented only on individual works, such as *The Last Days of Mankind*. For non-Marxists or "mechanistic materialists" the phenomenon Karl Kraus can only be "an object of hysterical love (*Liebe*), hysterical hatred (*Haß*), or superhysterical *Haßliebe*" (63). Leschnitzer discerns many contradictions in Kraus's partly pseudorevolutionary, partly conservative or reactionary, partly rationalistic or metaphysical-mystical, partly realistic, partly unworldly thinking and writing. The early *Fackel* coincided with the beginning of the monopolistic and imperialistic phase of capitalism. Kraus's fetishistic belief in the independence of linguistic form (*Sprachgestalt*) is linguistic fetishism and the ideological counterpart of the fetishism connected with the production of merchandise. As a thinker Kraus remained under the spell of metaphysics, antirationalism, and irrationalism. As an "espouser of ancient Christian doctrines" (65) Kraus critiqued not the structure of bourgeois society as such but its culture. A bourgeois was to him not so much a member of a propertied class as an exemplar of an intellectually reprehensible type. Kraus's rebellion against the bourgeois world was not based on any insight into the anarchic nature of capitalism but constituted a purely emotional, albeit idealistic and ethical, opposition to certain symptoms of its superstructure (*Überbau*), such as self-satisfaction, self-righteousness, and spiritual emptiness. Leschnitzer goes on to say that Kraus failed to see larger connections, which led him to attack press czars rather than tycoons, bankers, or stock-exchange magnates and to rail against the intellectual terror of the print media rather than against physical and social outrages. Commenting on Kraus's poem "Mein Widerspruch" (My Contradiction), Leschnitzer says that Kraus could imagine progress only in terms of capitalistic technology. The author believes that to Kraus *Ursprung* signified an ideal, primitive community with a simplistic culture. Moreover, Kraus's satiric critique of bourgeois culture may be regarded as a kind of self-critical stance. The very titles of his major works (*The Last Days of Mankind, Destruction of the World by Black Magic, Last Judgment*) are indicative of the wrong track taken by the satirist, who equated the downfall of the bourgeoisie with the downfall of mankind. Leschnitzer does praise *The Last Days of Mankind* as a magnificent, courageous documentary drama, and yet it is not realistic — because the catastrophic development of bourgeois class society is identified with the development of mankind as a whole and also because there are many pacifist, utopian, nihilistic, apocalyptic, and phantasmagoric touches. The play's main insight, the imperialistic nature of the war, is not sufficiently emphasized. What is unduly stressed, however, is the role of the press — and Leschnitzer regards this as but another instance or variant of Kraus's language fetishism. Both culturally and politically, then, Kraus was deeply rooted in the weltanschauung of the 1880s. He did condemn monopolistic capitalism and champion free competition. But when he later became acquainted with Austro-Marxism, chiefly through his reading of the *Arbeiter-Zeitung* and primarily in the form of "Max Adler's grotesque synthesis of Marxism and Kantianism" (71), he satirized this as well. Living in self-styled insularity, Kraus had little knowledge of, or interest in, the Soviet world. While he never betrayed the revolutionary movement, he was at no time a true revolutionary. Leschnitzer lashes out at Heinrich Fischer, who in turn polemicized against those who want to force Kraus onto a Procrustean bed of political doctrines. With his espousal of Dollfußian Austro-Fascism and his opposition to the revolutionary press of the antifascist emigrants, Kraus, hitherto an occasional "enemy of our enemies," became "our enemy" (71).

The foregoing remarks by Leschnitzer were culled from a section entitled "The Cultural Critic." Leschnitzer has less to say about Kraus as a poet, but he does make the point that Kraus's lyric poetry has been appreciated by relatively few and gives two reasons for it. For one thing, Kraus always described his prose as artistry and equated it with his poetry. His linguistic metaphysics led him to do so, but journalism is not art and not a substitute for it. For another, his poems are versified polemics; most of his poetic subjects are already known from his prose writings and only have a different rhythm. However, Kraus is a master in his *Gedankenlyrik* or *Reflexionslyrik* (lyric poetry carrying a cargo of cogitation in the tradition of Friedrich Schiller) and at times also in his recitals. In "Fazit," a section in which Leschnitzer sums up his insights, he states that Kraus concerned himself with symptoms, with excrescences rather than roots. He was aware of the contradictions and conflicts in capitalism, but he was unable to lay these bare. Language became his fetish and gave rise to verbal play, jokes, rhymes, and rhythms. Words were and remained his weapons — but against what? Basically only against the press. He did attack other manifestations of imperialistic decadence — literary decline, hypocrisy, charlatanry, a narrow clerical mindset, psychoanalytic quackery — but it was a fight limited to language, metaphysics, and linguistic fetishism. He went downhill in the postwar period, tending toward clerical conservatism, equating the temporary paralysis of the working class with the bankruptcy of all political activity, and maligning communism. Leschnitzer compares Kraus's fate to that of Henry Louis Mencken, his "American intellectual/spiritual brother" (82), whose personal tragedy was his inability to comprehend the mission of the working class.

Edwin Timms's wide-ranging, magisterial, and provocative study *Karl Kraus, Apocalyptic Satirist* (1986), deserves consideration as a book that has attracted wide attention and favorable criticism as a great panorama of Austrian culture over a period of a half-century and an exhaustive treatment of Kraus's cultural milieu that is enhanced by numerous well-chosen and properly placed illustrations.

Taking issue with those who regard the satirist's life and work as all of a piece, but without wishing to debunk or deconstruct, Timms sets out to show a duality rather than a unity, to demonstrate that the man who did so much unmasking wore many masks himself and engaged in role-playing and a histrionic heightening of his own existence as he kept silent about such things as his affluence, his baptism, and his loves. The author is aware that critics generally have attributed the power of Kraus's satire to his exceptional moral qualities, but he feels impelled to provide an alternative reading. Concentrating on the rift between the facade of Austrian life (and that of its greatest satirist) and its inner reality as well as trying to provide a much-needed corrective to the overly aestheticized picture of fin-de-siècle Vienna that is so frequently encountered in the literature, Timms is primarily concerned with the parameters, paradigms, paradoxes, and parallels of Krausian satire, his imaginative and archetypal transformations of actual persons, places, and conditions, and the relationship between the satirist's public and private worlds. With reference to Count Buffon's celebrated dictum, in this instance the style was *not* the man. "The relationship between Kraus's authorial position and his narrative voice is far more oblique than is generally supposed" (170). Timms has many cogent things to say about the nature of satire, the psychological and artistic impulses that form the satirist's persona and underlie the writing of satire. For example, he discusses the role of Nietzsche and Oscar Wilde in shaping Kraus's self-image as an embittered, embattled, and misunderstood heroic artist — and yet those who knew him personally describe him as warm-hearted, kindly, life-affirming, sensitive, and sociable rather than crabbed, aloof, and misanthropic. Commenting on Kraus's efforts to construct an authentic identity for himself, Timms writes: "He was a Jew by birth, an Austrian by nationality, a Viennese by residence, a German by language, a journalist by profession, bourgeois by social status, and a *rentier* by economic position. Amid the ideological turmoil of Austro-Hungary, all of these ascribed identities seemed like falsifications" (182–83).

In a chapter entitled "Between Jerusalem and Rome: The Dilemma of the Baptized Jew," the author regards as "the most perplexing aspect of Kraus's career the dichotomy between satirical discourse and religious conviction" and states that "his conversion to Catholicism is perhaps the most surprising event of his whole career" (237, 240). Rather than using the by now standard designation "Jewish self-hatred," Timms speaks of a "desire to liberate the self from compromising affiliations" (237), though "like Otto Weininger, [Kraus] seems to have internalized the antisemitic tendencies of his age" (239). In an excursus on the symbolism of beards, the author concludes that "being clean-shaven was part of his attempt to divest himself of all traces of Jewish identity" (134). Commenting on Kraus's baptism, Timms believes that "the position of satirist and Christian are incompatible. One cannot simultaneously serve two masters — Jesus and Juvenal," for "satire is by definition uncharitable" (244). In this connection he compares Kraus with other Christians who adopted a satiric persona: Erasmus, Pope, Swift, and Kierkegaard. In a chapter on Kraus's relationship with Sidonie Nádherný, the author outlines Kraus's multifarious satiric and poetic strategies of concealment, sublimation, and elegiac affirmation, and in dealing with Kraus's attitude toward Freud and his followers, Timms concludes that the satirist never attacked the "sorcerer" but only his "apprentices." He points out that Freud and Kraus were "the two greatest critics of the discontents of civilization to emerge from Habsburg Vienna, and their diagnoses are essentially complementary" (94) and that Freud's *Jokes and Their Relation to the Unconscious* contains a wealth of observations relevant to the strategies of satire — for example, Freud's notions of "compression" (*Verdichtung*) and "conflation" (*Mischwortbildung*).

Timms's excellent study, which is based on his 1967 Cambridge dissertation, does not go beyond 1920, but a second (and concluding) volume is scheduled to appear shortly.

Last but definitely not least, cognizance must be taken of Burkhard Müller's magisterial and uncommonly stimulating study *Karl Kraus: Mimesis und Kritik des Mediums* (1995). The author has succeeded in his endeavor to turn his Würzburg dissertation into a book that is as readable as it is innovative. In three major sections Müller deals with the literary and satirical uses of the photograph, acoustical aspects of Kraus's writings, and the impact of the cinema on Kraus's dramatic works. Paying tribute to Leo Lensing's pioneering studies in this field, the author identifies mimesis, critique, and hyperbole as primary methods of Krausian satire. Müller concentrates on the period between 1908 and 1919, a fertile decade that witnessed the advent of development of expressionism, cubism, futurism, the automobile, the telephone and telegraph, the airplane, illustrated journals and wartime techonology; and he begins with the minor earthquake of February 1908 that occasioned the quintessential *Grubenhund*.

Pointing out that the visual aspects of Kraus's work have been largely neglected, Müller discusses physiognomic aspects of the satirist's writings — acts of identification, uncoding, and unmasking — and demonstrates that the "clipping" of his time was increasingly added to Kraus's method of copious quotation, or putting the word between quotation marks. Among the photographs and caricatures that he presents (in necessarily poor reproductions) and discusses is Kraus's photomontage "Der Sieger" (The Victor), the first photo to appear in *Die Fackel* (July 1911).

Exemplifying both the mimetic and the hyperbolic aspects of Kraus's satire, it show Moriz Benedikt, the editor-proprietor of the *Neue Freie Presse*, standing in front of the Austrian parliament building and indicating the victory of liberalism in the election. This picture foreshadows Kraus's multifarious depictions of "das österreichische Antlitz," the face of Austria, in wartime, including the famous mordant depiction of the type of the jolly hangman.

To demonstrate the basic polarity of mimesis and hyperbole in Kraus's work, Müller includes a section about the physiognomy-based anti-Semitism of his satire, presenting the "Little Cohn" of song and caricature as well as the German cartoonist Wilhelm Busch's "Schmulchen Schievelbeiner."

Curiously enough, the erudite author has little to say about the radio, which became important to Kraus in his last years, but he does not neglect the linguistic aspects of Krausian satire, as witness his section on "The Birth of the Cliché from the Spirit of the Metaphor," in which he demonstrates that Kraus used wit and jokes as a weapon against clichés. The author argues that the wonderful lightness of Offenbach's operettas provided for Kraus a counterpoise to the gravity and drudgery of his satire. Müller believes that "Kraus recognizes music not as an independent art but as a potential inherent in sound [*Geräusch*] and a mystery inherent in language" (337). Like Friedrich Torberg, Müller believes that *The Last Days of Mankind* is unperformable, and on the basis of the ditties sung by Ganghofer, Roda Roda, Wahnschaffe, and Emperor Franz Joseph, he attempts to demonstrate that Kraus's play "tends toward the operetta whenever it abandons the naturalistic mimesis of newspaper parlance and changes to rhymed language. . . . Over all bloody horrors of *The Last Days* hovers the spirit of the operetta" (342, 368).

While the early Kraus had no use for the cinema, he took cognizance of battle films and other documentaries in the wartime *Fackel* and used film as a hyperbolic resource in his play. Pointing to cinematic techniques and phantasmagoric elements, including dreams and nightmares, in Kraus's play, the author identifies certain scenes that could be imagined in silent films.

Müller's study, in turn, may be imagined as a textbook in an advanced, though of necessity small and exclusive, interdisciplinary university seminar on Karl Kraus.

Conclusion

Adam Phillips concludes his review of Edward Timms's magnum opus with these words: "Timms's book will be indispensable when we have that most unlikely thing: an English Kraus" ("How to be Viennese," *London Review of Books*, May 3, 1987, 29). Does this mean that the book is doomed to be *dispensable* until a miracle of translation and publication happens, that it is fated to be a road map to an exotic or arcane territory that can only be glimpsed through a glass, darkly, an intriguing and stimulating entertainment for intellectual armchair travelers? But perhaps this is Timms's own fault, for his book marks a milestone in Kraus research precisely because he shows shades of gray, and of course other hues as well, in the spirit of the German poet Stefan George, who once described the dying decades of the Austro-Hungarian Empire and the Habsburg dynasty as "der farbenvolle Untergang" (a colorful sunset, or decline), whereas many other critics have contented themselves with viewing the life and work of Karl Kraus as a study in black and white. This variegated view is in the spirit of the satirist as well, for he once defined an artist as someone who can turn a solution into a riddle. But what Phillips may have meant is the fact that even though Timms quotes copiously from German sources and provides entirely serviceable English translations, his book lacks the backing of a major portion of Kraus's writings readily available in reliable English translations. As long as there is no such support system, too much of what critics have to say about Kraus will have to be conveyed to too many readers through a filter and taken on faith, as it were. Surely it is significant that no important selection from Kraus's writings has appeared in English translation during the last twenty years, nor has there been a comprehensive and authoritative critique of existing translations or a practical assessment of the satirist's translatability or untranslatability. Just what is it about Kraus's subject matter or style that impedes a proper translation and militates against an "English Kraus"? Is it easier to render him into French or other languages, and if so, for what reason? Perhaps it would be a good idea to convene an international conference of translators for that purpose. Such a conference might address, among other things, problems of rendering Kraus into the "world pidgin" of our time from a particular viewpoint. Should a writer like Karl Kraus be made to conform to a contemporary reader's sense of style, clarity, smoothness, and readability even if such qualities are achievable only at the expense of his stylistic uniqueness? In his book Timms briefly comments on the two existing abridged English translations of *Die letzten Tage der Menschheit*, pointing out that the Gode-Wright version (1974) "eliminates from the play antisemitic and anti-capitalistic utterances which might give offence to American readers" and that "a similar tendency to transpose the complex ruminations of the satirist into the idiom of democratic antimilitarism mars the translation of selected scenes by Max Knight and Joseph Fabry, included in *In These Great Times*" (429).

International conferences on Kraus have been convened in Vienna, London, Albany, Poznan, and other places, and the proceedings of some of these have been published in book form. The latest of a number of Kraus exhibits (with catalogues) was presented at the Literaturhaus in Vienna in the summer of 1996. Over a period of several decades dozens of dissertations have been written on Kraus in a number of countries; the satirist's biography appears in numerous reference works; and his aphorisms may be found in such compilations as *Bartlett's Familiar Quotations*, *The Viking (Faber) Book of Aphorisms*, *The Crown Treasury of Relevant Quotations*, *The New Penguin Dictionary of Quotations*, and, most recently, *The Columbia World of Quotations* on CD-ROM. However, those Anglo-American scholars who have written on satire and/or compiled anthologies of satirical writings for use in academic courses have, with virtually no exceptions, failed to take cognizance of Kraus. Yet there is much evidence that Kraus belongs in the pantheon of great satirists, and it would be desirable for scholars to investigate the special nature of his satire as compared to that of Swift, Pope, Heine, Mark Twain, Ambrose Bierce, H. L. Mencken, Kurt Tucholsky, and other important satirists of the past few centuries.

Perhaps this will come about through word of mouth, for it is apparent that Kraus, for whatever reason, has become fashionable in some circles and even entered the realm of popular culture. If a letter printed in the *Boston Globe* (April 24, 1994) quotes a Kraus aphorism ("There is no more unfortunate creature under the sun than a fetishist who yearns for a woman's shoe and has to settle for the whole woman") inaccurately as "Pity the poor shoe fetishist who, falling in love with a woman's foot, is compelled to marry the entire woman", this may be regarded as a positive development. The same can hardly be said of an excerpt from *Freud on Women: A Reader*, edited by Elizabeth Young-Bruehl (New York: W. W. Norton, 1990), which contains this excerpt from Freud's 1908 essay "Civilized Sexual Morality and Modern Nervous Illness": "In the phantasies that accompany satisfaction the sexual object is raised to a degree of excellence which is not easily found again in reality. A witty writer (Karl Kraus in the Vienna paper *Die Fackel*) once expressed this truth in reverse by cynically remarking: 'Copulation is no more than an unsatisfying substitute for masturbation'" (177–78). Here is a plain translation of what Kraus actually wrote: "A woman is, occasionally, quite a serviceable substitute for masturbation. It takes an abundance of imagination, to be sure." Such instances of misinformation or misinterpretation seem like illustrations of Rainer Maria Rilke's dictum that fame is the sum total of the misunderstandings that form around a big name. And what excuse was there for the late Ernst Pawel, a serious scholar, to "punish" Kraus for his early persiflage of political Zionism by writing that "he converted to Catholicism, turned Protestant, and eventually gave up on religion"? (*Theodor Herzl: The Labyrinth of Exile*. New York: Farrar, Straus & Giroux, 1989, 396).

In his book *Karl Kraus und die Presse* (1974) Helmut Arntzen gives a useful corrective "wish list" for future research on Kraus. For example, the factual and literary contents of Kraus's major polemics (against Harden, Kerr, Békessy, Schober, and others) need to be analyzed, and it should be shown how all of Kraus's writings aim at a satire in which even ephemeral material is presented artistically and thus rendered significant. Kraus's lyric poetry and his aphorisms need to be interpreted to a greater extent than they have been. The method of montage in Kraus's theater and the relationship of his plays to the documentary dramas of the 1920s and 1960s should be investigated. The *Fackel* needs to be read as "history" that dissolves obvious connections and illuminates hitherto unsuspected ones. (In this regard it might be added that individual issues of the journal need to be examined for form, symmetry, variety, and other aspects of composition. Also, what changes did Kraus make in the book editions of *Fackel* satires?) Arntzen goes on to say that the structure and intention of Kraus's public readings should be researched, and the satirist should be presented as a productive advocate of Liliencron, Wilde, Strindberg, Wedekind, Altenberg, Lasker-Schüler, Trakl, and others. According to Arntzen, Kraus is still insufficiently investigated and appreciated as an editor, translator, and resuscitator of Shakespeare, Nestroy, and Offenbach as well as a rediscoverer of German preclassical poetry (of the seventeenth and early eighteenth centuries). While a few of these topics have been addressed during the past two decades, Helmut Arntzen wrote me in a letter dated July 1, 1996 that he finds the situation virtually unchanged today and is bothered by the "Scheinrezeption" of Kraus today. Everyone talks and writes about him, but few really come to terms with his issues and points. Linguists do not concern themselves with his conception of language and journalists fail to deal with his view of the press in any meaningful way. Even though unprecedented attention is paid to the media today, once again the source of Kraus's critical reflections is ignored.

In her book *Paul Celan* (1991) Amy Colin mentions as one of the seminal factors in the poet's cultural background that remains unexplored "the impact of Karl Kraus on the development of twentieth-century Bu-kovinian literature with its strong emphasis on tradition" (5). The American scholar Jay F. Bodine, who has long been interested in investigating the parallels and divergences in approach between the satirist and such thinkers as Walter Benjamin, T. W. Adorno, and the Frankfurt School generally, wrote me on July 15, 1996: "It has until now simply not been recognized to what an extent Ludwig Wittgenstein justifies Karl Kraus's views on language and his '*sprachkritische Praxis*' — and to what extent the Krausian aspect in Ludwig Wittgenstein, i.e., the consideration and estimation by Wittgenstein of Kraus's praxis, enhance an understanding of Wittgenstein's language theories and philosophy." In a personal communication the versatile Bodine also came up with this interesting twenty-first century idea: "It would be an immensely important scholarly aid to have *Die Fackel* and Kraus's *Schriften* — those edited by Wagenknecht as well as, perhaps, those edited by Heinrich Fischer — scanned into an electronic format and made available to at least Kraus scholars on a CD-ROM. The text retrieval and analysis possibilities then made possible, even with only the software currently available, would be amazing." This may come about sooner than anyone could reasonably expect, for a committee of the Austrian Academy of Sciences under the direction of the Germanist Werner Welzig has been working, on the basis of a "digital *Fackel*," a scan of each of its 22,578 pages, on a *Wörterbuch der Fackel*, a three-volume dictionary of Kraus's journal, the first volume of which is scheduled to appear on the occasion of its hundredth anniversary in 1999. Scholars are already arguing about access to this databank.

Leo Lensing, another noted American Kraus scholar, has pointed out (in a letter to me dated September 3, 1996) that "there is nothing in print which even approaches a reliable chronicle of Kraus's literary life, much less a comprehensive critical biography." He takes issue with Timms for not dealing with Kraus's early anti-Zionist pamphlet *A Crown for Zion* and his quite complex relationship to Theodor Herzl, or, for that matter, with the pre-*Fackel* phase of the satirist's life and work. Lensing continues:

> Another serious lacuna in Timms's study is the intense interaction with Herwarth Walden and the *Sturm* circle of expressionist writers and artists, including Oskar Kokoschka. . . . A critical biography of Kraus will have to make many such corrections as well as fill in these gaps and others pertaining to Kraus's extensive network of aesthetic and intellectual contacts. A central issue of such a study will be the satirist's Jewish identity. This question should not be reduced, as it often has been in the past, to whether or not Kraus can be denounced and dismissed as an anti-Semite or a self-hating Jew, nor will it be sufficient to separate satirical achievement from the use of anti-Semitic motifs. It will be essential instead to fo-

cus on the complex, ambivalent ways in which Kraus expressed his own Jewish background and those of his fellow Jews, friend and foe alike, in the construction of a satirical discourse of great rhetorical power. . . . No one has yet brought the rich resources of the Karl Kraus Archive of the City Library of Vienna, with its vast store of personal and professional correspondence, especially letters to Kraus, to bear on this and other central biographical issues. *Die Fackel* itself, for all its attention to social, literary and political issues, has an important biographical dimension to which Kraus alluded frequently; in one memorable phrase he referred to the "novel of my literary life" (*Fackel* 484–88, 1918, 140). This formulation demands a critical narrative attuned to a much more complex interaction between the life and the work than the neat "duality" between private person and satirical persona which has hitherto served as the predominant paradigm of biographical interpretation.

Given the nature of satire in general and that of Krausian satire in particular, a truly dispassionate and comprehensive appraisal of Kraus may never be possible. However, the eventual publication of the critical commentary on Kraus's oeuvre that is being prepared at the University of Innsbruck under the direction of Sigurd Paul Scheichl, the author of a legendary 1500-page dissertation on Kraus (Innsbruck, 1971), will undoubtedly provide fresh scholarly impulses. Meanwhile, the international "Kraus and . . . " industry is likely to flourish and produce interesting and worthwhile results.

Works Consulted

The standard reference work is *Karl Kraus-Bibliographie* by Otto Kerry (Munich: Kösel, 1970). This 478-page compilation was preceded by a 12-page pamphlet issued in 1954 in Vienna under the imprint of Kerry, who was an actor and sometime book dealer. Kerry published supplements in *Die Pestsäule* 6 (April-May 1973, primary sources) and *Modern Austrian Literature* 8, 1–2 (special Kraus issue, edited by Donald G. Daviau, 1975, secondary sources). A *Kommentierte Auswahlbibliographie* by Sigurd Paul Scheichl is contained in the special Kraus issue of *text+kritik*, edited by Heinz Ludwig Arnold (Munich: edition text+kritik, 1975). Scheichl continued his critical bibliography in the *Kraus-Hefte*, 72 issues of which were published by edition text+kritik from 1977 to 1994 under the editorship of Scheichl and Christian Wagenknecht. In 1994 Wolfgang Hink published *Die Fackel: Bibliographie und Register 1899 bis 1936* (Munich: K. G. Saur, 2 vols.). A chronological checklist of Kraus's public readings by Christian Wagenknecht may be found in *Kraus-Hefte* 35–36, October 1985.

Writings of Karl Kraus

Die Fackel. (1968–76). Photomechanical reprint in 39 volumes (plus a supplementary volume containing *Die letzten Tage der Menschheit* as printed in special issues of the journal) by Kösel Verlag, Munich.

Die Fackel. 1977. Photomechanical reprint in 12 volumes by Zweitausendundeins, Frankfurt (with an index of persons by Franz Ögg). Contains the so-called Akt-Ausgabe of the above-mentioned play.

Books:

Die demolirte Literatur. 1897. Vienna: A. Bauer.

Eine Krone für Zion. 1898. Vienna: Moriz Frisch.

Sittlichkeit und Kriminalität. 1908. Vienna: Leopold Rosner.

Sprüche und Widersprüche. 1909. Munich: Albert Langen.

Die chinesische Mauer. 1910. Munich: Albert Langen.

Heine und die Folgen. 1910. Munich: Albert Langen.

Pro domo et mundo. 1912. Munich: Albert Langen.

Worte in Versen. (vol. 1, 1916; 2, 1917; 3, 1918; 4, 1919; 5, 1920). Leipzig: Verlag der Schriften von Karl Kraus.

Worte in Versen. (vol. 6, 1922; 7, 1923; 8, 1925; 9, 1930). Vienna and Leipzig: Verlag "Die Fackel."

Nachts. 1918. Leipzig: Verlag der Schriften von Karl Kraus.

Weltgericht. (vols. 1, 2, 1919). Leipzig: Verlag der Schriften von Karl Kraus.

Ausgewählte Gedichte. 1920. Leipzig: Verlag der Schriften von Karl Kraus.

Literatur oder Man wird doch da sehn. 1921. Vienna and Leipzig: Verlag "Die Fackel."

Die letzten Tage der Menschheit. 1922. Vienna and Leipzig: Verlag "Die Fackel."

Untergang der Welt durch schwarze Magie. 1922. Vienna and Leipzig: Verlag "Die Fackel."

Traumstück. 1923. Vienna and Leipzig: Verlag "Die Fackel."

Wolkenkuckucksheim. 1923. Vienna and Leipzig: Verlag "Die Fackel."

Traumtheater. 1924. Vienna and Leipzig: Verlag "Die Fackel."

Epigramme (compiled by Viktor Stadler). 1927. Vienna and Leipzig: Verlag "Die Fackel."

Die Unüberwindlichen. 1928. Vienna and Leipzig: Verlag "Die Fackel."

Literatur und Lüge. 1929. Vienna and Leipzig: Verlag "Die Fackel."

Zeitstrophen. 1931. Vienna and Leipzig: Verlag "Die Fackel."

Die Sprache (edited by Philipp Berger). 1937. Vienna and Leipzig: Verlag "Die Fackel."

Adaptations, editions and translations by Kraus:

Nestroy, Johann Nepomuk. *Das Notwendige und das Überflüssige,* adapted by Kraus (Vienna: Lányi, 1920).

Nestroy, Johann Nepomuk. *Der konfuse Zauberer oder Treue und Flatterhaftigkeit,* adapted by Kraus (Vienna: Lányi, 1927).

Offenbach, Jacques. *Madame L'Archiduc,* adapted by Kraus (Vienna: Lányi, 1927).

Shakespeares Sonette, translated by Kraus. (Vienna and Leipzig: Verlag "Die Fackel," 1930).

Shakespeare, William. *Timon von Athen,* adapted by Kraus (Vienna: Lányi, 1930).

Offenbach, Jacques. *Perichole,* translated and adapted by Kraus (Vienna: Universal-Edition, 1931).

Altenberg, Peter: Auswahl aus seinen Büchern, edited by Kraus (Vienna: Schroll, 1932).

Offenbach, Jacques. *Vert-Vert,* translated and adapted by Kraus (Vienna: Verlag "Die Fackel," 1932).

Shakespeares Dramen: Für Hörer und Leser bearbeitet, teilweise sprachlich erneuert, adapted by Kraus, 2 vols. (Vienna: Lányi, 1934, 1935).

Postwar Collections (edited by Heinrich Fischer):

(Volumes 1 to 10 were issued by the Kösel Verlag, Munich; volumes 11 to 14 bear the imprint of Albert Langen-Georg Müller, Munich)

1.   1952. *Die Dritte Walpurgisnacht.*
2.   1954. *Die Sprache.*
3.   1955. *Beim Wort genommen.*
4.   1956. *Widerschein der Fackel.*
5.   1957. *Die letzten Tage der Menschheit.*
6.   1958. *Literatur und Lüge.*
7.   1959. *Worte in Versen.*
8.   1960. *Untergang der Welt durch schwarze Magie.*
9.   1961. *Unsterblicher Witz.*
10. 1962. *Mit vorzüglicher Hochachtung.*
11. 1963. *Sittlichkeit und Kriminalität.*
12. 1964. *Die chinesische Mauer.*
13. 1965. *Weltgericht.*
14. 1967. *Dramen.*

Annotated and illustrated paperback edition by Christian Wagenknecht issued by Suhrkamp, Frankfurt.

First series:

1.   1987. *Sittlichkeit und Kriminalität.*
2.   1987. *Die chinesische Mauer.*
3.   1987. *Literatur und Lüge.*
4.   1989. *Untergang der Welt durch schwarze Magie.*
5.   1988. *Weltgericht I.*
6.   1988. *Weltgericht II.*
7.   1987. *Die Sprache.*
8.   1986. *Aphorismen.*
9.   1989. *Gedichte.*
10. 1986. *Die letzten Tage der Menschheit.*
11. 1989. *Dramen.*
12. 1989. *Dritte Walpurgisnacht.*

Second series:

13. 1994. *Jacques Offenbach.*
14. 1992. *Johann Nestroy. Zeitstrophen.*
15. 1994. *William Shakespeare.*
16. 1991. *Brot und Lüge.*
17. 1992. *Die Stunde des Gerichts.*
18. 1993. *Hüben und Drüben.*
19. 1994. *Die Katastrophe der Phrasen.*
20. 1994. *Kanonade auf Spatzen.*

Briefe an Sidonie Nádherný von Borutin, 1913–1936, 2 vols., edited by Heinrich Fischer and Friedrich Pfäfflin (Munich: Kösel, 1974)

Frühe Schriften 1892–1900, 2 vols., edited by Johannes J. Braakenburg (Munich: Kösel, 1979); vol. 3, Commentary (Frankfurt: Suhrkamp, 1985).

Karl Kraus contra . . . Die Prozeßakten der Kanzlei Oskar Samek, 2 vols., edited by Hermann Böhm. Vienna: Wiener Stadt- und Landesbibliothek, 1995.

Briefwechsel Karl Kraus — Otto Stoessl, edited by Gilbert J. Carr. Vienna: Deuticke, 1996.

Volumes in English translation:

Poems, edited and translated by Albert Bloch (Boston: Four Seas, 1930).

The Last Days of Mankind, abridged and edited by Frederick Ungar, translated by Alexander Gode and Sue Ellen Wright (New York: Ungar, 1974).

In These Great Times: A Karl Kraus Reader, edited by Harry Zohn, with translations by Joseph Fabry, Max Knight, Karl F. Ross and Harry Zohn (Montreal: Engendra, 1976; Manchester: Carcanet, 1984; Chicago: University of Chicago Press, 1990).

Half-Truths and One-and-a-Half Truths: Selected Aphorisms of Karl Kraus, edited and translated by Harry Zohn (Montreal: Engendra, 1976; Manchester; Carcanet, 1986; Chicago: University of Chicago Press, 1990).

No Compromise: Selected Writings of Karl Kraus, edited by Frederick Ungar, with translations by Albert Bloch, Sheema Z. Buehne, Marcus Bullock, Michael Bullock, Edward Mornin, Helene Scher, Frederick Ungar, and D. G. Wright (New York: Ungar, 1977). Includes several scenes from the Ungar edition of *The Last Days of Mankind.*

Secondary Sources

This bibliography is limited to works discussed in this book.

Eisenberg, Ludwig, ed. 1893. *Das geistige Wien.* Vienna: C. Daberkow.

Scheu, Robert. 1909. *Karl Kraus.* Vienna: Jahoda & Siegel.

Jelusich, Mirko. 1910. "Die Wiener Vorlesung Karl Kraus." *Der Sturm* (Berlin) May 19.

Albrecht, Adalbert. 1911. "Sittlichkeit und Kriminalität." *Journal of the American Institute of Criminal Law and Criminology* 1, 6.

Michaelis, Karin. 1911. "En Karl Kraus Aften." *København* 23, 315, November 14. German translation in *Die Fackel* 336–37.

Ende, Amalie von. 1913. "Karl Kraus." *Bookman,* October.

Studien über Karl Kraus. 1913. Innsbruck: Brenner.

Steed, Henry Wickham. 1914. *The Hapsburg Monarchy.* London: Constable.

Kocmata, Karl F. 1916. *Karl Kraus, der Krieg und die Helden der Feder.* Vienna: Neue Bahnen.

Ficker, Ludwig von, ed. 1917. *Rundfrage über Karl Kraus.* Innsbruck: Brenner.

Kreuzig, Fritz. 1919. *Ave Karl Kraus!* Vienna: F. Lang

Liegler, Leopold. 1920. *Karl Kraus und sein Werk.* Vienna: Richard Lányi.

Viertel, Berthold. 1921. *Karl Kraus: Ein Charakter und die Zeit.* Dresden. Kämmerer.

Rychner, Max. 1924. *Karl Kraus.* Vienna: Richard Lányi.

Kuh, Anton. 1925. *Der Affe Zarathustras.* Vienna: J. Deibler.

Benjamin, Walter. 1928. "Kriegerdenkmal." In *Einbahnstraße.* Berlin: Rowohlt.

Lessing, Theodor. 1930. *Der jüdische Selbsthaß.* Berlin: Jüdischer Verlag.

Benjamin, Walter. 1931. "Karl Kraus: Allmensch-Unmensch-Dämon." *Frankfurter Zeitung,* March 10. Reprinted in Benjamin, *Schriften* 2. Frankfurt: Suhrkamp, 1955. English translation in Benjamin, *Reflections.* New York: Harcourt Brace Jovanovich, 1978.

Schütz, Arthur. 1931. *Der Grubenhund: Eine Kultursatire.* Vienna: Jahoda & Siegel.

Bin Gorion, Emanuel. 1932. *Der Fackelreiter.* Berlin: Morgenland.

Flatter, Richard. 1934. *Karl Kraus als Nachdichter Shakespeares.* Vienna: Berger & Fischer.

Křenek, Ernst. 1934. "Karl Kraus und Arnold Schönberg." *23. Eine Wiener Musikzeitschrift,* October. (Also in Křenek, *Zur Sprache gebracht.* Munich: Langen Müller, 1958. English translation in Křenek, *Exploring Music.* London: Calder & Boyars, 1966).

Stimmen über Karl Kraus. Zum 60. Geburtstag von einem Kreis dankbarer Freunde. 1934. Vienna: Richard Lányi.

Bickel, Shlomo (Sloime). 1936. *Inzich un Arumzich.* Bucharest: Editura Salom-Aleichem.

Liegler, Leopold. 1936. *In Memoriam Karl Kraus.* Vienna: Richard Lánui.

Bloch, Albert. 1937. "Karl Kraus's Shakespeare." *Books Abroad* 11, 1.

Pollak, Oskar. 1946. "Die Kraus-Legende." *Arbeiter-Zeitung,* August 18.

Kraft, Werner, ed. 1952. *Karl Kraus.* Wiesbaden: Franz Steiner.

Jones, Ernest. 1955. *The Life and Work of Sigmund Freud,* vol. 2. New York: Basic Books.

Kraft, Werner. 1956. *Karl Kraus.* Salzburg: Otto Müller.

Leschnitzer, Franz. 1956. "Der Fall Karl Kraus." *NDL (Neue deutsche Literatur)* 4, 11, November.

Mittler, Franz. 1956. "Es war nicht leicht, aber schön." *Forum* 3, 30, June.

Heller, Erich. 1957. "Karl Kraus: The Last Days of Mankind." In Heller, *The Disinherited Mind.* New York, Farrar, Straus & Cudahy.

Mayer, Hans. 1957. "Karl Kraus und die Nachwelt." *Sinn und Form 9.*

Mautner, Franz H. 1958. "Kraus: Die letzten Tage der Menschheit." In *Das deutsche Drama,* vol. 2, edited by Benno von Wiese. Düsseldorf: Bagel.

Hahnl, Hans Heinz. 1961. "Der Satiriker zwischen Vision und Wirklichkeit." *Wort in der Zeit 7,* 6, June.

Sperber, Manès. 1961. "Nach Jahr und Tag." *Forum* 8, 90, June.

Kohn, Caroline. 1962. *Karl Kraus, le polemiste et l'écrivain, défenseur des droits de l'individu.* Paris: Didier.

Kohn, Hans. 1962. *Karl Kraus, Arthur Schnitzler, Otto Weininger. Aus dem jüdischen Wien der Jahrhundertwende.* Tübingen: J. C. B. Mohr.

Schlamm, William Siegmund. 1964. *Wer ist Jude? Ein Selbstgespräch.* Stuttgart: Seewald.

Torberg, Friedrich. 1964. "Das Wort gegen die Bühne." *Forum* 11, 128, August.

Adorno, Theodor W. 1965. "Sittlichkeit und Kriminalität." In *Noten zur Literatur* iii. Frankfurt: Suhrkamp.

Jenaczek, Friedrich. 1965. *Zeittafeln zur* Fackel. Gräfelfing: Edmund Gans.

Schick, Paul. 1965. *Karl Kraus in Selbstzeugnissen und Bilddokumenten.* Reinbek: Rowohlt.

Schönauer, Emil. 1965. "Über Karl Kraus: Eine Einführung." In Friedrich Jenaczek, *Zeittafeln zur* Fackel. Gräfelfing: Edmund Gans.

Wagenknecht, Christian Johannes. 1965. *Das Wortspiel bei Karl Kraus.* Göttingen: Vandenhoeck & Ruprecht.

Canetti, Elias, 1966. "Warum ich nicht wie Karl Kraus schreibe." *Wort in der Zeit.* 12, January.

Kohn, Caroline. 1966. *Karl Kraus.* Stuttgart: Metzler.

Stern, J. P. 1966. "Karl Kraus's Vision of Language." *Modern Language Review* 61, 1, January.

Alff, Wilhelm. 1967. "Karl Kraus und die Zeitgeschichte *1927–1934.*" In Kraus, *Die Dritte Walpurgisnacht.* Munich: Kösel.

Ficker, Ludwig von. 1967. *Denkzettel und Danksagungen.* Munich: Kösel.

Field, Frank. 1967. *The Last Days of Mankind: Karl Kraus and His Vienna.* New York: St. Martin's Press.

Hatvani, Paul. 1967. "Versuch über Karl Kraus." *Literatur und Kritik* 15, June.

Iggers, Wilma Abeles. 1967. *Karl Kraus: A Viennese Critic of the Twentieth Century,* The Hague: Martinus Nijhoff.

Spalter, Max. 1967. *Brecht's Tradition.* Baltimore: Johns Hopkins University Press.

Wittels, Fritz. 1967. "The Fackel Neurosis." In *Minutes of the Vienna Psychoanalytic Society 1908–1910,* edited by Hermann Nunberg and Paul Federn. New York: International Universities Press.

Hartl, Edwin. 1968. "Das Ja und Nein zu Karl Kraus." *Literatur und Kritik* 24, May.

Kohn, Caroline. 1968. *Karl Kraus als Lyriker.* Paris: Didier.

Raddatz, Fritz J. 1968. "Der blinde Seher. Überlegungen zu Karl Kraus." *Merkur* 22, June 6. Reprinted in Raddatz, *Verwerfungen.* Frankfurt: Suhrkamp, 1972.

Snell, Mary. 1968. "Karl Kraus's *The Last Days of Mankind.*" *Forum for Modern Language Studies* 4, July.

Weigel, Hans. 1968. *Karl Kraus oder Die Macht der Ohnmacht.* Vienna: Fritz Molden.

Naumann, Michael. 1969. *Der Abbau einer verkehrten Welt: Satire und politische Wirklichkeit im Werk von Karl Kraus.* Munich: Paul List.

Borries, Mechthild. 1971. *Ein Angriff auf Heinrich Heine: Kritische Betrachtungen zu Karl Kraus.* Stuttgart: W. Kohlhammer.

Frühwald, Wolfgang. 1971. "Kritik der Phraseologie. Sechs Thesen zu Karl Kraus's *Dritte Walpurgisnacht.*" In *Interpretationen zur österreichischen Literatur.* Vienna: Ferdinand Hirt.

Zohn, Harry. 1971. *Karl Kraus.* New York. Twayne. Reprint New York: Ungar, 1979. German edition Frankfurt: Anton Hain, 1990.

Kayser, W., and Gronemayer, H., eds. 1972. *Max Brod-Bibliographie.* Hamburg: Hans Christians.

Liptzin, Sol. 1972. "Christianized Jews." *Jewish Spectator* 37, 8, October.

Fischer, Jens Malte. 1973. *Karl Kraus: Studien zum "Theater der Dichtung" und Kulturkonservatismus.* Kronberg: Scriptor.

Heller, Erich. 1973. "Dark Laughter." *New York Review of Books* 20, May 3. Reprinted in Heller, *In the Age of Prose.* New York: Cambridge University Press, 1984.

Janik, Allan, and Toulmin, Stephen. 1973. *Wittgenstein's Vienna.* New York: Simon & Schuster.

Kaufmann, Walter. 1973. "On Karl Kraus." (Response to Heller's article). *New York Review of Books* 20, August 9.

Lilienfeld, Robert. 1973. "Reflections on Karl Kraus." *Nation* 296, 17, 18, April 23, 30.

Mautner, Franz H. 1973. "Karl Kraus's *The Last Days of Mankind.* In Kraus, *The Last Days of Mankind.* New York: Ungar.

Neumarkt, Paul. 1973. "Kraus, Tucholsky, F. Mendelssohn: A Trio of Apostates." *Jewish Currents* 27, 11, December.

Reich-Ranicki, Marcel. 1973. "Außenseiter und Provokateure." In *Über Ruhestörer.* Munich: R. Piper.

Bohn, Volker. 1974. *Satire und Kritik: Über Karl Kraus.* Frankfurt: Athenaion.

Fischer, Jens Malte. 1974. *Karl Kraus.* Stuttgart: Metzler.

Kraft, Werner. 1974. *Das Ja des Neinsagers: Karl Kraus und seine geistige Welt.* Munich: edition text+kritik.

Mitscherlich-Nielsen, Margarete. 1974. "Sittlichkeit und Kriminalität. Versuch einer Psychoanalyse." *Basler Nachrichten,* May 4, 11, 18. Reprinted in special Kraus issue of *text+kritik,* edited by H. L. Arnold. Munich 1975.

Arntzen, Helmut. 1975. *Karl Kraus und die Presse.* Munich: Wilhelm Fink.

Fischer, Jens Malte. 1975. "Affe oder Dalai Lama? Kraus-Gegner gestern und heute." In Kraus issue of *text+kritik,* edited by H. L. Arnold. Munich.

Hatvani, Paul. 1975. "Karl Kraus und die totale Satire." *Modern Austrian Literature* 8, 1–2.

Iggers, Wilma Abeles. 1975. "Karl Kraus and His Critics." *Modern Austrian Literature* 8, 1–2.

Kohn, Caroline. 1975. "Der Wiener jüdische Jargon im Werke von Karl Kraus." *Modern Austrian Literature* 8, 1–2.

Kohn, Caroline. 1975. "Lexique viennois dans l'oeuvre de Karl Kraus." In Kraus issue of *L'Herne*, edited by Eliane Kaufholz. Paris.

Stern, J. P. 1975. "Karl Kraus and the Idea of Literature." *Encounter* 45, 2, August.

Zohn, Harry, 1975. "Karl Kraus: 'Jüdischer Selbsthasser' oder 'Erzjude'?" *Modern Austrian Literature* 8, 1–2.

Kruntorad, Paul. 1976. "Karl Kraus." In *Die zeitgenössische Literatur Österreichs*, edited by Hilde Spiel. Munich: Kindler.

Pfabigan, Alfred. 1976. *Karl Kraus und der Sozialismus: Eine politische Biographie*. Vienna: Europaverlag.

Stieg, Gerald. 1976. *Der Brenner und die Fackel*. Salzburg. Otto Müller..

Szasz, Thomas S. 1976. *Karl Kraus and the Soul-Doctors: A Pioneer Critic and His Criticism of Psychiatry and Psychoanalysis*. Baton Rouge. Louisiana State University Press. Reissued as *Anti-Freud*. Syracuse University Press, 1990.

Hartl, Edwin. 1977. "Karl Kraus und die Psychoanalyse." *Merkur* 31, February 2.

Reich-Ranicki, Marcel. 1977. "Karl Kraus: Sein Haß, seine Liebe." In Reich-Ranicki, *Nachprüfungen: Aufsätze über deutsche Schriftsteller von gestern*. Munich: Piper.

Steiner, George. 1977. "Corruption at the Core." *London Times Literary Supplement*, May 27.

Zohn, Harry. 1977. "A Case of 'Translation Envy' or Shrinking a Shrink." *ATA Chronicle* 6, 1, January-February; 6, 3, April-May.

Zohn, Harry. 1980. "Karl Kraus im Bewußtsein österreichischer Schriftsteller der Gegenwart." In *Österreichische Gegenwart*, edited by Wolfgang Paulsen. Berne: Francke.

Bilke, Martina. 1981. *Zeitgenossen der Fackel*. Vienna: Löcker.

Goldschmidt, Hans E. 1981. *Von Grubenhunden und aufgebundenen Bären im Blätterwald*. Vienna: Jugend und Volk.

Grimstad, Kari. 1982. *Masks of the Prophet: The Theatrical World of Karl Kraus*. University of Toronto Press.

Lensing, Leo A. 1982. "'Kinodramatisch': Cinema in Karl Kraus's *Die Fackel* and *Die letzten Tage der Menschheit*." *German Quarterly* 55, 4, November.

Stremmel, Jochen. 1982. *Dritte Walpurgisnacht: Über einen Text von Karl Kraus*. Bonn: Bouvier.

Wagner, Nike. 1982. *Geist und Geschlecht: Karl Kraus und die Erotik der Wiener Moderne*. Frankfurt: Suhrkamp.

Carner, Mosco. 1983. *Alban Berg*. New York: Holmes & Meier.

Worbs, Michael. 1983. *Nervenkunst: Literatur und Psychoanalyse im Wien der Jahrhundertwende*. Frankfurt: Europäische Verlagsanstalt.

Bodine, Jay F. 1984. "Heinrich Heine, Karl Kraus and 'die Folgen': A Test Case of Literary Texts, Historical Reception and Receptive Aesthetics." *Colloquia Germanica* 18, 1–2.

Knepler, Georg. 1984. *Karl Kraus liest Offenbach: Erinnerungen, Kommentare, Dokumentation.* Berlin: Henschelverlag; Vienna: Löcker.

Steiner, George. 1984. "Karl Kraus's Fear and Loathing in Vienna." *London Sunday Times,* August 12.

Feingold, Michael. 1985. "A Kraus Divided. German Literature's Best-Kept Secret." *Village Voice Literary Supplement* 38, September.

Perle, George. 1985. *The Operas of Alban Berg.* Vol. 2: *Lulu.* Berkeley: University of California Press.

Horowitz, Michael, ed. 1986. *Karl Kraus und seine Nachwelt: Ein Buch des Gedenkens.* Vienna: Christian Brandstätter.

Scheichl, Sigurd Paul. 1986. "Der Stilbruch als Stilmittel bei Karl Kraus." In *Karl Kraus in neuer Sicht,* edited by Scheichl and E. Timms. Munich: edition text+kritik.

Schuh, Franz, and Vogel, Juliane, eds. 1986. *Die Belagerung der Urteilsmauer: Karl Kraus im Zerrspiegel seiner Feinde.* Vienna: Edition S.

Smith, Joan Allen. 1986. *Schönberg and His Circle.* New York: Schirmer.

Timms, Edward. 1986. *Karl Kraus, Apocalyptic Satirist: Culture and Catastrophe in Habsburg Vienna.* New Haven: Yale University Press.

Wimmer-Webhofer, Erika. 1986. "Zur Überlieferung der *Dritten Walpurgisnacht.*" *Kraus-Hefte* 39, July.

Scharang, Michael. 1987. "Zur Dritten Walpurgisnacht." *Literatur und Kritik* 213–14, April-May.

Wagner, Nike. 1987. "*Incognito ergo sum.* Zur jüdischen Frage bei Karl Kraus." *Literatur und Kritik* 219–20, November-December.

Gay, Peter. 1988. *Sigmund Freud: A Life for Our Time.* New York: W. W. Norton.

Rode, Susanne. 1988. *Alban Berg und Karl Kraus.* Frankfurt: Peter Lang.

Bodine, Jay F. 1989. "Karl Kraus, Ludwig Wittgenstein and Poststructural Paradigms of Textual Understanding." *Modern Austrian Literature* xxii, 3–4.

Colin, Amy. 1990. "Karl Kraus und die Bukowina: Ein unbekanntes Kapitel in der Kraus-Rezeption." In *Karl Kraus: Diener der Sprache, Meister des Ethos,* edited by Joseph P. Strelka. Tübingen: Francke.

Kully, Rolf Max. 1990. "Die erotische, die polemische und die poetische Verwendung der Eigennamen in den Werken von Karl Kraus." In *Karl Kraus,* edited by Joseph P. Strelka. Tübingen: Francke.

Le Rider, Jacques. 1990. *Modernité Viennoise et crises de l'identité*. Paris: Presses Universitaires de France. (German edition: *Das Ende der Illusion: Die Wiener Moderne und die Krisen der Identität*. Vienna: Österreichischer Bundesverlag, 1992. American edition: *Modernity and Crises of Identity: Culture and Society in Fin-de-Siècle Vienna*. Translated by Rosemary Morris. New York: Continuum, 1993).

Ribeiro, António. 1990. "Karl Kraus und Shakespeare: Die Macht des Epigonen." In *Karl Kraus*, edited by Joseph P. Strelka. Tübingen: Francke.

Colin, Amy. 1991. *Paul Celan: Holograms of Darkness*. Bloomington: Indiana University Press.

Glatzer, Nahum, and Mendes-Flohr, Paul, eds. 1991. *The Letters of Martin Buber*. New York: Schocken.

Kostelanetz, Richard. 1991. "Another Father for Us All." *New England Review* 14, 1. Fall.

Schroeder, David P. 1991. "Opera, Apocalypse and the Dance of Death: Berg's Indebtedness to Kraus." *Mosaic* 25, 1, Winter.

Timms, Edward. 1991. "Kraus's Shakespearean Politics." In *Austria in the Thirties: Culture and Politics*, edited by K. Segar and J. Warren. Riverside, Calif.: Ariadne.

Wolff, Kurt. "Karl Kraus." 1991. In *Kurt Wolff: A Portrait in Essays and Letters*, edited by Michael Ermarth. University of Chicago Press.

Dolmetsch, Carl. 1992. *"Our Famous Guest": Mark Twain in Vienna*. Athens: University of Georgia Press.

Lang, Ulrike. 1992. *Mordshetz und Pahöl: Austriazismen als Stilmittel bei Karl Kraus*. Innsbruck: Innsbrucker Beiträge zur Kulturwissenschaft.

Lensing, Leo A. 1992. "Heine's Body, Heine's Corpus: Sexuality and Jewish Identity in Karl Kraus's Literary Polemics Against Heinrich Heine." In *The Jewish Reception of Heinrich Heine*, edited by Mark H. Gelber. Tübingen: Max Niemeyer.

Mittler, Franz. 1993. "It Wasn't Easy, But It Was Nice." In Diana Mittler-Battipaglia, *Franz Mittler*. New York: Peter Lang.

Carr, Gilbert. 1994. "Karl Kraus und die Moderne." In *Erscheinungsformen literarischer Prosa um die Jahrhundertwende* (vol. 1 of *Die Literarische Moderne in Europa*), edited by Hans Joachim Piechotta, Ralph-Rainer Wuthenow, and Sabine Rothermann. Opladen and Wiesbaden: Westdeutscher Verlag.

Kranner, Georg. 1994. *Kraus Contra George: Kommentar zu den Übertragungen der Sonette Shakespeares*. Vienna: WUV Universitätsverlag.

Krolop, Kurt. 1994. *Reflexionen der Fackel*. Vienna: Verlag der Österreichischen Akademie der Wissenschaften.

Merkel, Reinhard. 1994. *Strafrecht und Satire im Werk von Karl Kraus.* Baden-Baden: Nomos.

Pizer, John. 1994. "'Ursprung ist das Ziel': Karl Kraus's Concept of Origin." *Modern Austrian Literature* 27, 1.

Baron, Frank, ed. 1995. *Albert Bloch: German Poetry in War and Peace.* Lawrence: University of Kansas.

Müller, Burkhard. 1995. *Karl Kraus: Mimesis und Kritik des Mediums.* Stuttgart: M & P Verlag für Wissenschaft und Forschung.

Ribeiro, António. 1995. "Karl Kraus and Modernism: A Reassessment." In *The Turn of the Century: Modernism and Modernity in Literature and the Arts,* edited by Christian Berg, Frank Durieux, and Geert Lernout. Berlin and New York: Walter de Gruyter.

Theobald, John. 1996. *The Paper Ghetto: Karl Kraus and Anti-Semitism.* Frankfurt: Peter Lang.

Index